Lobbying for Freedom in the 1980s

Lobbying for Freedom in the 1980s

A Grass-Roots Guide to Protecting Your Rights

Edited by Kenneth P. Norwick

A Wideview/Perigee Book

Perigee Books
are published by
G.P. Putnam's Sons
200 Madison Avenue
New York, New York 10016

Library of Congress Cataloging in Publication Data

Main entry under title:

Lobbying for freedom in the 1980s.

1. Lobbying—United States.   2. Civil rights
—United States.   3. State governments.   4. Local
government—United States.   I. Norwick, Kenneth P.
JK2498.L63   1983   328.73'078'0202   82-21398
ISBN 0-399-50718-3 (pbk.)

First Perigee printing, 1983
Printed in the United States of America
1   2   3   4   5   6   7   8   9

Acknowledgments

This book is a revised and substantially expanded version of a book entitled *Lobbying For Freedom: A Citizen's Guide to Fighting Censorship at the State Level*, which was published in 1975. Like its predecessor, this book was made possible in part by a grant from the Playboy Foundation, which recognized the need for a current and comprehensive resource for citizens who want to join the fight to preserve individual freedom in the United States in the 1980s. I am pleased to acknowledge the assistance and support of the Foundation in this project. I also wish to acknowledge with gratitude the encouragement and support of various members of the Playboy organization, including especially Burt Joseph, to whom this book is dedicated, Christie Hefner, Howard Shapiro, Mary Ann Stuart, and Anne Harrison.

I am also grateful to Tom McCormack, president of St. Martin's Press, the publisher of the 1975 version of the book, for graciously allowing us to proceed with this one. I also wish to acknowledge the contributions of Joanne Kaufman, who had a major hand in the preparation of the chapter on censorship; Alan S. Chartock, who provided material for the sections on lobbying; and Rochelle Leib, who cheerfully and most expertly typed and retyped the various drafts of the book.

Finally, I am most grateful to my wife, Susan, and my children, Rebecca and Daniel, for their patience and understanding while this book was being prepared.

—K.P.N.

For Burt Joseph, a true champion of individual freedom, without whom this book would not have been possible

Contents

Introduction

One of the most important ways we as individuals can influence the kind of government and laws we have—which, after all, is what democracy is all about—is to lobby our state and local legislatures. Nevertheless, few of us know very much about our legislatures or even who our legislators are. And far too few of us ever even consider lobbying for something we believe in.

For a variety of reasons, the term "lobbyist" has come to have a negative meaning to many people. To some, the term brings to mind suspicious characters lurking in the halls of legislatures trying improperly to influence legislation for the benefit of selfish special interests. To others, the term connotes rich and powerful "political action" groups that attempt to influence legislation by offering legislators financial and other support for their next election campaigns or by threatening to give such support to their opponents. Unfortunately, such connotations are not wholly without foundation.

At the same time, however, the term "lobbyist" has a much different meaning, and one that goes to the heart of our democratic form of government. The First Amendment is properly revered by most Americans as the source of our precious guarantees of free speech and press and for its separation of church and state. But the First Amendment also contains another guarantee, less well known but just as important: "the right of the people peaceably to assemble, and to petition the Government for a redress of grievances." In the truest sense, the lobbyist is the embodiment of that fundamental First Amendment right: a person petitioning the government, in this case the legislature, for a redress of grievances. And it is in that sense that the word, and the person, must be understood.

This book has been written for a very special kind of lobbyist—individual citizens who care enough about an issue to want their legislators to know how they feel and to reflect those feelings in the legislation they enact. In short, it is for the "citizen-lobbyist," the person who gives the word "lobbyist" its most noble definition and who embodies the essence and genius of our democratic form of government.

This book is especially needed today. As a result of the election of President Ronald Reagan in 1980, and the emergence of the political philosophy and climate he represents, our nation is undergoing dramatic and fundamental changes, not only in the way the laws that govern our everyday lives are established but in the content of those laws as well. Prior to 1980, the trend in this country was for more and more of those laws to be enacted, enforced, and interpreted at the federal level—by the United States Congress, the national administration, and the federal courts, including the Supreme Court—with the result that our state and local governments had less and less control over the nature and content of those laws. By the early 1980s, however, to a significant extent that trend has been reversed, with governmental power over our lives being systematically returned from the national government to the states.

This is especially true with respect to the kinds of issues that involve our ability to live our lives as freely as possible without the interference, control, or discrimination of government. Beginning in the 1960s, our nation witnessed remarkable advances in many areas of individual freedom, including among others the right of women and minorities to be free from arbitrary discrimination, the right of individuals to decide for themselves whether to bear children, the right to consume recreational drugs such as marijuana without the risk of dire criminal consequences, and the freedom to read and view materials without intrusive governmental censorship. Today, however, the dominant political climate throughout the United States is clearly less sympathetic to the cause of individual freedom than it has been in many years. The result is that those freedoms are in very serious trouble indeed, and that the battles to preserve them will now take place in the various state legislatures across the country and not just in Washington.

The contributors to this book are committed to protecting and enhancing those freedoms as fully and as vigorously as they can, and they have all lobbied in numerous legislatures toward that goal. They have written this book as a guide to those individuals who share that commitment and who wish to do their part to lobby for freedom at the state and local level.

In every legislature there are professional lobbyists who seek to influence the course of legislation on every conceivable subject. Issues involving individual freedom are no exception, and there will be professional lobbyists actively fighting for and against such freedom wherever those issues are presented. It is not the purpose of this book to turn you into a professional. It is our goal to show you how to work most effectively alongside them.

Part I of this book consists of two chapters, the first of which describes what a state legislature is and how it functions, including a discussion of the kinds of people who are legislators, the factors they consider in deciding how to vote on a controversial issue, and how they function. The second chapter describes how the individual citizen-lobbyist can most effectively bring his or her views to bear on the legislature concerning the kinds of issues that are discussed in this book.

Part II of the book consists of five chapters, each of which discusses the background and current status of a major area of individual freedom: reproductive freedom, women's rights, gay rights, drug laws, and censorship.

Part III provides appendices and other background information on these issues, as well as on each of the fifty state legislatures, together with sample materials that the individual citizen-lobbyist can use in connection with his or her lobbying efforts.

We hope this book will assist all citizen-lobbyists in the never ending battle for freedom.

Kenneth P. Norwick

PART I

Lobbying on the State and Local Level

by Kenneth P. Norwick

1 / THE LEGISLATURE AND THE LEGISLATIVE PROCESS

What Is a Legislature?

Under this country's system of government, it is the function of the legislative branch—on the local, state, and national levels—to write the laws under which we are expected to live.

Every state, and most cities and counties, have legislative bodies. In some states, the state legislature has almost all the legislative power within the state, with the cities and counties having very limited powers. In other states, the cities and counties possess much more legislative power—sometimes called "home rule"—and the state legislatures exercise much less. In almost every state, the state legislature has the power to preempt city and county legislation, although it does not always exercise that power.

People interested in lobbying on an issue should first learn where the legislative power lies in their own state. If your city or county legislature has no power to legislate on the issue, it would be a waste of time to lobby there. On the other hand, if they do have that power, or share power with the state, it is essential to know that too. Chapter 2 suggests how to learn where the legislative power in your state lies. For the sake of simplicity, the discussion in this chapter focuses on how state legislatures function. But much of the information will apply to city and county legislatures as well.

Unlike the national Congress, which is in session throughout the year every year, the various state legislatures are part-time legislative bodies. Some meet only every other year, and then only for a month or two, while others meet every year for sessions that extend anywhere from a few months to most of the year. Except in the closing days of a session, most state legislatures meet for only two or three days a week. If you are interested in lobbying your legislature, you should first determine when its sessions begin and end. Table 1 in Part III lists the duration of a normal session for each state legislature.

With only one exception—Nebraska, which has America's only "unicameral," or one-house, legislature—every state legislature consists of two houses, which are called the senate and the house of representatives (or assembly). In each of these legislatures, the two houses have equal legislative power, and before a bill can become law it must be passed by both. In every state the senate is the smaller house, ranging in membership from nineteen in Delaware to sixty-seven in Minnesota, while the house or assembly is usually much larger, numbering from thirty-nine in Delaware to four hundred in New Hampshire. Table 2, also in Part III, lists the size of each house of every state legislature.

Prior to 1964, at least one house of virtually every state legislature was apportioned according to factors other than population. In that year, however, in the case of *Reynolds v. Sims,* the Supreme Court declared that such apportionment violated the Constitution's guarantee that every citizen is entitled to the equal protection of the law; it ruled that every legislature must be apportioned so that every citizen has an equal voice in the selection of the members of both houses. This rule, called "one man, one vote," has revolutionized every state legislature, and today every member of each house represents substantially the same number of people.

Every member of every state legislature is elected directly by the people of the district he or she represents. Some state legislatures have single-member districts, with one legislator elected to represent each district, while others have multimember districts, which means that the voters of a district elect several legislators to represent the district. In many states, elections for every member of the legislature are held every two years, while in other states the legislators' terms are for four years. And in some states the members of one house are elected every two years and the members of the other every four years. Table 2 also shows whether a legislature has single-member or multimember districts and what the legislators' terms of office are. It is essential for people interested in lobbying to be familiar with these aspects of their own state legislature.

In any state, no bill can become law until it is passed by both houses and signed by the governor, or, if it is vetoed by the governor, until that veto is overridden by the legislature. (This is not true in North Carolina, where the governor has no veto power.) In some states, it is fairly common for vetoes to be overridden, while in others this almost never happens. In some states, only a simple majority is needed to override a veto, while in others a two-thirds or three-fourths vote is necessary. Some states have special sessions of the legislature just to consider possible overrides of vetoes, while no such sessions are possible in many others.

Although all state legislatures have much in common, they are also very different from each other in many important ways, and anyone interested in lobbying must learn as much as possible about his or her own legislature. Chapter 2 includes several suggestions on how to do this.

How Does a Legislature Function?

Probably the most important thing citizen-lobbyists must know about their legislature is how it functions. Here too, all state legislatures have much in common, but are also very different.

As indicated, the timing of each legislature's session varies from state to state. In many states, the legislature convenes in early January and adjourns in late spring or early summer, while in others it convenes in midspring or in the fall and adjourns several months later. Some states have several special sessions during the year, while others rarely do. To understand how a legislature functions, it is obviously necessary to know when and for how long it is in session.

In every state, every member of the legislature has the power to introduce proposed legislation on any subject. Although each legislature has its own rules in this regard, usually these bills can be prefiled beginning shortly before the session starts and can be introduced until a previously announced cutoff point some time during the session. Almost every legislator introduces at least some bills during every session, although some legislators seem to introduce far more bills than others. These bills usually represent the legislators' own views on the subject, but sometimes legislators will introduce bills simply as a courtesy to a constituent or interest group. Sometimes the legislators themselves work very hard on the research and drafting of these bills, and sometimes the bills are prepared and drafted by others without involving the legislator.

Just because a legislator has introduced a certain bill on a certain subject, however, does not mean that he or she is committed to it or that the bill will be taken seriously or given a fair hearing during the session. Many bills are introduced for "show" or personal political reasons—for example, to demonstrate that the legislator has his or her own legislative program—with no intention on the part of the legislator to try to have them enacted into law. Also, in every legislature there are members who—for reasons such as politics, personality, or lack of seniority—find it virtually impossible to have a bill taken seriously, much less passed.

In preparing to lobby your own legislature, it is not enough to know that a bill you are for or against has been introduced. You must also know whether its sponsor truly stands behind it, and whether it has a chance of being taken seriously by the legislature. Some pointers are provided in the next chapter.

Every legislature consists of several committees, whose function is to study the bills that have been introduced by the individual members. Each committee handles a specified area of legislation, although the jurisdiction of such committees will frequently overlap. Some state legislatures have a great many committees, while others have much fewer. Every member of the legislature is assigned to one or more of these committees, with the political party in the majority in the particular house having a majority of the members, including the chairperson. Usually the leadership of the respective parties in each house determines which members are assigned to which committees, with the members themselves sometimes but not always being assigned to the committees of their choice.

In many states, every bill that is introduced is automatically referred to a committee, usually by the leadership of the house or by a special committee controlled by the leadership. In other states, such references to committees are not automatic but require a special request from the sponsor and/or the specific approval of the leadership or the reference committee. In those states, if a bill is not referred to a committee, it is dead for the session.

The referral of bills to committees is one of the most crucial steps in the whole legislative process. Obviously, if a bill is not referred at all, that alone seals its fate. But frequently the selection of which committee a bill is referred to can be just as significant. In many legislatures committees have overlapping jurisdiction, and it is not uncommon for one to have an entirely different outlook from another on a particular issue. As a result, sponsors of bills will often do whatever they can— especially in the drafting and titling of the bills—to ensure that their bills are assigned to the most receptive committees. It is essential for citizen-lobbyists to learn as much as possible about the committee to which a bill they are following has been referred.

Once a bill has been referred to a committee, the next step in the legislative process begins. In most states, every bill referred to a committee will get a "hearing"—or be considered in some other way— sometime during the session. In other states, whether or not a bill is considered at all is decided by the chairperson, who has the sole power to determine which bills shall be considered by the committee at every meeting. In most states, all committee meetings are open to the public and the press, but in others they are closed to all. In most states, the bills to be considered by the committee at each meeting are publicly announced several days prior to the meeting, while in others they are not made public at all, or not until after the meeting has been held.

In those legislatures where every bill is given an open committee hearing, the hearing usually begins with the sponsor testifying in support of it, explaining why it was introduced and how it would affect the problem it deals with. Then other witnesses, who may include other legislators, public officials, lobbyists, interested parties, and ordinary citizens, are given the chance to testify for or against the bill. During these hearings, the committee's members or staff may ask questions of these witnesses, and when all the testimony is completed the committee will vote on whether to "report" the bill to the full house for its consideration. Such a report by the committee usually indicates its approval of the bill and is the first step toward passage. If the bill is reported, it is then either referred to another committee for further study, especially if it has serious fiscal consequences, or it is referred immediately to the full house. If the committee refuses to report the bill, or if it reports the bill with a recommendation that it not be passed, that usually means the bill is dead for the session.

In those states that do not give every bill a full hearing, the process is different. First, the sponsor and other supporters of the bill must try to have it brought before the committee for consideration. On the other hand, those who oppose the bill will try to keep it from ever being considered. Second, if the bill is put on the committee's agenda, or if there is no way of knowing whether it is or not, both the proponents and opponents of the bill will communicate their views to as many members of the committee as they can prior to the meeting. This is most often done through the submission of written memoranda on the bill and through individual discussions with the committee's members. Also, the proponents and opponents will try to ensure that those members of the committee sympathetic to their views are present at the meeting and prepared to discuss the bill. After the bill is discussed by the committee, a vote will be taken on whether it should be reported.

It is important to understand the dynamics that underlie the operations of the committee system. The role of the chairperson, in particular, must be appreciated. In most states, the chairperson is appointed by the majority leadership of the house, and these appointments usually go to senior members of the majority party who are closely aligned with the party leadership. Thus, committee chairpersons often speak not only for themselves and their constituents, but also for the majority leadership of the house. (Because of their power to appoint committee chairpersons, among many other reasons, the leaders of every legislature are almost always the most important and powerful members of their legislatures, and it is desirable from a lobbyist's point of view to have the leadership on your side or at least neutral on your issue.) Particularly in those states where the chairperson alone determines whether and when bills will be considered by the committee, but in all states to one extent or another, the chairperson wields considerable influence over the fate of most bills that come before the committee. As a result, most proponents and opponents of a bill will concentrate their efforts on persuading the chairperson to adopt their point of view.

Among the committee members as well, there are usually some who are far more influential than others. They may have developed a special expertise on the subject covered by the bill, or they may have political power wholly unrelated to the committee or the subject matter of the bill (for example, if they are officials of their political parties). Also, legislators will often try to accommodate their friends and colleagues in the legislature. Thus if the sponsor of the bill is a committee member, or if the sponsor tells the members that the passage of the bill is particularly important to him or her, the committee members will often cast their votes for personal reasons having nothing to do with the merits of the bill. Such political favors are not usually forgotten, and legislators will often vote for a colleague's bill solely in exchange for his or her vote on a different bill.

One final, but most important, factor should be noted about the functioning of a legislative committee. In many cases a bill that is unacceptable to a majority of the committee can be made acceptable by negotiating a compromise on some of its provisions. Knowing when and how to compromise in a legislature, as anywhere else, requires not only a knowledge of the subject matter but also a sense of how strong the other side is and how far it is willing to go to achieve the compromise. In lobbying for or against a bill, it is essential to know who is authorized to negotiate on behalf of your position, and how far that person is authorized to go. Once a compromise bill is agreed upon, it is usually assumed that those persons and groups who took part in the negotiations will go along with the compromise bill. It is almost always much easier to negotiate a compromise while a bill is still in committee than after it has been reported to the floor.

Once a bill has been reported from committee, it can be considered by the entire house. In most states, the bill appears on a printed calendar that indicates when it is likely to be taken up. In other states, there may be no printed calendar at all, or if there is one there may be no way of knowing from it when the bill will be brought up for debate. Also, in some states the fact that a bill has been reported from committee does not necessarily mean that it will in fact be brought up for debate, since in those states the house leadership alone has the power to determine whether and when the bill will be considered.

In some states, it is common for bills to be amended from the floor, while in others that almost never happens. Also, in some states it is possible for opponents of a bill to filibuster it to death, or use other parliamentary tactics to keep it from ever coming to a vote, while in others the debate and parliamentary maneuvering are tightly controlled. For those who are lobbying for or against a bill, it is essential to know whether these tactics are possible in your state, and if so, how best to utilize or defend against them. It is also essential to know when the bill is likely to be brought up, what the prospects for the vote are, and who the important swing votes may be. At this stage in the legislative process, the job of the citizen-lobbyist is to reinforce those legislators who agree with you and to persuade those who do not. How that is best accomplished is discussed in Chapter 2.

In some states, a majority of the total membership must vote for the bill for it to pass, while in other states all that is required is a simple majority of those members actually voting. In many states, even if a bill is defeated the first time it is brought to a vote, that vote can be reconsidered and the bill brought back at a later date for a second try. Indeed, in many states it is not at all uncommon for bills that were defeated the first time to come back and be passed the second.

If a bill is finally defeated in one house, it is usually dead for the session in both. If, however, a bill is passed by one house, that only means that it must go through and survive the same process in the other. Moreover, it is important to realize that in many states one house will pass a bill—usually for political reasons—on the clear understanding that it will be killed in the other. These understandings are rarely admitted or publicly reported, and are difficult for the citizen-lobbyist to discover. However, it is most important in every case to learn as much as you can about the reasons a bill you are following was passed in one house so you can best be able to lobby on it in the other.

Finally, of course, it must be remembered that even if a bill is passed by both houses, it still must be signed by the governor of your state before it can become law, except in North Carolina.

Who Are Legislators?

In many ways, legislators are like the population at large. Some are intelligent and conscientious, and some are not; some have strong views on many subjects, and some do not; some are informed, and some are not; some are young or rich, and some are not; most are honest, but some are not.

In many ways, however, legislators are very different from the population at large. Perhaps the most significant difference stems from the fact that they *are* legislators, which means they are politicians whose continued success depends in large part on their ability to satisfy major segments of their constituents, and especially the most powerful and best-organized forces among those constituents. As such, they are usually far more accessible and gregarious than the average person, and far more likely to try to be known and liked. For example, most legislators consider it their responsibility to attend as many community functions as they can and to make themselves available to as many of their constituents, and others, as possible.

In other ways, too, legislators tend to be different from the rest of us. They are far more likely to be lawyers by profession, and they usually have far more knowledge and experience in public affairs than the general population. Also, they are almost always thinking about their next election campaign, and are often considering races for higher political office, which may lead them to try to become known to and to please constituencies broader than and different from those which elected them.

The vast majority of state legislators have other employment or businesses in addition to their legislative jobs, most in or near the districts they represent. Indeed, in some cases at least, legislators will use their outside employment to enhance their political roles, and vice versa. It is important for citizen-lobbyists to be aware of the outside employment of each legislator, especially their own, and how that might relate to the legislator's performance in his or her legislative role.

Within every legislature there are members who represent the more liberal political points of view as well as the more conservative. And, of course, there are many who represent the political "center." Usually legislators accurately reflect the political climate of their own districts, although it is not uncommon for legislators to be somewhat more liberal or conservative than their districts. In most cases, as will be discussed below, the degree of political independence—that is, deviation from the general political climate of their districts—legislators show depends largely on how much that independence is likely to hurt at the next election. Also, legislators frequently act far more independently behind the scenes, especially in committee and in the process of negotiating compromises, than in the ultimate debate and roll-call vote.

In many legislatures, one or both of the major political parties are extremely strong and unified, with the members of that party generally expected to go along with the party leadership, regardless of their personal views. In other legislatures, the parties are much less powerful, with the individual members almost always free to go their own way on a bill. And even in those legislatures with strict party control, there are always mavericks who will defy the party leadership from time to time. Citizen-lobbyists should learn as much as they can about the role of the political parties in their legislature, and who the "regulars" and "mavericks" are likely to be.

The nature and volume of the bills introduced into every legislature prohibit any legislator from reading, much less studying, all of them. Indeed, most legislators have time to read and study carefully only a small number of the bills that are introduced. As a result, most legislators specialize in only a few legislative areas and depend on others for information and advice in all other areas. In some states, legislators have their own assistants or counsels, and they rely heavily on them for research and assistance. In other states, most legislators do not have such individual staff assistance, and they must depend on the assistance provided by the staff of their party leadership and by others. In those states, this further concentrates legislative power in the hands of the leadership.

Among the most important sources of such additional information are the legislature's lobbyists, who are almost always experts on their own legislative subject areas. In some legislatures, such lobbyists are highly regarded and fully utilized by the legislators, while in others they are treated with suspicion and distrust. Citizen-lobbyists should learn how their own legislatures regard such professional lobbyists, and who those lobbyists are who are most directly involved in the issues with which they are concerned. A description of lobbyists and how they function is provided below.

What Motivates a Vote?

Although it is often tempting to categorize state legislators with labels and to assume they will respond in knee-jerk fashion on most controversial issues, many legislators are in fact more complex and unpredictable than such labels or assumptions indicate. Most usually want to do the right thing—to act responsibly on legislation so that the best interests of their constituents and the people of the state are served—and they will occasionally cast votes inconsistent with their political images if they are persuaded of the rightness of that course.

As with anyone who has to make a difficult decision, many important and often conflicting factors are considered when a legislator decides how to cast his or her vote on a controversial issue. The less controversial the issue, the easier it usually is for the legislator to make that decision, since far fewer political consequences can result from it. Also, on such issues it is more likely that the legislator's decision may be motivated by personal self-interest or the interests of special groups to which the legislator is particularly beholden or responsive. It is the responsibility of all lobbyists—indeed, probably their most important responsibility—to understand and utilize this decision-making process when attempting to persuade legislators to vote the lobbyist's way.

On many issues, of course, legislators have no difficulty reaching their decision. They may be sponsors or co-sponsors of the bill, or the bill may so clearly benefit, or injure, their own constituents that there can be no doubt how they will vote. In the vast majority of cases, however—including on occasion when the legislator is a sponsor of the bill—the legislator's vote should not be taken for granted. The factors legislators consider in deciding how to vote differ from issue to issue, with some factors being far more important on some issues than on others. Here are some of the most common:

Constituents' Views

Probably the single most influential factor to most legislators in deciding how to vote on a bill is the wishes of their constituents, and especially those who have the most influence and power. It is the essence of all legislators' jobs to represent their constituents in the legislature. Many legislators believe this means it is their duty to reflect the viewpoint of a majority of their constituents on every issue, regardless of all other considerations. Others believe they were elected not just to reflect their constituents but also to exercise independent judgment and to lead and educate those constituents. In either case, all legislators take very seriously the views of their constituents—particularly the best-organized and most vocal elements—and they will try to reflect those views as often and as accurately as they can.

Even though state legislatures constantly deal with matters that vitally affect the daily lives of every citizen in the state, most citizens either are unaware of what their legislature is doing or have decided that they can have no influence over it. On most vital issues most legislators hear from no more than a small minority of their constituents, and they rarely really know what their constituents are thinking. As a result, most legislators proceed on assumptions regarding the sentiment in their districts or they take steps themselves to discover that sentiment. In addition, they may also be guided by the few communications they do receive on an issue, even though those communications may not in fact reflect the prevailing view in the district.

On some issues, organized interest groups promote letter and telegram campaigns, often on prepared forms, so that legislators are deluged with communications from their constituents on those issues. Most legislators, however, realize that such communications are not spontaneous expressions of opinion but are instead inspired by others who are directly interested in the outcome of the bill, and they evaluate such communications accordingly. On the other hand, most legislators take much more seriously communications from constituents that do seem to be spontaneous, since they believe such constituents are much more likely to be sincere in their views and feel deeply about them. Most legislators and professional lobbyists agree that individually written communications from constituents are given far more weight than dozens, and perhaps hundreds, of form letters or petitions. Because of this, lobbying groups that are able to generate seemingly spontaneous communications from constituents can often have an impact far beyond their actual numbers or political influence.

To ascertain local viewpoints on an issue, many legislators circulate questionnaires or polls to their constituents, and they attend community functions where the issue can be discussed. Here, too, legislators give considerable weight to what they believe to be the sincerely held beliefs of their constituents, and most lobbyists try to make sure their point of view is fully expressed through responses to such questionnaires and polls and through attendance and participation at such community functions.

Political Consequences

A second factor legislators consider, and one that is closely related to the views of their constituents, is the extent to which a vote for or against a bill will help or hurt during their next election campaigns. Incumbent legislators have many advantages over their challengers, but they also have the disadvantage of having to explain and defend every controversial vote they cast. As a result, many legislators try to avoid controversial issues whenever they can, and it is an unfortunate fact of political life that legislators will sometimes cast a vote solely to minimize its political consequences or to avoid giving their next opponents an issue to use against them. This is particularly true in such sensitive areas as those discussed in Part II of this book. Lobbyists must understand the likely political consequences to a legislator of any given vote and be prepared to deal effectively with that problem. In particular, citizen-lobbyists should always remember that their power to deliver or withhold votes on Election Day, or their ability to make legislators think they have that power even if they do not, can often be the most potent weapon in their lobbying arsenal.

Personal Philosophy

Many legislators have their own philosophies or approaches to most social problems, and in many cases their positions on legislation will largely be influenced by those philosophies. A legislator who believes it is the responsibility of the state to set moral standards and to protect people from themselves, for example, is likely to favor legislation that restricts individual freedom, while one who believes the state has no business legislating private morality, and that people should be given as much individual freedom as possible, is likely to oppose such legislation. In both cases, however, their votes on the bill should never be taken for granted, since it is entirely possible that other considerations will persuade the legislator to vote the other way. In every case, citizen-lobbyists should learn as much as they can about the personal political philosophies of each legislator, and especially their own. Such knowledge can be crucial in determining how best to persuade and lobby the legislator.

The Bill's Effectiveness

Another factor legislators consider is whether the proposed bill can actually achieve its goal—whether it can work—and what its full and perhaps unintended consequences will be. In many cases, legislators will agree with a bill's objective and have no political problems supporting it, and yet vote against it because they do not believe the bill can work, or because they believe it will have undesirable consequences that outweigh the good the bill can do. For example, legislators who favor strict censorship laws may still oppose some censorship bills because they consider the standards too narrow to accomplish the desired goal or so broad as to authorize the censorship of works they believe should not be censored. Whenever possible, lobbyists should emphasize the practical shortcomings of a bill they are opposing, including the possibility that the bill is not tough enough, if that will help defeat the bill. In fact, sometimes a bill can be defeated simply because it is badly drafted.

Fiscal Implications

Another factor considered by legislators is that of the likely fiscal consequences of the bill. Legislators are always conscious of the resentment most citizens feel about the taxes they have to pay, as well as the fact that government never has enough money to do everything it would like, and they are therefore always concerned about what any given bill or program will cost. As a result, legislators will frequently oppose a bill solely because of its fiscal implications, even though they otherwise fully support it. It is essential for all lobbyists—whether for or against a bill—to understand fully its fiscal implications and to use that knowledge to further their lobbying causes.

Constitutionality

Another factor that is particularly relevant to the kinds of issues discussed in this book involves the constitutionality of the bill. Every legislator takes an oath to uphold the Constitution, and many take that oath seriously. Moreover, legislators also realize that if a bill they pass is subsequently struck down by the courts as unconstitutional, the result may be that there will be no law at all on the subject. For these reasons, the possible unconstitutionality of the bill should always be forcefully asserted, although some legislators may still vote for a bill because it is politically advantageous to do so even though they believe it is unconstitutional and will be struck down by the courts.

Personal Considerations

Another important factor legislators consider is who the sponsor is and what position is taken on the bill by the different political parties.

As indicated above, legislators may promise a vote to a colleague for personal reasons or in exchange for a similar promise on a different bill, or they may be bound by their party's position—or the position of their party's leaders—on the bill. Further, many legislators are influenced by the views of those legislators who are experts in the area covered by the bill or who represent a particular political point of view. Whenever possible, lobbyists should try to win over—or at least neutralize— these opinion-leaders in their own legislatures.

Organized Support or Opposition

A final factor legislators consider in reaching their decision on a bill involves the nature and identity of those who support and oppose it. In every state there are numerous interest groups concerned with particular issues, including the most controversial. In addition, in many cases different agencies of government, and various public officials and community leaders, will be directly concerned about a bill. And, of course, local newspapers, magazines, and radio and television stations frequently express opinions on bills before the legislature. Sometimes legislators will be closely associated with these groups or forces, or want to please them, and thus be motivated to agree with their positions on the issues concerning them. (Unfortunately, it is still true in most state legislatures that the votes of some legislators will be motivated primarily by the direct or indirect financial benefit they did or expect to receive for their votes, and there is probably little the citizen-lobbyist can do to influence those votes.) Similarly, some legislators will want to remain as distant as possible from such forces. In either case, most legislators consider the nature of the bill's supporters and opponents, as well as its own merits, in reaching their final decision. As a result, it is always important for citizen-lobbyists to identify and organize those forces on your side of the issue which will have the greatest impact on each legislator.

The Floor Debate

After considering some or all of these factors, most legislators at least tentatively decide how they will vote on the bill. In many cases, legislators will announce in advance how they intend to vote, but frequently they will keep their own counsel until the vote is actually held. In either event, there remains one final factor that can still influence the vote: the floor debate on the bill. For although it is undoubtedly true that most legislators decide how they will vote on most controversial issues before the debate begins, it is always possible, and sometimes happens, that a legislator will change his or her vote as a result of the debate. Accordingly, advocates of a position, including legislators and lobbyists, will prepare the most persuasive debate they can on the bill.

As this discussion shows, the decision-making process for most legislators on most issues is hardly as simple as any label would indicate. Citizen-lobbyists, armed with an understanding of what these factors are and how they relate to their own legislators, can and often will influence these legislators on many vital issues, and they will certainly help the professional lobbyist toward that goal. We shall now take a look at those lobbyists.

What Is a Lobbyist?

As with legislators, there is no "typical lobbyist." They are young and old, male and female, paid and volunteer, conscientious and undependable, honest and dishonest. Indeed, lobbyists are probably even more "representative" of the great diversity within the population at large than are legislators. As with legislators, however, lobbyists do have several common characteristics.

The one thing all lobbyists have in common is that it is their job to represent a particular interest or point of view to the legislature and to see to it that those interests and viewpoints are protected as fully as possible in the legislation that is enacted. Lobbyists are usually experts on the subjects they follow, and as such they provide a much-needed source of information to the legislators. Because of this role, they are sometimes called the "third house" of the legislature.

Lobbyists represent business, labor, professional, religious, good-government, consumer, and civil liberties organizations. In addition, many government agencies, and many cities and counties, have their own lobbyists, as do the governor and the judicial branch of government. In fact, it is hard to imagine an interest that does not have a lobbyist of one kind or another. And this, of course, is precisely what the right to "petition the government" is all about.

There are several different kinds of lobbyists, and every legislature has some of each. First, there is the full-time professional lobbyist for a particular company or association. These lobbyists are permanent employees or officials of their employers, with part or all of their duties being to represent their employers' interests in the legislature. These lobbyists represent only the interests of their particular employers, and they rarely, if ever, get involved in legislation that does not concern those employers. Usually, they concentrate their efforts on those legislative committees that have jurisdiction over the subject matters they are most interested in, although when necessary they will seek to influence the legislature as a whole. In large part because of their special expertise, these lobbyists often exercise considerable influence over the legislation that concerns them. Sometimes, however, and especially when these lobbyists represent minority or unpopular causes, they have less influence, although they still have some.

A second kind of lobbyist is the person who is retained on a part-time professional basis to represent a particular group or interest. These persons are often lawyers in private practice, former legislators, or public-relations consultants, usually with offices near the Capitol, and they frequently represent several different clients at the same time. These lobbyists also become experts in the areas they are involved in, and they usually work closely with more committees and legislators than their full-time counterparts. These lobbyists can have considerable influence—again, of course, depending on the political power of their clients and their clients' causes.

The third kind of lobbyist is an employee of a company, or a member of a group, who monitors the legislature and lobbies in addition to all his or her regular responsibilities for that employer or group. For example, a company treasurer or vice president may be assigned the job of following the legislature. These lobbyists maintain only sporadic contact with the legislature, and usually have less influence than the others. Nevertheless, on specific issues even these lobbyists can have a definite impact.

The final kind of lobbyist—the one to whom this book is addressed—is the concerned citizen, the individual who does not have a commercial or professional interest in the legislation but who nevertheless feels strongly enough to want to do what he or she can to influence its fate. These citizen-lobbyists often have the potential to accomplish a great deal in the legislature, but they are often much too unfamiliar with the legislature and its procedures and practices to utilize that potential. They are also usually scattered, unorganized, and without financial resources, and thus unable fully to use their potential influence and lobbying power. This book has been developed to help these citizen-lobbyists overcome such problems.

What Do Lobbyists Do?

One of the hardest questions lobbyists are asked is to describe exactly what they do. In fact, most lobbyists function on many different levels and in many different ways, with each having his or her own special methods of operation. In large part, the choice of methods lobbyists use depends on the nature and political makeup of the legislature and on the popularity and clout of the causes they are espousing. In general, however, the functions of most lobbyists can best be described as being on two distinct levels: the "inside" and the "outside."

On the inside level, the lobbyist attempts to influence the course of legislation by working directly with key legislators and committees, without attracting public attention. On this level, the lobbyists may actually draft the legislation they want passed (or help interested legislators draft it), arrange to have the legislation introduced by the best possible sponsor, try to have the legislation referred to the most receptive committee, and then try to persuade the committee to report it favorably to the whole house. On the inside level, too, lobbyists prepare research and background material in support of the bill; answer questions about it from legislators, including those raised by the bill's opponents; and help determine the timing and strategy for the bill's progress through the legislature. These lobbyists also arrange for others to testify for, and otherwise support, the bill, and they try to anticipate and head off the bill's opposition. If the bill is reported to the floor, lobbyists then undertake to persuade other key legislators, and perhaps the entire membership, of the merits of the bill. In most cases, however, lobbyists operating on this level accomplish their missions once they successfully steer their bills through committee, since the membership as a whole usually follows the recommendations of those committees, especially on technical and complicated legislation.

On the inside level, also, lobbyists use their access to the relevant committees to persuade those committees to kill legislation they oppose. Here too, lobbyists provide research and background information and materials, this time against the bill, and they try to answer the arguments put forward by the bill's supporters. In opposing legislation, as when supporting it, lobbyists help determine the timing and strategy of the bill's opposition and arrange for others to oppose it. If the bill is nevertheless reported to the whole house, the lobbyists then seek to persuade other legislators, and the membership as a whole, to defeat the bill, and they help plan the strategy to do so.

The essence of the inside approach is that the lobbyists exploit their special expertise and goodwill with key legislators and committees without appealing to the public or otherwise drawing attention to themselves or the bill on which they are lobbying. Usually, the lobbyists who most effectively use this approach are those whose causes are already greeted with sympathy by the pivotal legislators and the legislature as a whole, as well as those who for other reasons, including previous or expected campaign contributions or other favors or support, are listened to with special interest. On occasion, however, even those lobbyists who represent less popular causes, or who do not provide political contributions or favors or support, can still utilize the inside approach effectively, depending in large part on the merits of their case and the political strength of their opposition to the bill. Typically, these inside lobbyists avoid the public spotlight and thus escape notice by most members of the legislature, other lobbyists, and the press.

Lobbyists who function on the outside level do so either because they do not have the access or clout to operate on the inside level, or because the causes they espouse are so controversial or sensitive that a much wider lobbying effort is required. On this level, lobbyists may still draft desired legislation, provide research and background information, and work as much as possible with the relevant committees. The outside lobbyists, however, do not stop there, but also try to generate as much other support as they can for their position on the bill. To this end, they may seek to inspire favorable press coverage, issuing press releases and calling press conferences when they deem it appropriate. They may also seek to mobilize other lobbyists and groups, and the public at large, to join their position on the bill. These lobbyists may also form coalitions of groups and individuals to enhance the effectiveness of, and appearance of solidarity for, their position, and to generate grass-roots support from such groups and individuals. Similarly, some of these lobbyists or the organizations or interests they represent may endorse or oppose legislators, or provide other campaign support when they run for reelection, and they may use the possibility of such support or opposition as a part of their overall lobbying effort.

As might be expected, there are almost always several lobbyists actively engaged on each side of most controversial issues. As might also be expected, whenever possible these lobbyists will try to reconcile their differences through behind-the-scenes negotiations so that the interests they represent can all be protected to some extent at least. Obviously, some issues are far more susceptible to such negotiation and compromise than others. In all cases, however, diligent lobbyists take whatever steps they deem necessary and appropriate to protect most fully the interests they represent. How the citizen-lobbyist can best support the efforts of the professional lobbyists on their side of the issue is discussed in the following chapter.

2 / HOW TO LOBBY ON A BILL

There are many ways the individual citizen can effectively lobby his or her legislature on an important issue. Obviously, not all of them will apply to every individual or state legislature, and some may have to be adapted to meet local needs and circumstances. If used with common sense and an understanding of the nature of politics and the legislative process, however, the following suggestions should prove helpful.

Know Your Legislature

The first thing potential citizen-lobbyists must do is learn as much as they can about their own state's legislature and its members, and especially their own representatives. Where does the legislature meet? When does its session begin and when is it likely to end? How many days a week is it in session? How does its committee system function? Who has the political power in the legislature? How strong are the political parties? Who are our own legislators and what kind of legislators are they?

The answers to most, if not all, of these questions are usually fairly easy to obtain. In fact, some of these answers may be found in Tables 1 and 2 in Part III.

Most state legislatures make available free of charge official guides or directories which include the names, districts, party affiliation, and committee assignments of each legislator, as well as such other information as the names of the legislative leaders, the timing of the session, and an explanation of the legislature's procedures. To find out if these materials are available in your state, and to obtain copies, write the clerk of your state senate or house of representatives—usually, the only address you need is the name of your capital city—or your own legislators at the same address.

In addition, such organizations as the League of Women Voters, Common Cause, and the American Civil Liberties Union, among others, have offices in almost every state and most large cities, and they should also be able to give you background information about your legislature or help you find it. In some states, these organizations publish booklets and other materials about the state legislature, as well as city and county legislative bodies, while in other states these materials may not be available. In any event, you should never hesitate to ask these organizations, or the clerks or other officials of your legislature, for information or assistance; they are usually set up to provide such help and welcome the opportunity to do so. If you are unable to locate the addresses or phone numbers of these organizations in your area, you should contact their national headquarters and ask them to help you:

League of Women Voters of the United States, 1730 M Street, N.W., Washington, DC 20036

Common Cause, 2030 M Street, N.W., Washington, DC 20006

American Civil Liberties Union, 132 West 43rd Street, New York, NY 10036

In addition, there is a national organization specifically concerned with the various state legislatures that might be able to assist you in obtaining information about your own. That organization is The National Conference of State Legislatures, with headquarters at 1125 Seventeenth Street, Suite 1500, Denver, CO 80202. It also maintains an office at 444 North Capitol Street, N.W., Washington, DC 20001.

Further, the major political parties in every state usually have branches or clubs in every city and county within the state, and sometimes even in local communities, and the party headquarters in your area should also be able to provide you with information about your legislature and especially your own legislators. However, because of the partisan nature of these organizations the information they give should always be evaluated with special care, and it might be useful to consult several different party organizations in your community to see how that information varies.

Still another source of information is provided by back issues of your local newspapers. Most papers maintain indexes to help locate articles on specific people and subjects, and back issues are usually available at the public library and the offices of the papers themselves. Especially in smaller communities, which send only a few legislators to the legislature, it is likely that the local paper publishes regular articles by and about those legislators, particularly on their positions on controversial issues and their campaigns for election. Such articles can be invaluable in understanding how these legislators think and vote.

A final source of information about your legislature and legislators are the legislators themselves, or their staffs. In most cases they will be more than happy to tell you about themselves and the legislature and to provide whatever further information you might want. In fact, there is no reason not to contact your own legislators just to get to know them, and it is often particularly useful for citizen-lobbyists to do so even before they begin their lobbying efforts. However, you should probably avoid discussing the specifics of an issue until you have had an opportunity to become familiar with the issue and how it is likely to arise in your legislature. A common mistake many people make is to try to discuss complicated issues with their legislators before they have done their homework on the issues. When this happens, the legislators can raise arguments and make assertions that those people may not be able to answer, with the result that the citizen won't persuade the legislator and the legislator may well persuade the citizen. Nevertheless, if you do find yourself discussing specific issues with a legislator before you have had a chance to study them, you should make it clear to the legislator that although you are not an expert on the issue you still have strong feelings on it, and want him or her to know what those feelings are. You may not persuade the legislator on the merits of the issue, but he or she will get your political message loud and clear. To repeat: By all means feel free to contact your legislators to learn about them and the legislature and to tell them you hope to maintain contact with them.

Know Your Issue

Most legislators have at least a working knowledge of most controversial issues, or think they do, and almost all have at least tentative opinions or positions on them. Before discussing such issues with legislators, it is best to be as knowledgeable as possible on them, both in general terms and with respect to how the issue will arise in your own state legislature. What does the state's present law provide? How has that law been interpreted by the courts? Is it likely that the legislature will address that issue in the near future, and if so, what kind of bill is it likely to consider? What is the local political climate on the issue? What have the leaders of the legislature, local public officials, and other opinion-leaders said? Have any bills already been introduced? If so, what do they provide?

Unlike the background information about your legislature discussed above, the answers to these questions may be more difficult to find. There are, however, several sources that should prove helpful.

First, of course, you can try to dig out some of the answers through your own research. However, unless you are a lawyer, or are familiar with the techniques of legal research, and unless you have the time to do extensive research on the nonlegal questions, this may prove difficult and time-consuming. Since it is likely that others have already done most of this work, you should do so yourself only if you really want to or if you determine that no one else has done it.

The people who are most likely to have already done this work are those who are most directly affected by the relevant laws in your state, including individuals whose business may be affected as well as people who are affected in their own personal lives. Frequently, they belong to organizations and associations on both the state and national levels, and it is likely that these groups have lawyers and lobbyists who are familiar with the law and the prospects for change in your state. If you can locate these lawyers or lobbyists in your area, and tell them you are interested in lobbying against repressive laws, they will probably give you the kind of specific information you need or tell you who else can.

A similar source for this information is the local office of the American Civil Liberties Union. In some states the ACLU has large state branches with full-time lobbyists, while in other states the branches are smaller and the lobbying done by part-time lobbyists or volunteers. In either case, the ACLU affiliate in your state should be able to give you useful information about the issue in your legislature. In any event, one of your first steps as a citizen-lobbyist on an issue involving individual freedom should be to contact your state ACLU affiliate, since it will undoubtedly be working on a lobbying program of its own on the issue and be able to help you maximize your own lobbying efforts.

Still another source for this kind of specific information may be those state legislators who you know agree with you on the issue. Once you learn who they are, you should inform them of your interest in the issue, ask for the specific information you need, and tell them you want to lobby against repressive laws. In all likelihood they will welcome your interest and provide as much help as they can.

In addition, there are several other organizations and associations dedicated to the fight against repressive laws in the various states. These organizations may not actually have offices or personnel in every state, but they probably will be familiar with the status of the issue in every state. For information and assistance about the issue in your state, you should feel free to contact these national groups. Their addresses are set forth in the appendices to this book.

On every controversial issue, many different bills will be introduced in every state legislature. Some of these bills will represent the most extreme points of view, while others will fall somewhere in between. To lobby most effectively against the passage of any repressive bill, it is essential first to determine which of the introduced bills are most likely to be considered seriously by the legislature and which are not.

How to make that determination will differ from state to state. In some states, the answer may be clear: The governor or the legislative leaders may introduce their own bills on the subject, and their political power may be such that those bills automatically become the serious ones. Similarly, in some states certain interest groups may be particularly powerful, so that any bills they support automatically become the serious ones. On the other hand, in some states it will be much more difficult to determine which are the most serious bills, and it may even be that the relevant committees will hold hearings on the issue and only then come up with the serious bill. To learn which are the serious bills in your state, you should contact the different sources mentioned above, and follow the issue in your local newspapers.

Once you identify the serious bills and learn what they provide, you should then become familiar with the major arguments for and against those bills. The most effective lobbyists must be able not only to support their own position but also to show why the contrary view should not be adopted. To be able to do this, lobbyists must know who their opponents are on the issue and what arguments they are using in support of their position.

In some cases it will be fairly easy to identify your opponents and their arguments, while in others it may be more difficult. As a rule, individuals and organizations who lobby on controversial issues do not do so secretly, and once you identify who they are you should feel free to ask them to give you their arguments and materials on the issue. In most cases they will cooperate, even if they know you are on the other side. However, when dealing with the opposition you should always be alert to the possibility of being misled, and you should never rely solely on what the other side says. Nevertheless, consulting the other side remains one of the best ways to learn as much as you can about their arguments and strategy and to prepare yourself to respond to them.

Whenever possible, you should address your lobbying efforts to the specific issues and bills that will be considered seriously by the legislature. If you are unable to pinpoint them, however, you should nevertheless lobby in favor of freedom and against all efforts to curtail that freedom. How to do that lobbying will be discussed in the following sections.

Know Your Lobbying Power

Although it is true that every citizen in every electoral district has the same voting power—his or her own vote—it does not follow that every citizen has the same political influence or lobbying power. In fact, quite the opposite is true. To be most effective, citizen-lobbyists must understand not only that they can have lobbying power far beyond their actual numbers or the popularity of their cause, but also how they can create and maximize that lobbying power.

All legislators who are considering running for reelection, or for other political office, must constantly be aware that every position they take, and every vote they cast, can potentially earn or lose them an unknown number of votes the next time they run. Because these legislators can never really know how many votes any given vote can mean, many successful lobbying forces make every effort to persuade those legislators that their votes on the issues most important to those forces will directly affect how their members will vote the next time they run for office.

The National Rifle Association, one of the most effective lobbying forces in Congress, is an excellent example. Its membership does not comprise a majority in any congressional district. But its influence wherever it has a substantial minority is large, because the members of Congress know that NRA members feel so passionately about gun control that they are likely to cast their ballots solely on the basis of their representatives' vote on that issue. There is no question that this emphasis on the importance of a single issue to a well-organized minority of voters can have a tremendous impact on all legislators.

In order to have this kind of lobbying power, it is essential that you organize others in your community to join with you in your lobbying efforts. For although every individual citizen can have some influence on his or her legislators, by banding together even a small minority of citizens can have a lobbying impact far beyond their actual numbers. Indeed, if such lobbying groups can be organized in your community, it becomes much less important that each member of the group be fully familiar with the legislature or the issue. If you can show your legislators that organized segments of their constituents feel very strongly on a particular issue—so strongly, in fact, that the legislators' votes on that issue will probably determine those constituents' votes at the next election—that will usually be enough to get your lobbying message across.

Organizing in the Community

Although we may not always be conscious of it, most of us belong to several different organizations and groups and know many people who belong to others. For example, many of us belong to unions or professional or business associations, PTAs and other school-related groups, fraternal and veterans' organizations, block associations and other community-betterment groups, and to a particular church or church-related group, and we all know others who belong to such groups. Many of these organizations take positions on public issues, and sometimes they even get actively involved in furthering that view. Often, however, these organizations will not take such steps unless they are specifically requested to do so, and then only after the issue has been fully considered and debated by the membership.

If you believe an organization you belong to might take a public position on an issue that concerns you, or if you know of other organizations that might do so, and if you believe that position would agree with yours, you should do everything you can to help that happen. Conversely, if you believe that position would disagree with yours, you should do everything you can to defeat it.

Every organization operates according to its own rules and procedures, and you should find out as early as possible what must be done to bring such an issue before your organization. It often happens that an organization—indeed, even a legislature—is unable to take action solely because required procedures were not followed. Once you learn these procedures and determine the best time to raise the issue, you should then take the necessary steps to have the issue considered by the organization. Before that actually happens, you should also make sure you are fully prepared to advocate your position, and that as many other members as possible who agree with you are present at the meeting and prepared to support that position. A sample resolution you might submit to your organization is provided in Part III of this book.

If you believe your organization is likely to adopt a contrary position, you should do everything you can to prevent it from doing so. Among the ways you can do this is to insist that all procedural rules be followed, be fully prepared to debate against the position, and make sure as many members as possible who agree with you are present at the meeting. Also, if your organization does take the opposite position, insist that the organization acknowledge that there was a minority view against that position. If possible, prepare a minority report and ask that it be announced by the organization at the same time it announces the majority's position. Sometimes a strong minority position from certain organizations can be even more effective than its majority position.

Another way you can organize in your community is to form a special group or committee solely on the issue. Suppose, for example, there are many people in your community who agree with you that discrimination based on sexual orientation should be declared illegal, and there is no organization or group to express or mobilize this view. In that case, and even if there are such groups in existence, it can be especially effective to form a special ad hoc group just to express this view and to lobby for it. It is usually fairly simple to form such a group, and its impact can be great. All you have to do is call a meeting on the issue (an announcement in your local newspaper, notices on community bulletin boards, and personal contacts are the best ways); invite as many people as you can who agree with your position, including public officials and other community leaders; establish certain minimum rules for the group; give it a name (for example, "The West Springdale Committee for Fair Play"); adopt your position on the issue; and then decide how to communicate that position most effectively to the legislature. (See the following sections for specific suggestions along these lines.) These committees can be formed without any significant effort or expense and yet can have a most important impact, especially on the legislators who represent the specific communities involved. A checklist for steps to be followed in forming such a community organization is contained in Part III of this book.

Still another way you can organize within your own community is to conduct petition-signing drives and to encourage others to express their views on the issue to their legislators. There are several ways to do this. First, you can go door-to-door in your community to discuss the issue, ask people to sign a petition (a sample petition is provided in Part III); and to write, call, or visit their legislators on it.

Second, you can go to meetings of various organizations and, without asking the organizations themselves to take action, ask the individual members who are there to do so. Third, you can place notices on your community bulletin boards (including those in stores and houses of worship), or in your local newspapers, expressing concern about the issue and advising people how they can communicate their own concern to the legislature. Each of these steps can also be accomplished without significant expense and can be extremely effective.

One final way you can help mobilize your community is to persuade the leaders of the community—public officials, businessmen, lawyers, doctors, clergymen, school officials, and librarians, among others—to speak out on the issue. These people are widely considered opinion-leaders and are often well known and respected by the local legislators, so that statements by them on controversial issues are often given considerable weight. Similarly, if you know members of the legislator's family, or people who are clients of or who do business with them, you should urge them to speak out on the issue, and to use their access to the legislator to persuade him or her to your view. In one classic case, when the New York State Assembly passed that state's first liberalized abortion law, the deciding vote was cast by a legislator who said he would not be able to face his family if he voted the other way.

Citizen-lobbyists should always be on the alert for ways to mobilize their community to take action on their issues and to exert as much lobbying pressure as possible on their local legislators. The suggestions set forth above, as well as others that can be derived from them, can be accomplished without undue difficulty or expense and really can change a vote.

What Is the Strategy?

In every legislature, both proponents and opponents of controversial bills will try to devise strategies to help their positions prevail. Usually, the legislators who are most closely identified with the issue, and who will lead the battle in the legislature for their side, will largely determine the strategy for that side, often in cooperation with the professional lobbyists directly associated with that position. Sometimes these strategies will be very detailed and carefully planned and carried out, while at others they may be much more generalized and undisciplined. And sometimes, of course, there may be several different strategies in effect at the same time, or none at all.

Whenever possible, citizen-lobbyists should be aware of the strategies on their side of the issue before they begin their lobbying efforts. Unfortunately, well-meaning lobbyists can often do their side more harm than good just because they are unaware of the strategy devised for that side.

There are many different kinds of strategies that may be employed in working for or against a bill. One of the most obvious is to try to create, and then emphasize, widespread public support for, or opposition to, the bill. Another strategy, especially where public opinion is likely to be aroused against your position, is to minimize the public's awareness of or concern about the bill. Still other strategies may be to mobilize public officials, civic leaders, and other prominent citizens to speak out on the bill, and to persuade powerful interest groups, like unions or trade associations, newspapers, and radio and television stations, to take public or editorial positions on it. Another technique may be to emphasize the bill's unworkability or cost or unconstitutionality, or the fact that it will have disastrous side effects not intended or desired by the bill's supporters.

Obviously, if such strategies have been devised, and if all citizen-lobbyists are aware of them, they can adapt their lobbying efforts accordingly and thus maximize their lobbying effectiveness. To learn what these strategies are and how you can most effectively work within them, you should contact the leading legislators and professional lobbyists on your side. They will usually be happy to tell you how you can be helpful on the issue.

In some cases you may determine that there are no particular strategies in effect on your side of the issue, or you may decide that you cannot go along with the strategies that have been devised. In those cases you should then be guided by your own judgment on the issue, together with the views of others you respect. However, you should not lightly disregard the strategies devised by the legislators and professional lobbyists on your side of the issue—in most cases, they are experts on the workings and foibles of your own legislature, and their strategies are based on that expertise. Nevertheless, if you feel strongly enough about it, you should always follow your own conscience and beliefs. If you do so, however, you should at least advise those legislators and lobbyists of your plans, so that your activities will not come as a complete surprise to them.

Using the Press

A crucial part of every lobbying effort is the coverage given the issue by the newspapers and radio and television stations within the state. On some issues, in fact, the nature and extent of that coverage can spell the difference between victory and defeat.

Sometimes legislators and professional lobbyists will try to get as much press coverage as they can on an issue, while at other times they may try to minimize that coverage. Or they may try to use the press as a part of their lobbying strategy, seeking to have the issue reported in the light most favorable to their point of view. At the same time, of course, the legislators and lobbyists on the other side of the issue will also be trying to use the press to their own advantage. And at all times the press itself will be aware of these strategies and will try not to be used by anybody.

Usually the press strategy for each side of an issue will be determined by the legislators and lobbyists who are deciding the overall strategy for that side. These people will designate the spokesmen who are authorized to discuss the issue with the press, and they will decide how they would like the press to cover the story. These people will also try to prepare or review all press releases and other public statements put out on their side of the issue, and decide when and where to hold press conferences or other press-oriented events.

In almost every case, of course, it is not really possible for these few people to control completely the press strategy for their side of the issue. Inevitably there will be other legislators or lobbyists, or other persons interested in the issue, who have their own ideas about press strategy or who may just want to see their own names or organizations mentioned in the papers. If these people insist on following their own press strategies, or if there is no one coherent strategy for a position, the result will often be confused and contradictory coverage, which can't possibly help the prospects for that position. Nevertheless, unless all the legislators and lobbyists on the same side can get together with respect to the press, there is probably nothing that can be done to prevent such a situation from happening.

In considering the role of a press strategy in any lobbying campaign, it is important to understand how the press functions in covering legislative issues. In most cases the reporters who cover the legislature are among the best in the state: sharp, experienced, and honest. It is their job to get to the essence of every important story and to report those stories as clearly and as fully as they can. And usually they do these jobs remarkably well, rarely being fooled or used in the process.

However, the very nature of these reporters' jobs necessarily prevents them from personally digging into or even covering every issue that comes before the legislature. Sometimes issues of overriding importance and news value—like a new state income tax or a new get-tough approach to crime, including perhaps the death penalty—will so dominate the reporters' time and available space that they will overlook most other issues. And sometimes an important issue may be hotly contested behind the scenes and yet not surface in a public way, with the result that the capitol reporters are not aware of it or do not realize its importance.

Because of these limitations, most reporters come to rely on certain sources and experts whom they know they can trust to give them accurate information and perspective on an issue. Of course, all legislators and lobbyists understand this, and they often try to become trusted sources for at least some of the reporters covering the legislature. If they do, they can usually expect that information they provide to their reporters will be reflected in the stories they write. However, they also know that if they mislead or take advantage of those reporters even once, they may never have access to them again. As a result, most experienced legislators and lobbyists will not lie about or otherwise seriously distort a story when dealing with the press, although they will try to put the story in the most favorable light.

Although the legislators and lobbyists directly responsible for the press strategy on their side of an issue will try to determine the nature and extent of the coverage given the issue from the legislature, citizen-lobbyists in their communities still have an important role to play with regard to their own local press. In fact, if they play that role effectively they can often have a greater impact than the pros at the legislature.

Probably the most traditional way citizens can use their local press on an issue is through the "Letters to the Editor" page. Such letters, especially if properly written, can accomplish at least four very important objectives. First, the letter can alert the community that the issue is before the legislature; second, it can persuade the reader to your position; third, it can make clear that there are responsible and articulate people in the community who share that position; and fourth, it can enlist others in your lobbying efforts. A sample "Letter to the Editor" is provided in Part III of this book.

In writing letters to the editor, as in all lobbying, several basic guidelines should always be borne in mind. Never—repeat never—lie about, distort, or even seriously exaggerate your arguments. If you do, the risk is great that your lie will be exposed and your credibility destroyed. Similarly, you should avoid personalizing an issue, so that you end up attacking the bill's sponsor, or supporters, instead of the bill itself. Such an approach is not persuasive and may well be offensive to the very people you are trying to win over. No matter how tempting it may be to do otherwise, you should always stick to the specific merits of the issue being discussed. In dealing with that issue you should be as forceful and persuasive as you can, using your best arguments and omitting your weakest, and citing as many specific examples, statistics, and facts as you can. Finally, your letter should be as clear and succinct as you can make it: Most papers have maximum word limits anyway, but it is always best to write the tightest letter you can.

A similar way to use the press is to submit longer "opinion" articles to them on the issue. More and more papers have adopted the so-called Op-Ed page, consisting of opinion articles by people not on the paper's staff, and if your paper has such a feature you should submit to it an article on your issue. In form and substance, such an article can simply be an extended version of a letter to the editor, with the same guidelines applying. Also, most radio and television stations have local talk shows and public-affairs programs dealing with current issues, and you should do everything you can—including calling and writing the stations—to have them devote some of these programs to your issue, especially if they will feature a prominent and articulate spokesman from your side.

Similarly, whenever a radio or television station takes an editorial position with which you disagree, they are required by law to allow opposing viewpoints to be aired through editorial replies. Whenever you disagree with a station's editorial position, you should make every effort to have your position expressed through such a reply. Likewise, many stations have phone-in programs in which people can express their views on such issues; you should also be sure your side is well represented on such programs.

A related way to generate press coverage on the issue is to write to the editors and columnists of your local papers, and the managers and broadcasters of your local radio and television stations, urging them to devote appropriate attention to it. Usually the people who decide what issues will be covered try to anticipate what the public is most interested in, and your letters will help them make that determination in your favor.

Another important way to generate press coverage for your side of an issue is to issue press releases or to hold press conferences to call attention to developments that you believe should be reported by the press. If you decide to do so, keep the following basic guidelines in mind.

First, most reporters—especially those who work for daily newspapers or radio and television news programs—usually work under constant deadline pressure, and they should never be interrupted or distracted from their work unless there are important reasons to do so. If reporters begin to feel that a particular lobbyist is likely to call for frivolous reasons, they may decide not to take any calls at all from that lobbyist. Similarly, if reporters come to believe that a particular lobbyist is likely to issue press releases or call press conferences without cause, they may decide to ignore all such releases and conferences.

As a result, citizen-lobbyists should always exercise restraint in seeking press attention for their cause. The most valuable asset any lobbyist can have is a reputation for reliability and credibility, and this is especially true when it comes to dealing with the press. If reporters know that when a lobbyist wants to talk or issues a release or calls a press conference there is a good chance that an important story may result, they are more likely to cooperate with the lobbyist and take him or her seriously.

A second, related guideline is that reporters are always most interested in uncovering "news," which means new developments that have not been announced or reported before. Lobbyists therefore should always try to have some news in any release they issue or press conference they call; they should never just restate old developments or positions in the guise of "breaking news."

A third basic guideline is that you should always be aware of the deadlines and schedules that all papers and broadcasts must meet. Except for the most important breaking news, the deadline for morning newspapers is usually sometime the previous afternoon, while the deadline for afternoon papers is sometime the previous evening. Similarly, the deadline for most radio and television news broadcasts is several hours before those programs go on the air. Most weekly papers and magazines have deadlines several days before they actually appear.

As soon as you think you may be issuing a press release, calling a press conference, or otherwise seeking press coverage, you should find out as much as you can about the deadlines and lead time of the papers and stations you are most interested in. The more time reporters have to consider and write their stories, the better that story is likely to be. By making sure you give these reporters sufficient time, you will also insure the best possible coverage for your story.

A fourth guideline, and one that is related to the third, is that you should always try to determine the best time for your story to appear, instead of just rushing to the press as soon as you think you have something worth reporting. In most cases you should try to arrange the timing of the story so that you receive the maximum possible coverage and reach the widest possible audience. For example, if another, more important story—especially one involving the legislature—is dominating the news, it would probably be a mistake to try to get your story in at the same time. Likewise, if a major holiday is coming up, during which a lot of people are likely to be out of town, it would probably be a mistake to have your story appear during that period. Also, most daily newspapers and most radio and television news programs have much smaller audiences on Saturdays than on any other day; as a result most professional public relations people avoid releasing news on Fridays whenever they can.

Similarly, you should always bear in mind the overall timing and strategy for your side of the issue in deciding when to seek coverage in your local press. If one of your goals is to awaken public interest in the issue and to encourage people to speak out and lobby on it, then try to time that coverage so that it neither appears too soon—for example, before the session begins, or before the specific legislative issues become clear—or too late—after the committee hearings have been held or after most of the lobbying has been completed. To be most effective, citizen-lobbyists should prepare a press schedule and strategy for their own local lobbying efforts so that they can be sure the major developments can be given to the press at the best possible times.

The final basic guideline that should always be remembered is the admonition we've seen before: Don't lie, distort, or unduly exaggerate your case. If you give your opposition the slightest opportunity to attack your credibility, you can be sure that opportunity will be exploited to the fullest.

Press Releases

By far the most common, and most effective, way to secure press coverage is through the issuance of press releases. Indeed, it is primarily through such releases that most "public" persons and groups—from the President of the United States to your local Chamber of Commerce or other community organization—communicate their news to the press.

The principal objective of a press release is to announce your news in a way that attracts the attention of the reporters you want to reach and provides them with the information they need to write good, complete stories reporting that news. As a rule, the better your press release, the better your coverage is likely to be. In most cases reporters will write their stories based almost entirely on your release, highlighting the same points emphasized in the release. In fact, in some cases the press may simply reproduce your release exactly as written. In any event, you should always prepare your release so that it tells your story precisely as you would like it to be reported.

Although there is no one right way to prepare a release, there are certain elements that all good releases should contain. Several sample press releases are provided in Part III of this book. As you will see, each of those samples contains the following features:

Release time. This establishes the official date and time that your news may be reported. For a variety of reasons, you may want to delay the appearance of your story to an hour or day after the issuance of the release. For example, your release may be ready on a Thursday but you may decide that the best time for your story to appear is in next Monday's papers. Or, and this is especially true if your local reporters are currently preoccupied with other issues, you may want to give those reporters an extra opportunity to study your release and prepare their stories. Normally you should not delay the release date more than a few days after you issue the release; if you do, the reporters may lose track of it in the flurry of other stories or some paper or station may break the release date and run the story earlier than you wanted, with the other papers then deciding not to use it at all because it might seem old news. In many cases, of course, you will not want to delay the appearance of the story at all, and in those cases you should designate your news "for immediate release." This means that the press can run their stories based on your release whenever they want to, including immediately after they receive it.

Headline. Most professionals who issue press releases use headlines to alert the press to the contents of the release. Here too, there is no right way to write such headlines; as long as they are brief and accurately reflect the essence of the release, they will serve their purpose.

The lead. Effective press releases, like effective news stories, set forth the most important ("newsworthy") part of the story in the opening sentences and paragraphs ("the lead"). In preparing your release, determine the most significant points and put them in your lead. If there are several points you consider equally important, summarize or list them all in your lead, and then return and discuss each of them separately in the body of your release. If the purpose of the release is to publicize a speech or testimony or other public statement, the lead should set forth the name of the person who made the statement, whom he or she was representing, the audience to whom the statement was made, and the most important points contained in the statement. The balance of the release could then set forth the entire statement.

The body. After you have set forth the most significant aspect of your story in the lead, the balance of the release should contain the remaining information of the story, including all relevant names and dates. However, your release should not include extraneous material—internal debates within your organization, plans that have not been formally decided on, or too much detail or analysis—that can only confuse and detract from the main purpose of the release. Press releases should be written as concisely as possible—your reporters may not have the time or patience to wade through extensive ones—and should rarely exceed two pages.

Contact. Every press release should contain the name of one or two people who can be contacted for further information about the story, with telephone numbers at which they can be reached. These people should be familiar with the issue and the lobbying efforts and strategy on your side of it, and, if possible, should be known to the reporters in your area. Reporters occasionally like to follow up a release in order to have something in their stories that the other reporters' stories won't have, and the contact persons should be prepared to deal with this possibility. In this connection, the contact persons should be especially careful not to say things to such reporters that would detract from the main point of the release.

Normally, you should make enough copies of your press release—photocopying is probably the most efficient way—so that every newspaper and radio and television station in your community gets a copy, as well as all reporters, columnists, and commentators whom you know or who you think might be interested in it. Your releases should be mailed or delivered so that they are received at the same time. If you have the time and if you don't think it would unduly interrupt or disturb them, you might call the city desks of your local papers or stations, or the reporters you know, to alert them that the release is on the way. If a newspaper or reporter knows in advance that a release is coming, they may include it in their plans for the next issue or at least keep a special lookout for it. Most papers and reporters receive many such releases every day, all competing for coverage, and you should certainly try to make sure yours is noticed and used.

In some cases you may decide not to announce your news through a general press release but instead to give one paper or reporter an exclusive on it. This means that only that paper or reporter would have the information necessary to report the story. Sometimes papers will promise extensive coverage for your news if they can report it exclusively, and in those instances you have to decide whether such coverage is preferable to the possibility of more widespread (but perhaps less extensive) coverage by all the local papers and news programs. If the paper or station offering the exclusive coverage reaches much of the audience you want to reach, such an arrangement can often be quite desirable for your purposes. In any event you should be aware of the possibility of such coverage, and even discuss it in general terms with friendly reporters to see if they would be interested in such an arrangement should the occasion arise.

Press Conferences

The second basic way to secure press coverage is through press conferences. Successful press conferences, however, are much more complicated, time-consuming, and risky than press releases, and most public relations professionals do not call them unless there are special circumstances that justify or require the extra time and effort.

Essentially, a press conference is a "live" press release, with the persons or groups announcing the news doing so in the presence of the reporters they wish to reach. Its chief advantages over press releases are that it provides radio and television stations with an event to cover in addition to the news contained in the release, and that it enables reporters to ask questions regarding the story and thus presumably get more information and a fuller understanding of it than they could from just a release. Its main disadvantages are that it requires careful planning and preparation, and even then you can never be sure the press will actually attend. Unlike a press release, which you know will get to every reporter, you always run the risk that the reporters you most want to reach will be unable (or not sufficiently interested) to attend your press conference, and if that happens you're clearly worse off than when you started: You wasted the time, effort, and expense involved in holding the conference, and you still haven't communicated your news to the press.

Press conferences are most appropriate when you have a major news development to announce—for example, the decision of your local chamber of commerce or similar civic group to reverse its earlier positions on a particular issue—or an important statement on the issue by one or more prominent citizens, whom you can expect the reporters will want to question at length and the radio and television stations to cover live. In such cases a press release really cannot convey the essence of the story and a full press conference is warranted. Except for such major events, however, you should resist calling press conferences and stick to issuing press releases.

If you do decide to hold a press conference, find a place that can accommodate all the people you expect and yet is convenient to the press—some possibilities are a local church, civic center, or school—and try to ensure that the time you pick does not conflict with other developments the reporters may have to cover. (One way to do this is simply to ask a friendly reporter.) Then, once you've set your time and place, give the reporters as much advance notice as you can; twenty-four hours is probably the minimum. In such notices tell the reporters enough about what will happen at the conference to make them want to come, without, however, revealing so much as to enable them to write their stories without actually coming. (A sample "press advisory" is provided in Part III.) In many cases, especially if a long statement is to be announced at the conference or if you are afraid the press won't attend, you should prepare full press releases as well, which can be distributed during or after the actual conference.

As with press releases, press conferences should be kept as brief and to the point as possible. Reporters always have many stories to cover and write, as well as ever-present deadlines to meet, and you should never detain them longer than is necessary to get your story across. And, of course, you should always give them ample opportunity to ask whatever questions they may have. You should not, however, let yourself be goaded or boxed into making statements that you did not intend to make, no matter how hard the reporters try. Remember, you called the conference to announce your news, and there is no reason to let reporters (or anyone else) take it over. You should also be careful that your opposition does not crash your conference and steal your thunder and publicity; such attempts are often made and are frequently successful.

Manufacturing News

As a rule you should issue press releases, or call press conferences, only if what you want to announce qualifies as "news," not merely to restate old developments that may or may not have been reported before. However, even if you do not have any real news to report, but would still like publicity on your side of the issue, there are various ways to manufacture news to get such publicity.

First, of course, you should be aware of what actually qualifies as news. Depending in large part on the size of your community and the amount of space available in your local papers and news broadcasts, the following may all be considered worth reporting: the formation of a local committee to lobby on the issue; the adoption of a resolution or position by a local organization; a visit by a group of local citizens to their legislators, especially if they go to the state capital to do so; the holding of a public debate or forum; the conducting of a petition-signing or letter-writing drive; and the giving of testimony to a legislative committee or the issuance of other public statements on the issue. If you think your local papers or news broadcasts might cover these events, by all means put out press releases or otherwise publicly announce them: You may just find that it was a slow news day, and that your story was the big news of the day.

But what if you don't have any such real news to announce? There still may be ways to get into the papers and on the air.

One of the easiest is to respond quickly and forcefully to the news of others on the issue. The press loves controversy, and it will almost always cover a person or group that heightens the controversial nature of a story. Let's suppose, for example, that your opposition has just won a preliminary skirmish in committee, or that it has just announced the introduction of a new bill or the formation of a new group on the issue. Normally, your opposition would get all the coverage based on these developments. But let's also suppose that as soon as you hear of these developments, or of your opposition's public statements about them, you issue a strongly worded response challenging or minimizing their significance. The chances are—if only to foster the controversy—the press will include your response in its coverage of those developments, and maybe even give it a major share of that coverage. In any event, it is certainly worth the try. On the other hand, if you believe your opposition's news will not be covered, or if so only slightly, then you should probably not respond at all, since any response you make could well result in increasing the coverage given to your opposition.

A second way to manufacture news is to issue a challenge to your opposition, either to participate in a debate or other public forum or merely to respond publicly to a set of questions or statements you have prepared. The very idea of such a challenge—carrying with it notions of conflict and controversy—may well generate some good press coverage and can also serve to put your opposition on the defensive.

Still another way to manufacture news is to grant an award or issue a proclamation hailing the contribution of a prominent legislator or local citizen on your side of the issue. Such awards or proclamations can be put together at a nominal expense and can often generate good press coverage. In fact, if time and resources permit you might even base a testimonial dinner or cocktail party on that award or proclamation and raise some money for your cause as well.

One final way to manufacture news is to announce the formation of new committees or subcommittees to lobby on the issue or to announce the addition of certain prominent citizens to your cause. A common tactic used by candidates running for office is to space out their endorsements from public figures to maximize the press coverage such endorsements receive and to create the appearance of a bandwagon or ground swell for those candidates. This tactic can work just as well for a lobbying position on a controversial issue. (Sample press releases for all the above kinds of news are contained in Part III.)

Working with the Press

In one sense, at least, the lobbyist and the reporter have a common goal: communicating to the public the essence and meaning of the lobbyist's news and activities. In that sense, the lobbyist and reporter usually work together to accomplish that goal. In another sense, however, the two are also adversaries, with the lobbyist trying to manipulate the coverage on the issue while the reporter is trying to see through such efforts and uncover and report the whole true story. In that sense the two will inevitably disagree from time to time about the way a particular story was covered, or about the fact that a story wasn't covered at all.

It is important for all lobbyists, including citizen-lobbyists, to develop strong personal relationships, based on mutual trust and respect, with the reporters they must deal with. When such a relationship can be established it will obviously be easier to work together to accomplish your common goal and to express whatever complaints or disagreements you may have. If you have such complaints, and if they are well-founded, tell them to the reporters involved. Chances are they will take those complaints seriously and be more careful the next time. But never treat reporters as though they owed you coverage or otherwise have to explain themselves to you—the result may just be that you'll get no coverage at all. On the other hand, if you work with the press on a responsible level you will almost certainly get your fair share of coverage, which, after all, is exactly the way it should be.

Lobbying the Committees

One of the most crucial parts of the whole legislative process is the consideration of controversial issues and bills by the various legislative committees. It is at this stage that the fate of an issue or bill is frequently determined, and it is therefore at this stage that all lobbyists, including citizen-lobbyists, must devote a considerable portion of their lobbying time and effort. As soon as the legislative session opens, and the relevant bills are introduced and assigned to committees, those lobbying efforts should begin.

To effectively lobby the committee, it is most important to learn as much as you can about it and its members. Who is the chairperson? How powerful is he or she? What is his or her position likely to be on the issue? Who are the committee members? What parts of the state do they represent? Have they expressed opinions on the issue? What are the committee's procedures? Will there be public hearings? Who are the committee's counsel and other staff aides? What are their positions likely to be on the issue?

Some of the answers to these questions will probably be found in the official guides or directories put out by the legislature, but others may take some digging. The leading legislators and professional lobbyists on your side of the issue should be able to give you most of the answers, and the office of the committee chairperson or counsel should also prove helpful. Even those legislators and lobbyists on the other side will probably cooperate if you need specific information and assistance.

Once you have found the answers to those questions, you should map out a specific timetable and strategy for your lobbying efforts. You should decide which members of the committee to concentrate your efforts on, what kinds of arguments or approaches will prove most effective on them, how you can most effectively reach them, and who else you should enlist in your lobbying efforts. If any of your own local legislators are members of the committee—especially if they are on the other side of the issue—you should concentrate your efforts on them. But if no local legislator is on the committee, or if those who are are safely on your side, you must then decide how else to proceed. Since you will probably have only a limited time to devote to your lobbying efforts, it will soon become necessary to make some hard decisions regarding what you can and cannot try to do in that time. How you make that decision must ultimately depend on the needs and circumstances of your own legislature at the time.

As soon as you can discover the preliminary position of each member of the committee on the issue, and the leading or most committed members on each side, you can then determine the likeliest targets for your lobbying efforts. If your time is especially limited, in most cases it would be a waste of time to concentrate your efforts on those members who are the most committed to their present positions. For although it is always possible to change their minds, and although it is always useful to let them know that there are people who strongly approve or disapprove of their positions, practical considerations dictate that they are the least appropriate targets for grass-roots lobbying efforts. Instead, in most cases you should concentrate your efforts on those members who are the least committed, or who claim to be neutral or to be keeping an open mind.

These are the members who usually determine the outcome of most close and controversial issues and who are most susceptible to all forms of lobbying. Nevertheless, you should not ignore completely those members who are the most committed: At the very least you should tell those on your side that you support and appreciate their position, and you should tell those on the other side that you strongly disapprove. Such communications may not change anything, but they certainly can't hurt either.

Whenever possible, the lobbying effort addressed to particular members of the committee should come—or at least appear to come—from their own legislative districts. All legislators are most concerned about and responsive to the views of their own constituents, and they are most likely to be affected by a lobbying campaign that seems homegrown. If none of the target members represent your own community, try to locate people in the districts they do represent who agree with you on the issue and work with them to lobby those members. Beyond question the most effective lobbyists are those who are knowledgeable about the issue, who are lobbying their own legislators, and who can mobilize others in their communities to do so.

There are several different ways to communicate with—to lobby—individual legislators, and each can be used to maximize your lobbying effectiveness. Some will obviously be more effective in some states or localities than others, and some may be impossible for one reason or another. Some of the most effective are:

Visits with Legislators

One of the best ways to communicate your views to your legislators is through face-to-face visits with them. Most legislators maintain offices within their districts, and many have regular office hours during which they make themselves available to their constituents. If you are firm (and, if necessary, persistent) in requesting an appointment, you will almost certainly get the opportunity to meet with your legislators in their district offices.

In addition, in most (but not all) states, legislators have offices in or near the state capitol building, and they also meet with constituents there. However, because of the unpredictable nature of most legislatures, with daily sessions, committee meetings, and party caucuses often scheduled on short notice, it is usually difficult to get firm appointments with legislators at the capitol. Nevertheless, if legislators know that constituents have traveled to the capital to meet with them, they will usually find some way—even if it means coming off the floor of the legislature or leaving a committee or party meeting—to do so. If you plan to visit your legislators at the capital—and such a trip is highly recommended as an effective lobbying tool—be sure to let them know in advance, and keep after them or their staffs once you get there.

If you are planning to visit your legislators, whether at their district offices or in the capital, there are several guidelines to bear in mind. First, be sure you know not only what the issues are, but also what you want your legislator to do about them. If the strategy on your side of the issue is to kill the bad bills in the committee, you should lobby your legislator accordingly. If the strategy is to press for a more acceptable compromise bill, urge that course. And if—and this is always possible—the strategy is to delay the issue from coming to an early vote, in the hope of killing the bill or at least forcing a better compromise later in the session, try to persuade your legislator to the wisdom of that course. Whatever the strategy, you should know exactly what you want from your legislators, so that they can know it too.

Second, be as firm and tough as you can in discussing the issue with your legislators, but don't try to force them into changing their positions or committing themselves if they clearly do not want to. Also, don't threaten them with any kind of reprisal—including voting them out of office—if they don't vote your way. Most legislators like to think they are immune from overt pressure and threats, and they may even decide to vote the other way just to prove it. Besides, the very fact that you are there pressing your views on them will usually be enough to tell them that *your* votes the next time they run may well depend upon *their* votes on this issue. If there have been petition drives in your community, such visits are the perfect time to present those petitions to your legislators. Especially if the signatures all come from their own districts, the legislators are bound to take them, and you, most seriously.

Third, always be courteous in dealing with your legislators, and never let your disagreement or displeasure with them lead to harsh or personal remarks. Further, although it is obviously important to get your own views across, it is also important to let your legislators have their say, and you should never prevent them from doing so. If you lose your temper or prevent them from speaking, they will feel justified in branding you a kook or crackpot and in disregarding everything you've said. Also, most legislators would never let it appear that they changed their minds or committed themselves on an issue just because a few constituents asked them to, and it may well be that you are having a greater impact on them than their responses to you indicate. Losing your temper, indulging in name-calling, or making threats won't contribute to that impact.

Finally, it is usually best to visit your legislators in small groups— five or six is probably the maximum—and to keep your visits as brief as you can. Larger groups tend to become unruly, especially if not everyone gets a chance to speak, and the legislators may find that they are able to play some of the members of the group off against others. On the other hand, going alone or with just one other person may also be unsatisfactory: The legislators may try to outtalk you, or you may find that you have reached an impasse too quickly. Visits by groups of from three to six can usually be kept under control and yet present a sufficient variety of people and points of view to keep the discussion moving along productively. However, even though six people may be the maximum for a visit, you should always try to convey the impression that these six are merely representative of many more. If each of the six represents a different organization or group, for example, their potential electoral power will maximize your lobbying impact on the legislators you are visiting. Unless you have something very new or different to say, you should probably not visit the same legislators more than once or twice on the same issue, but you should help as many others as you can to do so. Such face-to-face visits may be the single most effective grass-roots lobbying tool available.

Letters

A second effective way to lobby individual legislators, especially at the committee stage, is to mobilize their constituents (and others) to write strong letters on the issue. As members of a committee, legislators are far more conspicuous than simply as members of the whole legislature, and they are therefore more likely to be sensitive to the expressed views of their constituents on any given issue. Also, as members of a committee, legislators usually believe their roles and responsibilities are more statewide than usual—at least as compared with just representing their own districts—and they are thus more likely than usual to respond to the views of people outside their districts. Accordingly, all members of the committee, and especially those you most want to keep or win over, should receive a constant barrage of letters, telegrams, and other written communications from their own constituents and others, all preferably sounding self-initiated and strongly motivated. Sample letters are contained in Part III.

As with personal visits to your legislators, several guidelines should be remembered in writing such letters. First, if you are a constituent, say so, preferably in your first sentence, and if you supported or voted for the legislator, say that too. (If neither, say nothing on those subjects.) Second, make clear what your position is and what you would like your legislator to do. (See discussion above.) Whenever possible, refer to specific bills and not just general issues. Third, if you are working with others on this issue, or if you are otherwise active in the community, say this too. However, don't say you belong to specific political or lobbying organizations, like a political party or the ACLU, since that may detract from the apparent spontaneity and effectiveness of your letter. Finally, keep such letters brief, and don't threaten or otherwise abuse the legislator.

The main purpose of such letters is to tell these legislators that their constituents are watching them on the issue and have strong feelings on it. These letters are not necessarily designed to persuade them to vote your way. But if the legislators receive enough sincere letters from constituents expressing firm views on the issue, the threat to their political futures will be clear enough.

Calls

Another way to communicate your views to your legislators is to call them at their offices and convey your message. In many cases you may not be able to speak with them directly, but in any event you should make clear to whomever you speak with that you are a constituent and that you want him or her to vote your way in committee. These messages will usually be relayed to the legislator, and they can only add to the overall impact of your lobbying effort. Here, too, however, remember: Identify yourself, be specific and brief, but don't be abusive and don't threaten.

Testimony

If the committee will be holding hearings on the issue and if members of the general public are permitted to testify, it is particularly appropriate and effective for citizen-lobbyists to make sure they are heard. At these hearings many legislators and other public officials, and professional lobbyists, are certain to testify, but it is not always certain that ordinary citizens will also be heard. Because those other, professional witnesses may all be somewhat predictable in what they have to say, it may well be that the citizen-lobbyists will be the most significant and persuasive witnesses of all.

As soon as you learn of the hearings and decide to testify, make sure you are placed on the witness list. Usually this can be done by calling or writing the office of the committee chairperson. Also, if at all possible, try to be given a specific time at which you will testify—otherwise you may find yourself waiting around all day never knowing when you may be called.

In preparing your testimony, don't try to be more of an expert than you actually are, and don't make arguments or assertions you are not prepared to prove and defend. For example, unless you are an expert on the Constitution, don't stress in your testimony that the bill under consideration is unconstitutional. Instead, emphasize what you are, in fact, an expert on: the views and feelings of an ordinary citizen who believes in individual freedom. Especially if other witnesses decry what they consider to be the "dangerous" or "immoral" nature of your position, but even if they don't, it will be particularly effective for you as an ordinary citizen to make clear that even though you may not personally be directly affected by the legislation in question, the risks and results of governmental restraints on freedom are inevitably worse.

Second, answer any questions from the committee as honestly as you can, but if you don't have an answer, say so. Third, bring with you enough copies of your testimony for each member of the committee and its staff, and also for the members of the press and others who may be attending the hearings. Finally, don't be nervous—if only for their own political interests, the committee members will do everything they can to make your appearance as comfortable and easy as they can. And try to enjoy the experience: It can and should be a most exciting and rewarding one.

The steps outlined above for lobbying the committees—if carried out in good faith and with common sense—can prove most effective in

influencing the course of legislation on a controversial issue. And, even
if your side does not succeed in committee, all is not lost: There is still
the legislature as a whole to be lobbied and won over.

Lobbying the Legislature

Let's now assume the appropriate committees have held their hearings
and taken their votes and that a bill you support, or oppose, has been
reported favorably to the full house. The next step in the legislative
process—and obviously the most crucial—is the consideration of the
bill by the legislature as a whole. Here too, the citizen-lobbyist has an
important role to play.

The various steps discussed in the previous section for lobbying the
committees are equally applicable to lobbying the legislature as a
whole. Indeed—for those legislators who are not on the committees—
such visits, letters, and calls are absolutely essential if you want them
to vote your way on the issue. The specific suggestions and guidelines
included in that discussion are just as relevant to lobbying the whole
legislature.

In addition to those specific lobbying suggestions, there are several
other lobbying possibilities you might consider. In each case, however,
there may be good reasons not to try them.

One such possibility is to organize a mass gathering of people from
all parts of the state at the capitol to lobby on the issue. Usually such
events include mass rallies in or near the capitol, with speeches and
pep talks from legislative and other leaders on your side, the group
then dispersing to visit and lobby their individual legislators and perhaps other pivotal legislators and the governor. Such an event, if carefully planned and successfully carried out, can create the impression
that an overwhelming number of people support your side of the issue,
and it can make a significant impression on undecided or wavering
legislators. However, such events can also be very risky, and can prove
seriously counterproductive to your cause. First, there is the risk that
the event may fail—that only a small number of people will turn out—
with the result that it will appear that there is actually very little public
support for your position. Secondly, even if your rally is successful and
you attract more people than you expected, you still run the risk that
the opposition will top you and produce even larger rallies for their
position. If they do, they may well convey the impression that far more

people actually support their position than yours. Finally, such events, to be successful, usually require extensive planning and at least some expense—particularly for buses to transport people to and from the capital—so unless you are sure the risks are worth taking you should probably avoid them.

If you decide against such a mass rally, you may decide that a smaller, more regionally oriented gathering would be worth trying. In this way you can attempt to bring large groups of people from just one part of the state to the capital to lobby their legislators, without the mass public rallies and their attendant risks. Such regional efforts will usually be played up in the local press, and they will certainly be felt by the local legislators. Here too, however, careful planning and some expense are required, and again you run the risk of being upstaged by your opposition. Nevertheless, such efforts may be easier to carry off successfully and you may decide that those risks are worth taking.

Another lobbying possibility you might consider—especially if you were dissatisfied by the hearings held by the committees, or if the committees did not hold hearings—is to conduct such hearings yourself. Particularly if sympathetic legislators and other officials and prominent citizens cooperate, and if there is appropriate press coverage (as there probably will be), such unofficial hearings can often be extremely effective in getting your views across to the legislature and the public. Again, though, careful planning is required, and you should probably not try to hold such hearings unless you are reasonably sure they will be successful.

Still another lobbying possibility, but one that should be used only rarely, is to maintain picket lines in front of the capitol to call attention to the issue and to get your message across. In most cases such picket lines tend to be ignored, if not ridiculed. But on occasion they can serve to remind the legislature—and the public—that an important issue is being considered and that some people feel strongly about it. Such tactics, however, should probably be used only if you feel the public is being excluded completely from the legislative development of the issue and that this is the best way to publicize what is actually happening.

In some states committees will hold hearings and vote on a major issue early in the session, so that the issue can be considered by the full houses during the balance of the session. In other states committees may not act until late in the session, with the full houses having only a very short time to consider the bills. In the former states, citizen-lobbyists can and should concentrate their lobbying efforts first on the committee and then on the legislature as a whole. In the latter states, however, the lobbyists may not have that luxury, and will have to lobby the committee and the whole legislature at the same time. Lobbying timing and strategy will vary from state to state, and here, as elsewhere, the legislators and professional lobbyists on your side of the issue should be able to help you decide how you can most effectively use your lobbying time and effort.

Lobbying the Governor

Let's now assume a bill you support, or oppose, has been passed by both houses of the legislature. That bill must still be signed by the governor before it becomes law (except in North Carolina). In every state, on almost any issue, the governor's signature should never be taken for granted, and this is particularly true for most highly controversial issues. Especially on such issues, citizen-lobbyists still have an important job to do.

In some states the governor maintains regular office hours, or is otherwise accessible to the public, while in other states it is virtually impossible to get to see him or her. Similarly, on some issues certain governors will go out of their way to solicit the views of the public, while on other issues the governor may not seem the least bit interested in such views. How best to lobby your governor on your issue will depend largely on what kind of governor he or she is, especially with regard to that issue. Nevertheless, in most cases the most effective lobbying devices are still those we've seen before for lobbying the committees and the legislature, and particularly the personal visits (either with the governor or with his or her staff), letters, and calls.

Unlike members of the legislature, governors are elected by, and are answerable to, all of the people of their state, and they usually feel less bound by local sentiment on an issue in any particular community than do individual legislators. In lobbying the governor, accordingly, it is important that people from all parts of the state be heard from, even if their local legislators voted the other way.

In lobbying the governor, also, it is especially important that as many groups and organizations—unions, PTAs, church and professional associations, libraries, and other civic and good-government groups—as possible submit letters or memoranda on your side of the issue. The governor is usually far more responsive to such groups and officials than are most individual legislators. This is especially true if those groups and officials have special expertise or experience on the issue. If you have any influence with such groups or officials, by all means urge them to lobby the governor on the bill.

Similarly, most governors are sensitive to the editorial positions of the major newspapers and radio and television stations across the state. Frequently such papers or stations will take positions on issues when they are before the governor even though they did not do so when the issue was in the legislature, and even more frequently they will reiterate earlier positions at that time. In either event, you should do everything you can to have your local papers and stations speak out on the issue on your side when the bill is before the governor.

Normally, mass rallies or other major events designed to attract attention to or mobilize support for an issue are not appropriate or feasible in lobbying the governor, but from time to time exceptional circumstances may justify such efforts. If you feel such events might be appropriate in your state, discuss them with the legislators and professional lobbyists on your side. But remember, such events always require careful planning and entail definite risks.

In all lobbying, you should always be on the alert for ways in your community and state to get your message across, and you should always be ready to adapt and revise the suggestions made in this book to your local needs and circumstances. By becoming active in a lobbying effort in your community you will provide the best possible proof of the genius of our democracy, and you will make a real contribution to the most important element of that democracy: individual freedom.

PART II

Lobbying for Specific Freedoms

1 / REPRODUCTIVE FREEDOM
by Janet Benshoof

No issue today is as hotly contested in the state and federal legislatures as is the right to an abortion. The Supreme Court abortion decisions of 1973 clearly declared that the right to choose abortion is part of our constitutional right to privacy, but this did not end the controversy. Although public opinion polls consistently show that the majority of Americans believe most abortions should be legal, powerful minority forces have influenced legislators to vote for legislation that would considerably weaken our existing right to decide whether and when to bear children.

Furthermore, the 1980 elections brought a President, a Republican party platform, and many new members of Congress all expressing support for a so-called "Human Life" amendment to the United States Constitution, an amendment that would make abortion a crime and give fertilized eggs more constitutional rights than now exist for human beings. Such an amendment would permit a degree of governmental interference in the lives of women and their families unprecedented in this country.

Although the term "reproductive freedom" brings to mind abortion, our constitutional right to privacy protects much more than the right to decide whether or not to have an abortion. It protects the freedom to make other kinds of important decisions as well, including those involving contraception and sterilization. What is ultimately at stake when these rights are threatened is our fundamental right to individual autonomy and freedom—the right to be let alone, which the Bill of Rights was designed to protect and promote.

The framers of the Constitution believed it was necessary to limit the power of government in order to protect individual rights. The Bill of Rights was intended to counteract the impulses of special interests and passions that might momentarily control the legislative or executive branches of government. In fighting to preserve our reproductive freedoms, it is important to remember that a government that is allowed today to exceed its constitutional limits and compel pregnancy would also have the power to compel abortion in the future. Protecting privacy rights ensures that all people are able to make personal decisions compatible with their own needs and beliefs.

Although the Supreme Court decisions in *Roe v. Wade* and *Doe v. Bolton* in 1973 established that the right to decide whether or not to bear children is protected by our Constitution, Congress and the states have been attempting to chip away at this right by passing various kinds of restrictive laws. Many of these laws have been declared unconstitutional by the courts, including the Supreme Court, yet it is critical that all persons concerned about preserving our privacy rights lobby against the passage of such laws. It is a mistake to depend exclusively on our judicial system to repeatedly strike down unconstitutional legislation.

This is because, first, our courts themselves are not completely immune to political pressure; recent political appointments have altered the Supreme Court and President Reagan's Attorney General, William French Smith, has repeatedly attacked the courts and even suggested that they should follow the election returns. Bills have also been introduced in Congress that would remove jurisdiction from the federal courts even to hear cases dealing with abortion. While these bills themselves may be unconstitutional, they have helped create a political climate intended to inhibit courts from giving vigorous protection to our constitutional rights, and there are signs that the Supreme Court has, indeed, been less vigorous.

The second reason it is urgent to lobby against such laws is that Congress often looks to the state legislatures as political barometers.

Members of Congress who see that their state legislatures are passing anti-abortion legislation are more likely to vote for federal anti-abortion legislation, such as a "Human Life" amendment or a restrictive Medicaid bill. The defeat of these bills in the state legislatures are signals that voting to preserve our constitutional rights is not a political liability.

This chapter is designed to provide background information for those persons who are lobbying on reproductive privacy issues at the state and local levels. The first section reviews the development of the law, including the right to privacy in the Constitution, its scope and meaning, the history of abortion laws, the Supreme Court decisions of 1973, and subsequent Supreme Court decisions which have further defined the constitutional limitations that state and federal legislation must follow.

The second section details the specific types of legislation that are being introduced in the state legislatures and local governing bodies. It discusses whether such laws are constitutional and describes some of the legal, medical, and social arguments that may be used against those laws which do interfere with our constitutional rights. It also covers laws on sterilization and the mentally retarded.

The third section discusses the campaign to have a "Human Life" amendment added to the Constitution, including the attempt by state legislatures to require Congress to convene a constitutional convention for the purpose of adopting such an amendment and why such a convention poses an unprecedented danger to our entire Bill of Rights. This part also explains how a "Human Life" amendment to the Constitution would not stop abortions but would instead create greater legal and medical problems in this area than ever before.

ABORTION: A CONSTITUTIONAL RIGHT

Opponents of the right to abortion are putting intense political pressure on state legislatures and local government bodies to impose governmental restrictions on the availability of abortions. Because such legislation interferes with intensely personal decisions involving procreation, childbirth, and the family unit, it violates our fundamental right to privacy as guaranteed by the United States Constitution.

This right to be free from governmental interference in making

certain decisions is not a "new" right, nor is it a right any less fundamental than our First Amendment right to free speech and religious
liberty or our Fourth Amendment right to be secure in the privacy of
our own homes from unwarranted government searches. But because
the word "privacy" does not explicitly appear in the Bill of Rights, the
right to privacy is less well defined than other rights and less understood as critical to our form of government. As a result, anti-abortion
activists try to portray the Supreme Court decisions on abortion as an
aberration in constitutional law rather than as the logical and inevitable
corollary of other Supreme Court decisions on privacy.

In lobbying to protect our privacy rights from unjustified governmental interference, it is essential to understand the basis and scope of
the right to privacy and how the 1973 abortion decisions flow from that
right.

The Right to Privacy

The Bill of Rights guarantees certain rights to individuals. However, its
enumeration of rights is not complete, nor was it intended to be by its
framers. The Constitution would not have been ratified without the
promise that a Bill of Rights would be adopted, even though some of
the framers considered such rights obvious and implicit in the Constitution itself and believed that additional guarantees were unnecessary.
But others considered it imperative that the Constitution include explicit legal limits on the power of the government, and their view
prevailed.

The proponents of a Bill of Rights, however, wanted to ensure that
the listing of several explicit rights would never be taken to imply the
exclusion of other rights. Accordingly, they added the Ninth Amendment: "The enumeration in the Constitution of certain rights shall not
be construed to deny or disparage others retained by the people."
Therefore, although the Constitution nowhere mentions a "right to
privacy" in those words, or a "right to marry," or a "right to raise one's
children," these rights, as well as procreative rights, are considered
fundamental. In fact, in 1974, when Congress passed a Privacy Act, it
specifically found that privacy is a personal and fundamental right
protected by the Constitution. Indeed, as early as 1891, the Supreme
Court recognized that a guarantee of privacy exists under the
Constitution:

No right is held more sacred or is more carefully guarded by the common law than the right of every individual to the possession and control of his own person free from all restraint or interference of others unless by clear and unquestioned authority of law.

The Supreme Court's most comprehensive definition of the right to privacy came in a unanimous decision in *Whalen v. Roe* in 1977. The Court there described the right as involving two kinds of interests, "the individual interest in avoiding disclosure of personal matters," and "the interest in independence in making certain kinds of important decisions." Of course, some cases—particularly abortion cases—involve both kinds of privacy. However, it is the second type of privacy interests that underlie the Court's rulings in the 1973 abortion cases and that form the basis for earlier privacy decisions involving marriage, procreation, contraception, family relationships, childrearing, and education. This right to privacy—basically, a right to personal autonomy—has been found by the Supreme Court in the Fourteenth Amendment's guarantee that individuals may not be deprived of "liberty" by the government without "due process of law."

The importance of an individual's control over reproductive matters was first recognized by the Supreme Court in 1942, when the Court invalidated an Oklahoma statute that mandated sterilization of certain felons. This concept was further developed in 1965 in *Griswold v. Connecticut* when the Court struck down a Connecticut law that prohibited the use of contraceptives even by married persons, declaring that the state could not interfere with "a relationship lying within the zone of privacy . . ." In 1972, in *Eisenstadt v. Baird,* the Court went one step further and struck down a Massachusetts law forbidding distribution of contraceptives to unmarried persons. The Court made clear that the right to use contraceptives was part of the individual's right of privacy:

If the right of privacy means anything, it is the right of the individual, married or single, to be free from unwarranted governmental intrusion into matters so fundamentally affecting a person as the decision whether to bear or beget a child.

The right of individuals to be free from governmental interference in making basic decisions about their lives was very much on the minds of the framers of our Constitution. The constitutional right to privacy, keeping the government out of our personal lives, has been recognized by the Supreme Court for over ninety years. The right to choose abortion is not a constitutional aberration but necessarily flows from these other privacy decisions.

The Legal Status of Abortion Prior to 1973

In order to appreciate the impact of the 1973 abortion decisions, it is important to understand the history of abortion laws in the United States prior to that year.

That history makes clear that abortion was never equated with murder, nor were prohibitions initially enacted because of a belief that fetal life was the equivalent of human life. Before 1800, abortions prior to "quickening" (the first feeling by the woman of fetal movement) were not considered crimes, which was also the case under English common law. In fact, there was considerable compassion for the woman involved.

Between 1821 and 1841, the first laws were passed that dealt specifically with abortion. Connecticut was the first state to enact an abortion law; it made abortion by violent purges illegal after quickening. It punished not the woman, but the person who provided the abortifacient. This was followed by similar laws in ten other states. In 1830, New York was the first state to make an explicit exception on behalf of the woman's health in its abortion law.

From 1840 to 1880 there was a great increase in the adoption of state abortion laws. Several factors contributed to this. Abortion had become more visible as a result of advertising of abortion services and press coverage of a few sensational trials involving botched abortions. The number of abortions was increasing, and the type of woman choosing abortion had changed: Abortion was increasingly chosen by white, married, Protestant, native-born, middle- and upper-class women. Finally, physicians for whom the Hippocratic Oath precluded the performance of abortions wanted to stop non-physicians, particularly midwives, from practicing medicine and, in particular, from performing abortions.

The first law prohibiting abortion was passed in Massachusetts in

1845. Soon after, in New York, the first law was passed which made the woman herself liable to punishment. By 1900, almost every state had made abortion illegal. Even as late as 1960, forty-four states allowed abortion only if the life of the pregnant woman would be endangered if the pregnancy were carried to term.

By the late 1960s and early 1970s, however, the political movement to decriminalize abortion was rapidly gaining ground. This was due to several factors: concern over overpopulation and for the quality of life, the growing political consciousness of women, the expanding legal doctrine of equal rights, medical data on the relative safety of abortion, the anti-poverty movement, the fact that most physicians no longer actively opposed abortion, and, perhaps most significant of all, the increasing number of women who continued to seek and have abortions even though it was unlawful. In 1967, Colorado became the first state to pass an abortion reform bill. Thought at the time to be quite liberal, it permitted abortion for physical or mental health reasons as well as for fetal defects or because the pregnancy resulted from rape or incest. By 1972, twelve more states had adopted similar reform laws and four had repealed their abortion laws altogether, permitting abortion whenever a woman and her doctor felt it was necessary.

The 1973 Abortion Decisions

On January 22, 1973, the Supreme Court, by a seven to two majority, ruled that a Texas criminal abortion law and portions of a Georgia abortion law were unconstitutional on the ground that they violated a woman's constitutional right to privacy. These cases, *Roe v. Wade* and *Doe v. Bolton,* also established a standard of review for courts to use when adjudging the constitutionality of abortion regulations. It is important to examine these cases in some detail because it is against the principles set forth in them that the constitutionality of legislation in this area is measured.

In *Roe v. Wade,* the Court struck down a Texas statute that prohibited abortion except when necessary to save the life of the woman. Justice Blackmun wrote the opinion of the Court:

This right of privacy, whether it be founded in the Fourteenth Amendment's concept of personal liberty and restrictions against state action, as we feel it is, or, as the District Court determined, in the Ninth Amendment's reservation of rights to the people, is broad enough to encompass a woman's decision whether or not to terminate her pregnancy.

However, the Court further held that the right to decide to have an abortion "is not unqualified and must be considered against important state interests in regulation." The Court ruled that the State *may*, but is not required to, regulate abortions in certain specified ways. The Court held that legitimate state interests that may be promoted by appropriate state or federal legislation are an interest in medical standards, an interest in maternal health, and an interest in potential human life.

These interests were deemed by the Court to become "compelling," enabling the State to regulate to promote them, at different points in the pregnancy. Those points are:

1. For the stage of pregnancy up to the end of the first trimester (approximately twelve weeks), the State has no compelling interest, and the abortion decision must be left up to a woman and her physician. However, a state interest in medical standards may dictate that abortions be performed by physicians.

2. The State may choose to regulate second-trimester abortions (from twelve to approximately twenty-four to twenty-eight weeks of gestation), but only in ways that are narrowly tailored to promote maternal health.

3. In the third trimester of pregnancy (at viability), the State may, if it chooses, regulate or proscribe abortion to protect fetal life, but even then such laws must contain exceptions that allow abortion when a woman's health or life is at stake.

This decision severely limits a state's ability to restrict abortions. During the first two trimesters, abortion cannot be prohibited for any reason, and even during the third trimester laws that prohibit abortion cannot stand when a woman's health or life is at stake.

Although many abortion opponents insist that the Supreme Court has never ruled or had opportunity to rule whether or not the fetus is a "human person," that is not true. In the 1973 cases, there was considerable evidence before the Court on fetal development and the biological processes of life—evidence that was fully considered but rejected by the Court as irrelevant to the constitutional questions before it. The Court held that it did not "need to resolve the difficult question of when life begins" because the fetus is not a "person" as used in the Fourteenth Amendment and Fourteenth Amendment protections do not extend to the unborn. Even Justice Rehnquist, in his dissent in *Roe v. Wade*, agreed that there is a right to privacy within the "liberty" guaranteed by the Fourteenth Amendment and that it would be unconstitutional for a legislature to protect fetal life at the expense of a woman's life. Thus, even the most conservative member of the Court considers it a violation of the Constitution for government to protect fetal life to the detriment of a woman's life, which is exactly what most versions of a "Human Life" amendment would do.

In *Doe v. Bolton*, the Court examined Georgia's 1968 reform abortion law and struck down four provisions on the ground that they violated the right to privacy. These provisions required that (1) abortions be performed only in hospitals accredited by the Joint Commission on Accreditation of Hospitals; (2) the procedures be approved by a hospital abortion committee; (3) two other doctors, as well as the attending physician, confirm the abortion judgment; and (4) only residents of Georgia might obtain abortions there. The Court upheld, on the other hand, the statute's requirement that the physician might only perform an abortion when "necessary," since, the Court held, such a medical judgment "may be exercised in the light of all factors—physical, emotional, psychological, familial, and the woman's age—relevant to the well-being of the patient."

Throughout the decision in *Doe v. Bolton*, the Supreme Court stressed that Georgia's abortion statute entailed restrictions that did not apply to any other medical procedures in the state, and that they therefore would not be tolerated. Although subsequent to *Doe v. Bolton* the Supreme Court has retreated from the position that abortion can never be singled out from other surgical procedures, the *Doe* holding remains a legitimate and supportable argument both in the legislatures and in the courts whenever abortion is singled out for special legislative treatment.

Supreme Court Decisions Subsequent to Roe and Doe

The 1973 decisions firmly established that the right to decide to have an abortion is protected by the Constitution. But this constitutional right is different from most other constitutional rights in two ways.

First, abortion involves serious medical, social, ethical, and religious questions. The 1973 decisions did not answer any of these questions, nor did they prevent abortion from becoming the most politicized and explosive social controversy of the day. Second, *Roe v. Wade* is unusual in constitutional law in that it creates a standard of judicial review that permits greater restrictions with the length of the pregnancy. The predicate for this was medical safety, i.e., the Court's belief that abortion becomes more risky for the woman as her pregnancy progresses, so that it is more reasonable to permit a state to regulate it more closely as that risk increases. With advances in medical technology, including the use of new abortion techniques, this basis becomes less compelling. For example, although second-trimester abortions were as risky as childbirth in 1973, new techniques have made most of them much safer than childbirth itself, eliminating the need for an in-hospital requirement which the Supreme Court thought might be medically indicated in 1973.

Although *Roe* and *Doe* overturned the state criminal abortion laws that existed prior to 1973, Congress and almost every state legislature in the years since have responded to pressure from anti-abortion groups by passing laws intended to curtail abortion to the greatest extent possible. The legislatures and the courts have thus been engaged since 1973 in an intense and continuing battle over the constitutionality of such legislation.

From 1973 through 1981, there were nine decisions by the Supreme Court involving state statutes regulating abortion and one decision on federal legislation. There were also two additional decisions which involved privacy rights and which reaffirmed the constitutional standards set forth in *Roe v. Wade*.

An examination of the Supreme Court decisions on abortion subsequent to *Roe v. Wade* is important for two reasons. First, many legal questions left open in *Roe* have been answered by these decisions. Second, by tracing the language, if not the actual rulings, of the various decisions by the Court since 1973 one can discern a subtle but definite retreat by the Court from its initially firm ruling that the right to decide to have an abortion enjoyed fundamental constitutional protection. This change over the years can be seen as one indication that the Supreme Court is not completely immune to political pressure, even though, as in the case of abortion, the pressure exerted represents the views of only a minority of Americans. Despite this change, however, *Roe v. Wade* and *Doe v. Bolton* remain surprisingly strong legal precedents and have been repeatedly reaffirmed. They remain the most important cases against which to measure state or local abortion legislation.

In 1976, in *Planned Parenthood v. Danforth,* the Court struck down portions of a Missouri abortion statute enacted in 1974. The Court declared unconstitutional a requirement that a married woman obtain her husband's consent prior to having an abortion. The Court held that since the state may not interfere in the decision to have a first-trimester abortion, neither could it delegate to a spouse power which not only interfered with the exercise of this right, but, in effect, could veto it.

Similarly, the Court invalidated a requirement that unmarried minors obtain at least one parent's consent. Since this could also, in effect, represent a veto, the Court struck down this section on the same grounds as it did the spousal consent provision. Further, the Court also struck down a prohibition on the use of saline amniocentesis, an abortion technique which was, in 1974, the most widely used method during the second trimester. The Court held this prohibition unconstitutional because it did not protect maternal health but rather prohibited abortion in the second trimester, since other second-trimester methods were unavailable in Missouri.

Finally, the Court ruled unconstitutional a requirement that a physician preserve the fetus's life and health at all stages of pregnancy. This was struck down because it was not limited to the third trimester, when state interests in fetal life may be promoted.

The Court upheld as constitutional the Missouri definition of viability, which is "that state of fetal development when the life of the unborn child may be continued indefinitely outside the womb by natural or artificial life-support systems." Also upheld was a requirement for prior written consent by the woman having an abortion, even though Missouri did not require such consent prior to other surgical procedures and even though this requirement applied to all abortions including first-trimester abortions. Various record-keeping and reporting requirements were also upheld; the Court ruling that because such requirements had no "legally significant impact" on either the abortion

decision or the patient-physician relationship, the strict rule enunciated in *Roe v. Wade* (that the state cannot regulate first-trimester
abortions) did not apply. Thus, regulations extending even to first-
trimester abortions may be constitutional so long as they do not "have
more than a [minimal] interference with the abortion decision."

In 1979, in *Colautti v. Franklin,* the Supreme Court agreed with a
lower court that part of a Pennsylvania abortion statute was unconstitutional because of its vagueness. The act imposed criminal penalties on
doctors who failed to use the abortion technique most likely to result in
live birth during the stage of pregnancy when the fetus "is viable" or
"may be viable." The Court found the statute's requirements to be
ambiguous and, therefore, possibly inhibiting to doctors' decisions to
perform abortions; such an inhibiting effect would, of course, restrict
access to abortions. *Colautti* is an important decision for two reasons.
First, because it reaffirms the principles of *Roe,* and second because it
serves as a warning to states that they cannot legislate to promote fetal
life if doing so impedes a woman's right to choose abortion by interfering with the freedom of doctors to exercise good faith medical judg-
ments without fear of arbitrary criminal prosecution. *Colautti* is also
important because it places the judgment of fetal viability and selection
of abortion technique with the doctor.

There have been three cases in the Supreme Court since 1973 which
involved state laws that require either parental consent or parental
notification before a minor may have an abortion. *Planned Parenthood
v. Danforth* established that teenagers, as well as adult women, have a
fundamental right to choose abortion, and that it is unconstitutional for
a state to condition the exercise of that right upon the consent of at
least one parent. However, this decision left many open questions, and
it has since been made clear that abortion statutes regulating minors
will not be judged by the Court with the same scrutiny as those involving adult women.

In 1979, in *Bellotti v. Baird,* the Court struck down a Massachusetts
parental consent law, holding that mature minors have the right to
make an abortion decision without parental involvement. However,
the Court went on to postulate the kind of parental consent statute a
state could constitutionally enact should it choose to do so.

In that case, the Justices disagreed on the extent of allowable parental involvement; one opinion, representing the views of four Justices,

suggested that some form of parental consent statute may be constitutional so long as (1) "mature" minors have a right to make their own decisions about abortion; (2) "mature" and "immature" minors have the opportunity, through an alternative judicial or administrative procedure, to obtain an abortion without parental consent *or* consultation; and (3) with respect to "immature" minors, that the sole test is their own best interests. Although *Bellotti v. Baird* establishes that "mature" minors have the right to make an autonomous decision about abortion, it does not make clear just who a "mature" minor is, as opposed to an "immature" minor.

In 1981, the Supreme Court decided *H. L. v. Matheson,* a case challenging a Utah statute which required that, prior to performing an abortion on any minor, a doctor notify, as opposed to obtain the consent of, the minor's parents. Although this particular parental notification statute was upheld, the decision was a very narrow one, since the opinion of the Court held that it was constitutional *only* as to a very narrow class of minors, namely those who are living with, and dependent upon, their parents; are not emancipated, by marriage or otherwise; and have made no claim that they are mature and informed enough to make the abortion decision or that their relationships with their parents provide some reason why notification would not be in their best interests.

Therefore, this decision does *not* mean that all (or even most) statutes requiring parental notification in all instances are constitutional, nor that parents have a constitutional right to be notified about their minor daughters' abortion decisions. In fact, five Justices indicated that, if the same Utah statute were challenged again by a "mature" minor or by a minor with a good reason why her parents should not be told, it would be held unconstitutional because it does not include a judicial or administrative bypass route for such minors to seek abortions without parental knowledge.

Since these decisions were handed down, opponents of abortion have made restrictions on minors a legislative priority, and many states have enacted new parental notification or consent statutes which attempt to comply with the standards set forth in *Bellotti v. Baird* and *H. L. v. Matheson.* Challenges to such new statutes on minors have not yet reached the Supreme Court. But it is clear that parents do not have a constitutional right to know about, or to approve of, their daughters' abortion decisions, and that states are not obligated to restrict minors' abortion rights in this way. It is also clear that if a state does pass a statute mandating parental notification or consent, such statute must contain a meaningful bypass mechanism whereby a minor can obtain an abortion without having her parents notified (or get their consent) if she is adjudged "mature."

Serious setbacks to the protection of abortion as a fundamental constitutional right occurred in 1977 in three Supreme Court decisions involving public subsidies for abortion. Two cases involved the refusal by Pennsylvania and Connecticut to pay for purely "elective" abortions under their state Medicaid programs; the third case involved the refusal of a public hospital staffed by Jesuit doctors who refused to perform abortions or hire staff doctors who would provide such services.

In *Maher v. Doe,* the Court upheld Connecticut's Medicaid scheme, holding that it is not a denial of equal protection for a state to refuse to pay for nontherapeutic or elective abortions while paying for childbirth. In arriving at this conclusion, the Court stated:

There is a basic difference between direct state interference with a protected activity and state encouragement of an alternative activity consonant with legislative policy.

The Court held that when dealing with state welfare schemes, as opposed to criminal laws, a state can abandon the neutrality that is usually required when fundamental rights are at stake and that a welfare policy that promotes "normal" childbirth over abortion was constitutional because it was rationally related to state interests, including the interest in the "potential life of the fetus."

In the hospital case, the Court did not detail its reasoning but it did uphold the refusal of the public hospital to provide elective abortions.

These cases signaled a retreat by the Supreme Court with respect to abortion legislation involving public funding. Most disastrously, the Court held that when public funding is involved, a state can legislate to "promote fetal life" throughout pregnancy, a position diametrically opposed to that in *Roe v. Wade* which held that fetal interests were "compelling" only in the third trimester of pregnancy.

In 1980, in *Harris v. McRae,* the Supreme Court upheld as constitutional the federal Hyde Amendment, which eliminates most federal

Medicaid abortions for poor women. This decision goes one step further than the 1977 funding decisions and holds that the federal Constitution does not require Medicaid to pay for abortions that are medically necessary, even when Medicaid pays for all other medically necessary procedures.

The Court there reiterated its position that abortion restrictions in the funding context are different from other abortion regulations, and held that it is permissible for the federal government to choose to promote fetal life by funding childbirth and not abortion even when a woman's health is sacrificed in the process. By making it legitimate for the government to accomplish indirectly by a withdrawal of funds what it cannot do directly, the decision radically undermines the protection which the Court will afford the poor. Although in *McRae* the Court stated that it was reaffirming *Roe v. Wade,* the fact that it upheld the state's ability to place fetal life over a woman's health or life in a funding scheme signals a retreat, at least in this type of case.

This decision does not mean, however, that states cannot fund Medicaid abortions, only that the federal Constitution does not require them to do so.

THE LEGISLATIVE ISSUES FOR THE 1980s

The availability of legal abortion in this country subsequent to 1973 has led to dramatic decreases in maternal deaths from illegal abortions and from unwanted pregnancies. Poor and minority women have particularly benefited. But despite these public health benefits, anti-abortion groups continue to work to restrict abortion. Their pressure has resulted in legislation ostensibly designed to "promote maternal health," although rarely, if ever, is this purported goal the actual one. In fact, early abortion is one of the safest surgical procedures in the United States and the real purpose of most abortion control legislation is to impede abortions. This is done by harassing women seeking abortions and by discouraging doctors from performing abortions at all.

Many states and localities are passing anti-abortion statutes or ordinances based on a model drafted by national "right-to-life" groups. Often called "Akron ordinances" (because the first in the country was passed in Akron, Ohio), these laws contain numerous restrictions on abortion. However, they do not address specific local health needs or problems; for example, the ordinance passed by the city of Akron forbade public hospitals from allowing abortions despite the fact that there are no public hospitals in Akron.

It is important for the citizen-lobbyist to recognize that these bills do not address any real health or medical problems but are intended instead to legislate the theological/moral belief that the fetus is a human being and that abortion is murder. We shall now examine the various types of anti-abortion bills that are being and will be considered in various state legislatures and local governing bodies. Besides the legal and constitutional arguments for or against such legislation, this part will also discuss other social, medical, and religious arguments which can be used. Although most of the following will focus on restrictions on abortion, the last section is on sterilization and the mentally incompetent, another current legislative issue involving reproductive rights.

Restrictions on Abortion Services in Public or Private Hospitals

Many states, local governments, and local hospital boards have adopted laws or policies eliminating or restricting abortion services in public and private hospitals. This presents a serious problem for women who need access to such facilities and for doctors who find their ability to treat their patients thwarted.

The number of hospitals performing abortions has declined steadily since 1976. This decline was primarily due to a drop in the number of public hospitals providing abortions. In fact, in five states no public hospital will allow abortions.

In 1978, 75 percent of all abortions were performed in freestanding clinics or in doctors' offices. Although abortions performed outside of hospitals are usually much less expensive than hospital abortions, the lack of hospitals performing abortions presents a serious hardship for women who rely on hospitals for their medical services or who need hospital abortions because of the stage of their pregnancy or for other health reasons. Some hospitals have even refused to treat abortion complications arising elsewhere or to enter into backup agreements with local clinics, even though without them the clinics may not get licensed.

When access to facilities is limited, the burden falls most heavily on poor women, minority women, and teenagers, the population which most needs hospital facilities and which can least afford to travel to distant hospitals or to private facilities. In 1978, 736,000 women were unable to obtain the abortion services they needed, and in eight out of every ten counties no physician, clinic, or hospital provided abortions.

Although in 1977, in *Poelker v. Doe*, the Supreme Court upheld the right of a public hospital in St. Louis, Missouri, to refuse to perform most abortions, that case did not address the question of whether health- or life-saving abortions can be prohibited or whether there could be a blanket restriction on the performance of abortions in public hospitals when the staff doctors want to perform them or are performing them on private patients. In 1982, a federal Court of Appeals distinguished *Poelker v. Doe* and held that a public hospital in Minnesota could not prohibit its doctors from using its facilities to perform abortions. The issue there did not involve subsidized abortions, since the doctors were using the facilities for abortions for their private patients. The court stressed the particular circumstances of the case, including the rural location of the hospital, the fact that the staff doctors wanted to perform abortions, and that without these hospital facilities abortion availability would be severely limited.

Although the *Poelker* case makes the legal situation difficult in terms of challenging public hospital restrictions under the United States Constitution, public and private hospitals may be required to permit abortions under state constitutions or other state law grounds. For example, in New Jersey, the policies followed by three private hospitals in prohibiting the use of their facilities for first-trimester, non-therapeutic abortions was overturned by the state Supreme Court based on state law. The Court held that in serving the public the hospitals constituted quasi-public institutions, and that under New Jersey law their policies must be rationally related to the "public good." The Court concluded that there was no rational relationship between the public good and the prohibition of non-therapeutic abortions and declared the policies invalid.

The hospital issue often arises when regional facilities are forced to consolidate certain medical services or when hospitals seek a "certificate of need" required by federal law before new hospitals can be built. It is important for local groups to fight against the granting of such "certificates of need" to hospitals with anti-abortion or anti-sterilization policies, since once such a certificate is granted other facilities may be foreclosed from operating in that region.

It is important to gather support from the medical community against these restrictions. Medical groups which might not otherwise be vocal on pro-choice issues are often the leading opponents of hospital restrictions because they constitute limitations on doctors' abilities to practice medicine and treat their patients.

Medicaid Abortions

The Medicaid abortion issue is one that arises in Congress and in most states every year. The federal Hyde Amendment, passed by Congress each year since 1976, currently limits the availability of federal funding for abortions to those situations in which the pregnancy is certified as "life-endangering." In 1980, The Supreme Court in *Harris v. McRae* upheld the Hyde Amendment as constitutional under the federal Constitution. However, the states are still free to fund Medicaid abortions if they choose to do so.

Subsequent to that decision, Congress passed an additional anti-abortion amendment, the Bauman Amendment, to the yearly appropriations bill. This amendment changes the states' obligations under the Medicaid program and permits them to make their Medicaid abortion restrictions even stricter than those of the federal government. Therefore, even though there are federal funds available for abortions in "life-endangering" pregnancies, the states, under the Bauman Amendment, do not have to provide that level of funding. This has not been challenged, since all states fund abortions at least to the federal level.

After the Hyde Amendment was upheld, some states voluntarily took over the funding of Medicaid abortions. As of early 1982, the District of Columbia and nine states—Alaska, Colorado, Hawaii, Maryland, Michigan, New York, North Carolina, Oregon, and Washington—were voluntarily paying for most Medicaid abortions with state funds. Also subsequent to that decision, challenges to restrictive state Medicaid abortion policies continue to be feasible in some states on state grounds; indeed, in five states—California, Connecticut, Massachusetts, New Jersey, and Pennsylvania—court orders were issued mandating the states on state law grounds to pay for all medically necessary abortions. As the Massachusetts Supreme Court observed:

> [We] deal in this case with the application of principles to which this court is no stranger, and in an area in which [Massachusetts']

constitutional guarantee of due process has sometimes impelled us to go further than the United States Supreme Court.

We think our Declaration of Rights affords a greater degree of protection to the right asserted here than does the Federal Constitution as interpreted in *Harris v. McRae*.

The Hyde Amendment has had the effect of eliminating 99 percent of Medicaid abortions in those states which do not supply their own funds. For example, in Texas, there were 290 publicly funded abortions per month when there was Medicaid funding for them; this has since been cut down to less than two. Since the states with the biggest Medicaid populations are still funding Medicaid abortions, about 75 percent of Medicaid-eligible women are still able to receive publicly funded abortions. However, the consequences of stopping such funding are already apparent. Some women have died, others have suffered increased risks because of delay forced by their having to come up with the money for abortions. Preliminary data from New Jersey show that during the time Medicaid abortions were unavailable there was an increase in childbirth, some of it presumably unwanted. In addition, statistics from Illinois show that, in 1980, the year government funds were cut off for most abortions there, the number of publicly funded sterilizations increased sharply, from 3,123 in 1979 to 6,219 in 1980.

Lobbyists should show legislators the enormous human costs that are paid when women are forced into compulsory pregnancy and childbirth, costs not only in terms of increased welfare but also in terms of perpetuating cycles of poverty, increased child abuse and neglect, damage to women's health, and dual standards of medical care.

Requirements That All Second-Trimester Abortions Take Place in Hospitals

A provision prohibiting all second-trimester abortions from being performed anywhere but in hospitals is part of the omnibus "Akron-type" ordinances that have recently been enacted in many states and localities. Other similar requirements are carry-overs from a time when medical safety dictated that hospital facilities be used. As of 1982, twenty-two states had laws limiting second-trimester abortions to hospitals.

In *Roe v. Wade*, the Supreme Court established guidelines which allow states to pass laws regulating second- and third-trimester abortions if such laws are necessary to protect maternal health. The Court's justification was that in 1973 abortion was safer than childbirth only during the first trimester. However, increased safety due to advances in abortion techniques have altered this situation. It is now undisputed that abortions performed by the "dilation and evacuation" technique up to at least the eighteenth week of pregnancy are twice as safe as childbirth itself. Medical experts agree that some second-trimester abortions may safely be performed in clinics, and some even believe that clinics are safer than hospitals. Clearly, in-hospital requirements greatly increase costs and often add travel distance for the woman, since few hospitals perform abortions. In states where no hospitals perform abortions such requirements may eliminate the availability of second-trimester abortion altogether. Courts in several states have recently enjoined in-hospital requirements as unconstitutional because they are not necessary to promote maternal health as required by *Roe v. Wade*.

There are two federal appellate court decisions on these laws but they are in direct conflict: one strikes down a Missouri hospital requirement as unconstitutional while the other upholds an Akron, Ohio, requirement as constitutional. The issue will be resolved by the Supreme Court in 1983.

If bills requiring that abortions after the twelfth week of pregnancy be performed only in hospitals are introduced in your state legislature, or if pro-choice lobbyists are seeking to repeal an existing law to that effect, it is important to present to your legislators the facts concerning the non-availability of hospital abortions, the safety of abortions performed outside a hospital, the abortion methods used in hospitals, and the increased costs of such abortions. The delay and costs of traveling to a hospital in another state that does perform abortions are not only burdensome to the abortion right but actually increase the risks to the health of the women seeking termination of their pregnancies. Moreover, unavailability of Medicaid funding exacerbates the problem; for the poor, the costs of traveling and of having a hospital abortion are prohibitive. Furthermore, data should be presented showing that outpatient methods of second-trimester abortions are less traumatic, cheaper, and just as safe as, or safer than, hospital abortions.

It is also important to point out that since 1979, the American Public Health Association, the American College of Obstetrics and Gynecology, the National Abortion Federation, and the Planned Parenthood Federation have all revised their medical policies and standards to recognize that changes in methods of abortion have rendered in-hospital requirements for all second-trimester abortions obsolete. The APHA Guide is crucial, since its abortion standards were cited with approval by the Supreme Court in *Roe v. Wade*.

Anti-Abortion and Other Restrictions on Family Planning and Other Funding Statutes

After the Supreme Court decision in *Harris v. McRae*, abortion opponents in state legislatures have expanded restrictions on abortion funding even beyond Medicaid. Anti-abortion restrictions are now being proposed on a variety of public funding programs, most commonly on family planning appropriations. As of 1982, seven states had passed legislation that put anti-abortion restrictions on appropriations bills: Arizona, Illinois, Minnesota, North Dakota, Ohio, Pennsylvania, and Utah. Some states, notably Utah and West Virginia, have attempted to require parental notice or consent when teenagers receive publicly funded family planning.

The restrictions aimed at chilling abortion rights contain two kinds of conditions. First, they penalize persons or agencies who perform, or even discuss, abortion by making them ineligible to apply for public monies, even if such monies are for other purposes. For example, a North Dakota criminal statute made any person or agency providing abortion referral services ineligible to apply for state, local, or federal family planning monies. Second, these statutes attempt to limit the conduct, including speech, of recipients of the grants: A statute passed in Illinois to fund counseling for problem pregnancies prohibited grantees from "referring or counseling for abortion."

These statutes have been enjoined by lower federal courts on several different legal grounds. For example, state statutes requiring family planning agencies to notify parents of minors who receive family planning services, or prohibiting family planning agencies from making abortion referrals, have been struck down because they violate the federal laws and related regulations governing these programs, such as Title X of the Public Health Service Act. Congress's purpose in enacting Title X was to make "comprehensive voluntary family planning services readily available to all persons desiring such services," and the regulations governing the Public Health Service Act have required that such family planning services be made available without discrimination based upon age. However, in February 1982, the Department of Health and Human Services proposed new regulations which would require that parents of adolescents be notified in almost every case when prescription birth control methods, including the diaphragm, are provided to minors under the Title X family planning program. Despite strong opposition to the proposed regulations from medical and health organizations, and despite the fact that the written comments submitted to DHHS oppose the regulations by an overwhelmingly large majority, the Department has not given any indications that it will abandon or make any significant changes in the regulations. If these regulations are promulgated, several court challenges will be brought against them in an effort to block their implementation.

There are also constitutional arguments against these anti-abortion funding restrictions. Those which attempt to limit the speech of doctors and other health professionals who receive public monies by prohibiting them from "counseling" or "referring" with respect to abortion interfere with free speech rights protected by the First Amendment. In addition, at least one court has found that limitations on referring and counseling, even in the funding context, constitute a direct and unconstitutional interference with abortion, since they distort the kind of information a woman receives and interfere with the abortion decision-making process protected by the Constitution. Another constitutional argument against this kind of statute is that its restrictions are vague. For example, many prohibit medical providers from "encouraging" or "promoting" abortion. Because these terms are not clearly defined, there is a good argument that the prohibitions violate the constitutional requirement that statutes be clear and not vague.

There are good medical and social arguments against these statutes as well. Many are aimed at defunding the largest family planning agencies in the state. If successful, the effect would be to reduce family planning services, which will inevitably lead to more unwanted pregnancies and to more abortions. If the aim of these statutes is to reduce the number of abortions by harassing abortion providers, the opposite will happen.

In addition, doctors and medical groups should be made aware of how restrictive these statutes are in limiting free speech and their ability to practice their professions freely. Many of these restrictive funding statutes try to stop family planning professionals from "referring or counseling for abortion" without any exception, even for women whose health or lives are at stake. This would have disastrous consequences; for example, if a woman becomes pregnant with an IUD in place, the Food and Drug Administration requires that doctors advise her that an abortion may be the safest medical option available to her. A doctor who did not comply might be subject to a malpractice suit and other penalties. These are good arguments to raise in a legislative context, and they can often be more effective than constitutional arguments.

Statutes Requiring Parental Notification or Consent

Subsequent to the Supreme Court's decision in *Bellotti v. Baird*, in which the Court indicated that a state statute that requires parental involvement in a minor's abortion decision could be constitutional, opponents of abortion have been pressuring state legislatures to enact statutes requiring that parents be notified, or that their consent be obtained, prior to the performance of abortions on their minor daughters.

As of 1982, twenty states and several localities had abortion laws requiring minors either to have parental consent or to notify their parents prior to obtaining an abortion. However, two of those statutes pre-date *Bellotti* and are not enforced, and another leaves the physician wide discretion to waive notification. In Nevada, Nebraska, Rhode Island, Maine, Kentucky, Missouri and Illinois, the requirements are not in effect because of court injunctions issued in pending challenges to the statutes. In Utah, Louisiana, Indiana and Minnesota there are also court challenges to these laws, but the laws have been put into effect. The notification or consent statutes in Massachusetts, Nebraska, Rhode Island, Indiana, Kentucky, Pennsylvania, Arizona, Minnesota, and Louisiana were enacted after 1979 and they all contain court bypass procedures which purportedly comply with the *Bellotti v. Baird* requirements. Of these nine statutes, six are in effect, while Pennsylvania's, Nebraska's and Kentucky's are under court injunction.

With respect to these kinds of bills, the first question to be considered is whether there is a difference between requiring parental consent and requiring notification. Several studies on the effects of such requirements on teenagers' behavior and willingness to seek medical care show that for many young people a requirement that parents be notified is as effective a deterrent to their seeking medical help as a consent requirement would be. For this reason, at least five members of the Supreme Court equate parental notification with parental consent, in that they would require such statutes to offer minors the ability to go to court and bypass their parents having to know about their pregnancy and desired abortion. In 1983 the Supreme Court will rule on two cases involving requirements that minors obtain either parental consent or court authorization prior to obtaining an abortion. Although the laws at issue in these two cases were enacted prior to the Court's decision in *Bellotti v. Baird,* the Court's ruling in these two cases should further clarify these issues.

Despite the fact that both types of statutes are extremely onerous to teenagers, a parental notification requirement is somewhat less so since it at least allows the teenager to get an abortion even without parental consent, whereas under a consent requirement she would have only the court option available to her. Similarly, it is less onerous if only one parent has to give consent or be notified.

Lobbyists often find that these are the most difficult anti-abortion laws to oppose. Some who support preserving freedom of choice and oppose other restrictive legislation hesitate when confronted with arguments that the purpose of these requirements is to preserve families or to help teenagers get good advice before they make a decision as important as abortion. But these arguments overlook the fact that such statutes are proposed by anti-abortion legislators who are not interested in seeing that minors get good advice and who will often admit that their purpose is to limit to the greatest extent possible the ability of teenagers to get abortions. These bills do not require physicians or teenagers to tell their parents whenever a pregnancy is discovered, but only when an abortion is sought. The concern is not that pregnant teenagers get help early so they can get advice on both abortion or continued pregnancy; to the contrary, the requirement applies only to teenagers seeking abortions and is intended to prevent them from doing so.

Legislators truly concerned about pregnant teenagers would require doctors to inform all such teenagers that the physical and emotional risks of early abortion are much less than those of childbirth. Moreover, it is clear that teenagers are generally reluctant to seek health care regarding sexual matters. For this reason, many states have passed laws specifically allowing teenagers to seek care for VD without having their parents notified. Further, many teenagers, particularly younger ones, do involve their parents in the abortion decision; those who do not usually have good reasons. These statutes will not change teenagers' relationships with their parents. They cannot force communication. They will only force teenagers into desperate situations.

Persons lobbying against this type of restriction on minors should be aware of the terrible impact these statutes have had in states where they have been implemented. Teenagers have been harassed and delayed; for some, the laws have resulted in forced childbirth. It is simply not feasible for teenagers who are reluctant to seek medical help in the first place to be expected to navigate their way through a state court system in order to be judged "mature" and then able to get an abortion. Teenagers not only lack the time and the money to do this, but the entire process is anxiety-producing, adding to the existing emotional upheaval of an unwanted pregnancy. Teenage girls realize that they are pregnant later than adult women, and usually seek help later. Statutes requiring judicial notice or consent add up to two or three weeks to this already built-in delay, making abortion much more risky for some teenagers and eliminating the option altogether for others.

Lobbyists should present data to legislatures showing that an early abortion is an extremely safe medical procedure that has no impact on future pregnancies. Furthermore, it is at least five times as safe as continued pregnancy and childbirth. Teenagers can least afford to have delay imposed onto their ability to get abortions, since they already tend to get them later in pregnancy. It should be made clear that eliminating the abortion option will not curb teenage sexual activity or lead to increased contraceptive use. The direct consequence will be more dangerous abortions for some and compulsory motherhood for others.

The only certain result of these statutes is to add a terrible toll to the health and lives of teenagers and to the children they may be forced to bear. Those who somehow make it through a court bypass system will have had to endure extra expense, harassment, mental anguish, and risks because their abortion will have been performed at a later stage. Those teenagers who live in rural parts of the state, where there is no available court bypass system, will have to seek illegal abortions or try to travel out of state or else be forced to carry a pregnancy to term because they can find no alternative to their dilemma. There is overwhelming evidence showing the detrimental social, mental, economic, and physical effects of compulsory motherhood on both the teenagers and their children.

"Informed Consent" Laws

Since 1978, "informed consent" abortion requirements have been proposed in almost every state legislature and have passed in fourteen states and four localities. Although such "informed consent" statutes contain many anti-abortion restrictions, they usually begin with a provision dictating the kind of information a woman must receive from her doctor prior to an abortion. Of course, obtaining the informed consent of patients before they undergo any medical procedure is an accepted and legally required practice. Instead of being passive recipients of any treatment, all patients should be well-informed about possible benefits and risks as well as about what will happen to them should they not have the proposed treatment.

However, the informed consent legislation that is currently being proposed involving abortion is unlike normal informed consent requirements in that it mandates that biased, harassing, misleading, or medically inaccurate information be given to a woman. Physicians are often required, under criminal penalties, to give their patients questionable and disturbing information, such as a statement that the fetus is a human being from the moment of conception. Some statutes require a detailed description of the appearance and characteristics of the fetus, including a showing of color pictures and a list of medical risks of abortion, many of which have not been proven or are misleading.

In 1976, the Supreme Court said that since the abortion decision is an important and stressful one some sort of limited informed consent for an abortion can be required. A permissible requirement can call for "the giving of information to the patient as to just what would be done and as to its consequences," but to require any more than that would not be allowed. Although the Court has upheld two very benign informed consent statutes, it has not yet ruled on the type of statute discussed here. In late 1982 the Court had before it a case challenging the constitutionality of an Akron, Ohio, anti-abortion municipal ordinance which contains numerous "informed consent" requirements, including those described above. The Court's decision is expected sometime in 1983.

Numerous lower courts have struck down as unconstitutional detailed mandatory information requirements, although some courts have upheld those portions which merely require the doctor to inform the patient of alternatives to abortion, of the risk to the individual patient, and of the procedure to be used. A federal appellate court, striking down portions of a Massachusetts informed consent statute that included mandatory fetal description, held that the statute violated not only privacy rights but First Amendment free speech rights as well. The Court found that the required information was not material to any medically relevant fact and that its impact on many women seeking abortion would be to cause distress, guilt, and in some cases increased pain, an "unwelcome and medically contraindicated state lecture." Furthermore, the Court recognized that the true purpose of the statute was "moral indoctrination," not to ensure that pregnant women receive information that is factually needed:

> To the extent that information may be imposed by the state it must be neutral and objective; coercive state indoctrination of particular values or ethical judgments is objectionable to First as well as Fourteenth Amendment principles. The state may not add to its) presentation of material facts such a moral overlay, an attempted imposition of ideas that is particularly objectionable in connection with the exercise of fundamental rights.

Lobbyists confronted with this type of statute should emphasize that many states already have informed consent laws covering all medical procedures, including abortion. Furthermore, state malpractice and licensure laws provide additional assurance that a woman will be informed. Doctors should not be used as state agents for moral indoctrination, and the danger these statutes create for First Amendment rights should be highlighted. Since these statutes attempt to impose one moral or religious viewpoint about abortion and the nature of fetal life, church groups with strong pro-choice positions should join in opposing these bills in the state legislatures.

Mandatory Waiting Periods

Many state legislatures and localities have passed a mandatory waiting period, usually of twenty-four or forty-eight hours, between the time a woman gives consent and the time the abortion may be performed. This requirement is clearly designed to discourage women from choosing abortion and to burden that choice once it is made. Numerous courts have held that such mandatory waiting periods are unconstitutional because they present a direct obstacle to women seeking abortions and because they are not supported by any compelling state interest. These decisions are based on factual findings proving that waiting periods would increase risks and burden women seeking abortions. The Supreme Court will consider such a law in 1983.

If a mandatory waiting period is proposed in your state, it is important to emphasize the burden that such a waiting period would have on women and doctors, including information on travel distances and cost increases as well as the psychological burden that such a mandatory waiting period imposes on women. Two detailed studies interviewing women on the effect of such a waiting period show that for some the combination of cost increases and delay would have the effect of stopping abortion altogether.

Furthermore, studies on the abortion decision-making process show that nearly all women have made up their minds to have an abortion once they come to an abortion provider. Many have sought advice from health professionals or other doctors. Therefore, the reality is that these women are not undecided and that a waiting period will not make them change their minds but will merely add physical, psychological, and economic burdens. It is also important to point out that most states do not require waiting periods for virtually all other surgical procedures, including many that are more serious and life-threatening than abortion.

Spousal Notification or Consent Provisions

Subsequent to *Roe v. Wade*, laws mandating that a husband give his consent prior to a woman's abortion were enacted in several states. But in 1976 the Supreme Court struck down a Missouri statute that required the husband's prior written consent to an abortion. The Court recognized that despite interests of the father in the fetus, the right to choose abortion is part of a woman's privacy right; it is she "who physically bears the child and who is more directly and immediately affected by the pregnancy period."

Nevertheless, this decision has not stopped states from enacting spousal notification requirements. Such statutes have passed in Illinois, Utah, Nevada, Kentucky, Rhode Island and Florida. Most of these laws have been preliminarily enjoined because they interfere with a woman's right of privacy under *Roe v. Wade*. However, a federal appeals court reached the opposite conclusion, preliminarily holding that a Florida criminal abortion statute requiring spousal notification may be constitutional because the state has a compelling state interest in helping the "authenticity" of the marriage, the basis of which is childbearing, and in promoting a husband's constitutional "right to procreate." However, the appeals court also found that the law might be unconstitutionally overbroad because it required notification even to husbands who had not necessarily fathered the fetus. The court sent the case back to the trial court for a factual determination as to whether abortion has more than a minimal impact on a woman's future childbearing capacity. After trial on this issue, the lower court found that legal abortion has less than a minimal chance of leading to infertility, spontaneous abortion, premature birth, low birth weight infants, or placenta previa (or unintended hysterectomy or death), and that legal abortion thus does not have a greater than minimal impact on a woman's future ability to bear children. Accordingly, the court found the statute to be unconstitutional. This decision is noteworthy because the court analyzed in detail numerous medical articles and the testimony of experts for both sides in reaching its conclusions about the safety of abortion. Thus, the decision will not only be an important precedent for cases challenging other husband notification laws but will also serve to refute the claims of anti-abortion groups that women who choose abortions need elaborate warnings about the "hazards" of the procedure.

If your state should propose such a restriction, it is important to stress that making it a crime for a woman not to give certain information to her husband constitutes direct state interference into marriage and the family. Furthermore, the restriction is sex discriminatory and may on that ground be contrary to state equal rights amendments or the federal constitution. A husband is not forced by the government to tell his wife when he has a vasectomy or when he contracts VD, both of which affect the "childbearing capacity" of a marriage.

In many situations, these laws could have a detrimental effect on a woman's mental and physical health. Some women, fearful of reprisals, may be foreclosed from exercising the legal abortion option at all; others will either delay until an abortion is much riskier or seek dangerous illegal abortions. In instances where the husband did not cause the pregnancy, the woman may be placed under special stress or danger. Spousal notification not only burdens a woman's privacy right but has serious First Amendment implications as well.

State Restrictions on "Wrongful Life" Actions

There has been an increasing tendency in the courts to uphold the right of parents to sue a physician or genetic counselor for the birth of an abnormal child needing special care when the doctor or genetic counselor did not properly detect and advise the parents of the risks of abnormality. Such lawsuits are called "wrongful life" actions. Since a predicate of these actions is that if forewarned the woman may have chosen a legal abortion, right-to-life activists have introduced legislation abolishing such lawsuits.

A typical bill provides that there shall be no right to sue on the claim "that but for the conduct of another, a person would not have been permitted to have been born alive," and "that but for the conduct of another he or she would not have been conceived or, once conceived, would not have been permitted to have been born alive." Such a law would preclude damage actions by a child or its parents as well as suits by parents who were deprived of the opportunity to choose to abort because the pregnancy was not properly diagnosed. Such bills redefine traditional legal notions of a doctor's duty to his or her patients and would declare instead that doctors owe no legal duty to parents or children to test for, diagnose, or counsel with respect to a deformed fetus and the possible effects of a disease on a fetus.

There are a number of arguments that can be made against such bills. First, the enactment of such a bill infringes on the prerogative of the courts. Courts should be able to decide whether conventional principles of negligence and medical malpractice would allow suits and recovery for "wrongful life." Second, such laws are contrary to general public policy favoring the compensation of injured parties and the general societal interest in proper medical care and advice, both of which are furthered by maintaining a right to sue for negligent conduct. Denial of such a right to sue in this context would succeed in its apparent goal of reducing abortions only if doctors are thereby encouraged to be negligent in detecting or in failing to disclose the risk of defects to their patients. A state legislature should not encourage negligence in any aspect of medical care, including prenatal care. Since more and more prenatally defective diseases are being treated, these laws would also adversely affect the chances of detecting treatable diseases.

Bills abolishing "wrongful life" suits may be unconstitutional. Several cases have suggested that the failure to recognize "wrongful life" claims impermissibly burdens the constitutional rights involved in conception, procreation, and other familial decisions. Such bills could also represent an unconstitutional infringement of equal protection rights, since it embodies legislative policy which allows recovery for all types of malpractice except "wrongful life."

Licensing Restrictions

Licensing laws that impose more stringent regulations on abortion facilities than on other medical facilities have been enacted by state and local governments. Such restrictions govern a multitude of items including clinic equipment, personnel, qualifications, building specifications, and hospital backup agreements.

A Louisiana law enacted in 1978 required abortion clinics to maintain a defibrillator—a completely unnecessary and inappropriate requirement since Louisiana abortion clinics do not use cardiac stimulants as an anesthetic. Similarly, a Michigan law required six-foot corridors in all abortion facilities. These are examples of burdensome regulations unrelated to health concerns. The primary objective of such regulations is not to protect women's health and safety but to hinder the operation of abortion clinics by imposing standards that are either costly or, in some cases, impossible to comply with. These regulations result in discouraging doctors and abortion clinics from providing abortion services, and, where abortions are still offered, higher fees for patients. Both effects interfere with a woman's right to choose abortion.

Many courts have declared such regulations unconstitutional under *Roe v. Wade*, holding that during the first trimester the abortion decision "may be effectuated without interference by the State." Other cases have held that states may regulate first-trimester abortions only to the same extent that they regulate similar surgical procedures.

Bills regulating abortion clinics should be read carefully—especially if introduced by anti-abortion legislators. Lobbyists should consult with health professionals and administrators of abortion facilities to determine whether the regulations would be burdensome and whether they are necessary to the performance of abortions, and especially first-trimester abortions, since many clinics do not perform second- or third-trimester abortions. The regulations should be compared to existing regulations applicable to facilities offering similar surgical procedures. Lobbyists should call attention to the low morbidity/mortality rate for abortion and present such statistics including the applicable state or local figures. It is important to keep in mind that some licensure laws which appear to be neutral as to abortion may be discriminatorily applied to facilities offering abortion services.

Zoning Restrictions

Another anti-abortion tactic to be watched for on the local level is the use of municipal zoning powers to prevent the building or remodeling of abortion clinics. These broad powers are sometimes arbitrarily applied to eliminate abortion services. For example, the City Commission in Deerfield, Florida, ignoring the Planning and Zoning Board's recommendation that an occupational license be approved for an abortion facility, denied the facility's application at a meeting crowded with anti-abortionists. A federal court of appeals granted the facility preliminary injunctive relief against the denial of the license, stating: "Any public interest in allowing zoning plans does not extend so far as to allow arbitrary and capricious actions that interfere with the exercise of a fundamental right." Similar challenges to discriminatory uses of zoning powers have also met with success.

It is important that hearings in which the application of clinics offering abortion services are considered not be one-sided events dominated by anti-abortionists. The pro-choice community should be mobilized to attend these meetings armed with relevant facts so that these decisions may be made in as fair a manner as possible. In light of the fact that there is a great unmet need for abortion services—in 1978, 736,000 women were unable to obtain the abortion services they required—it is essential that new providers of abortion services not be precluded from operating.

Anti-Abortion Regulations on Health Insurance

Anti-abortion statutes regulating health insurance have been enacted in Rhode Island, Pennsylvania, Illinois, Massachusetts, Kentucky, North Dakota, and Nebraska. In Illinois, Nebraska, and Rhode Island, these restrictions apply only to insurance coverage for state and municipal employees. The North Dakota, Massachusetts, and Kentucky statutes go much farther in restricting insurance coverage; they attempt to apply to every insurance policy issued or delivered in those states.

As of early 1982, these laws have not been challenged in court. The Supreme Court decision in *Harris v. McRae* makes it difficult to argue that the statutes that apply only to public employees are in conflict with the United States Constitution. Nor do these statutes appear to violate Title VII of the 1965 Civil Rights Act, which prohibits sex discrimination in employment, including state employment. However, in those states with a state equal rights amendment, or where the state's guarantees of equal protection and/or due process are interpreted more broadly than are the federal constitutional guarantees, it is possible that these statutes violate those state guarantees.

However, there are even stronger arguments that state insurance statutes preventing public or private insurance policies from covering abortion unless a separate premium is paid are unconstitutional. Clearly, the practical effect of these laws is to increase the cost of insuring against the cost of abortion. Thus, unlike the elimination of Medicaid abortions—which, according to the Supreme Court in *McRae*, left women no worse off than before the state intervened—this legislation constitutes an affirmative interference with the ability of women to exercise their right to choose abortion by making it more costly. Further, health insurance is an important item in collective bargaining for union members. By restricting coverage, the states are interfering with the bargaining rights of both employees and employers, and labor unions should be strong allies in opposing these restrictive statutes.

Statutes Governing Viability

Right-to-life literature is rife with ghoulish stories of live aborted fetuses. But, in fact, late abortions are rare occurrences. Over 91 percent of all abortions performed in the United States in 1978 were performed before the twelfth week of pregnancy, with only 1 percent performed after the twenty-first week. Late abortions almost always involve situations in which continuation of the pregnancy would severely threaten the woman's life or health or in which serious fetal abnormalities have been detected through the use of amniocentesis.

The Supreme Court in *Roe v. Wade* observed that a fetus is generally considered viable when it is "potentially able to live outside the mother's womb, albeit with artificial aid," adding that the potential life must be "meaningful" and not just a matter of momentary survival. The Court further stated that "viability is usually placed at about seven months (twenty-eight weeks) but may occur earlier, even at twenty-four weeks." *Roe v. Wade* has been interpreted to allow states to act to protect potential fetal life from about the twenty-fourth week of pregnancy. This means that the states may regulate, or even prohibit, abortion after that point, although at no point can they do so at the expense of the woman's life or health.

The Supreme Court has emphasized in subsequent decisions that the determination of viability is a medical judgment which must be made by the attending physician and that statutes which interfere with this process are unconstitutional. Therefore, statutes which fix viability at a specific point during pregnancy unduly restrict the physician's judgment and are unconstitutional.

Another type of statute by which states have sought to regulate late abortions concerns the standard of care which physicians must exercise during these procedures. Often these bills will require the doctor to perform the abortion in a way "best calculated" to preserve the life of the fetus. Or they require that life-support systems be available and the fetus treated as if it were to be delivered rather than aborted.

The Supreme Court has addressed some of these issues. In *Colautti v. Franklin* the Court struck down a statute requiring that where a fetus was viable, or where there was sufficient reason to believe that the fetus may be viable, the doctor was to "preserve the life and health of the fetus [as though] intended to be born." The Court observed that it was not clear whether the doctor's primary duty was to the woman or the fetus, and that since doctors were subject to criminal penalties this vagueness was impermissible. Under *Roe v. Wade*, the physician's primary obligation is to the woman. If the interests of the fetus conflict with those of the woman, the woman's interests must prevail.

Another type of statute requires that there be a second physician in attendance whose primary responsibility is to the fetus. The courts have recognized that these statutes present serious ethical questions. For instance, whose judgment would prevail in a situation in which one method of abortion would be preferable for the woman's health but another would be more likely to produce a live fetus? Most statutes of this type have been declared unconstitutional.

The Supreme Court has specifically left the concept of viability flexible, so as to accommodate advances in medical technology. As a result, states have the right to take into account new developments which may allow viability to occur at an earlier stage of pregnancy. Although most medical experts agree that such advances are not likely in the near future, some states have already taken advantage of this flexibility. The Pennsylvania legislature, for instance, recently passed a bill providing that annual hearings be held by the state medical board to determine at what point viability is likely to occur in light of advancing technology. Fortunately, the governor vetoed the bill. Had it gone into effect, doctors could have been subject to criminal penalties for violating viability standards under constant reassessment. It is easy to imagine that few doctors would be willing to perform late abortions under such circumstances.

The medical community is an important ally in fighting restrictions on abortions performed after viability. The performance of late abortions involves considerable medical skill and judgment and state attempts to interfere in this process are direct attacks on physicians' rights to practice medicine.

Sterilization Abuse

There is a well-documented history of sterilization abuse in the United States. Until very recently, access to sterilization was limited for many women, and was conditioned on arbitrary criteria such as a woman's marital status, the consent of her husband, her age, and the number of her children.

Thousands of persons were involuntarily sterilized under state eugenics statutes enacted during the early part of this century. More recently, the use of public funds to involuntarily sterilize poor and minority women resulted in the federal government's adoption of stringent regulations governing federally funded sterilization. But coerced sterilization of women, particularly minority women, continues through policies and practices of physicians and hospitals rather than through statutory authority.

Current state sterilization legislation primarily involves the sterilization of the mentally incompetent, a subject which involves complex and troubling legal and ethical considerations. There are many cases in which judges have authorized the sterilization of minors who are allegedly "mentally retarded" at the request of the minor's parents, only to have the woman later deeply regret what was done to her. There is no consensus as to the conditions, if any, under which sterilization of such individuals should be permitted.

In light of the tragic legacy of eugenic sterilization in the United States, however, and the fundamental nature of the rights at stake, any legislation in this area should provide maximum safeguards and not permit further abuse by giving third parties authority to consent to sterilization.

Standards outlined by the New Jersey Supreme Court for the sterilization of the mentally incompetent provide a useful guide for such legislation. Those standards include the requirement that a court, and not the parents or guardian, must determine the need for sterilization and whether sterilization is in the best interests of the incompetent; that there be procedural safeguards for the court hearing, including the appointment of a guardian *ad litem* for the incompetent, as well as proof, cross-examination, court review of independent medical and psychological evaluation by qualified professionals, and court access to the incompetent; that the court must find, by clear and convincing evidence, that the person lacks capacity to consent and that this is unlikely to change; and that there is clear and convincing proof that sterilization is in the incompetent's best interests, taking into account factors such as possible psychological damage from pregnancy or birth, the feasibility of other forms of contraception, and the good faith of those requesting the sterilization.

ANTI-ABORTION CONSTITUTIONAL AMENDMENTS

The anti-abortion measures described above are efforts on the part of state legislatures and local governing bodies to circumvent the Supreme Court's 1973 decisions legalizing abortion and to curtail to the greatest extent possible the performance of abortion. But the ultimate goal of the anti-choice movement is to outlaw all abortions altogether.

To this end, since 1973, the anti-abortion movement has been vigorously pushing for an amendment to the United States Constitution that would completely eliminate the availability of legal abortions.

In this country, there are two ways to amend our Constitution: one is for Congress, by a vote of two-thirds of both houses, to propose such an amendment; the second is for thirty-four states to call for a constitutional convention at which amendments can be proposed. In either case, the proposed amendment must be ratified by three-fourths (thirty-eight) of the states before it becomes part of the Constitution.

Until the November 1980 elections, congressional enactment of a so-called Human Life Amendment did not seem likely. But with the shift of power in Congress, including the election of a Republican majority in the Senate, enactment of such an amendment has become a real threat.

During the latter part of 1981, the Senate Judiciary Subcommittee on the Constitution, chaired by Senator Orrin Hatch, held hearings on anti-abortion constitutional amendments. Before the subcommittee were three "traditional" versions of a Human Life Amendment, as well as a new approach, the "Human Life Federalism Amendment."

The "traditional" Human Life Amendment that seems to have the broadest support from anti-abortion forces provides as follows:

Section 1. With respect to the right to life, the word person as used in this article and in the Fifth and Fourteenth Articles of the Amendments to the Constitution of the United States applies to all human beings irrespective of age, health, function or condition of dependency, including their unborn offspring at every stage of their biological development.

Section 2. No unborn person shall be deprived of life by any person; provided, however, that nothing in this article shall prohibit a law permitting only those medical procedures required to prevent the death of the mother.

Section 3. The Congress and the several states have power to enforce this article by appropriate legislation.

The implications of this proposed amendment are frightening. It would overturn the Supreme Court's 1973 decisions and give unprecedented legal protection to fertilized eggs; it would not only outlaw all abortions, it might also prohibit the use of IUDs and some birth control pills since they act as abortifacients rather than contraceptives by inhibiting the implantation of the already fertilized egg. Women who abort could conceivably be charged with murder, and women who miscarry or who are thought to have acted improperly during their pregnancies might be subject to charges of manslaughter or prenatal "child abuse." Any action that carries even a risk of causing fetal damage could be construed as a crime. A woman with cancer could be prohibited from continuing radiation therapy; women of childbearing age could be excluded from heavy work or toxic environments; the physical activities, travel, and other normal routines of pregnant women could be regulated.

As of early 1982, there was not enough support in the Congress for passage of an amendment such as this one. Indeed, it is for that reason that the "Human Life Federalism Amendment"—also known as the "Hatch Amendment"—has been proposed. That Amendment provides as follows:

A right to abortion is not secured by this Constitution. The Congress and the several States shall have the concurrent power to restrict and prohibit abortions.

Anti-abortion forces, conceding that they cannot secure passage of a Human Life Amendment, have turned their energies to this new "compromise" measure, which was first proposed in September 1981.

Passage of this amendment would not outlaw abortion itself, but it would give Congress and the states the power to criminalize the act by simple majority votes, thus transforming abortion from a constitutionally protected right to a matter controlled by a simple majority of any legislature. A myriad of state criminal abortion laws can be expected if this amendment is enacted. And even in states where the right to choose abortion seems secure, such as New York where abortion was legalized in 1970, the abortion right could be taken away by Congressional legislation.

During the Senate subcommittee hearings, constitutional scholars testified that this proposed Amendment would give government unprecedented power to intrude into private decisions by individuals, and, in so doing, would misuse the process for amending the Constitution in a way that would have profound implications for all constitutional rights.

Although the Hatch Amendment has caused a great deal of dissension among anti-abortion activists, it did receive the endorsement of the National Right to Life Committee and the National Conference of Catholic Bishops. It was approved by the Senate Judiciary Subcommittee in December 1981, and by the Senate Judiciary Committee, chaired by Senator Strom Thurmond, in March 1982. Consideration of this bill by the full Senate was expected in 1982. However, on September 15, 1982, the day the amendment was to be considered by the Senate, Senator Hatch, conceding that it lacked the votes needed for passage, withdrew the proposal. Although this was a significant setback for the anti-abortion forces, this proposal is by no means dead; Senate Majority Leader Baker has promised full debate on it during the spring of 1983.

Opponents of the right to abortion suffered another major setback in 1982 with the defeat of an omnibus anti-abortion bill proposed by Senator Helms. This proposal, known as the Helms "super bill," which unlike a constitutional amendment only requires a simple majority vote in Congress, would have permanently banned the use of federal funds for the performance of abortions and abortion-related activities such as referrals and training medical personnel in abortion techniques; prohibited insurance coverage of abortion for federal employees; and created a special expedited appeal to the United States Supreme Court for abortion cases. In addition, it contained "findings" by Congress that the Supreme Court erred in *Roe v. Wade* and that "scientific evidence demonstrates the life of each human being begins at conception." Immediately after the bill was introduced in August as an amendment to a pending debt limit bill, pro-choice senators began a filibuster. Several attempts to break the filibuster were unsuccessful, and despite last-minute lobbying efforts by President Reagan the Senate voted to table the bill by a very narrow vote.

In addition to these proposed constitutional amendments and statutes, anti-abortion activists have also been pushing for a constitutional convention. In June 1978, the National Right to Life Committee expressed approval of this amendment process and declared resolutions calling for a constitutional convention on abortion a top priority. As of early 1982, nineteen states have passed such resolutions—Alabama, Arkansas, Delaware, Idaho, Indiana, Kentucky, Louisiana, Massachusetts, Mississippi, Missouri, Nebraska, Nevada, New Jersey, Oklahoma, Pennsylvania, Rhode Island, South Dakota, Tennessee, and Utah. In addition, thirty-one states have passed resolutions on the issue of a balanced budget, only three short of the thirty-four needed to compel Congress to call a convention. This is significant because it is not clear if such a convention were called that it could be limited to just one issue. There is no deadline by which time the total of thirty-four states must be reached.

The legal issues involved in connection with a constitutional convention are complex, but the political impact is clear. If opponents of reproductive freedom should even approach success in the call for a constitutional convention on abortion, the likelihood of Congress passing a Human Life Amendment would become greater, since it would want to avoid the chaos of a constitutional convention.

The convention issue is a matter of great concern in itself. No one knows whether a convention could be limited to one issue, since there are no available procedures or precedents. The only constitutional convention in our history was the one that created the Constitution in the first place, nearly two hundred years ago. Every amendment to the Constitution since then has been the result of congressional initiative. Once a convention is called, it could decide to do away with any or all of the individual rights now guaranteed by the Bill of Rights. For this reason as well, it is important that pro-choice lobbyists oppose all resolutions calling for a constitutional convention.

One of the most effective means of defeating these calls is to alert the general public to the dangers of a constitutional convention. Where resolutions do not receive much attention, they are more likely to pass. In 1981, pro-choice activists in states where such resolutions were expected to be raised were prepared to work for their defeat. As a result, not one state passed such a resolution that year. Successful strategies included emphasizing the dangers of a constitutional convention rather than the abortion issue itself, since this may persuade a legislator who might normally vote anti-choice to vote against the amendment, and seeking the involvement of organizations not usually associated with abortion rights but which oppose the convening of a constitutional convention for other reasons. Also, where passage seems likely, resolutions that simply request Congress to propose an amendment, without the need for a constitutional convention, should be substituted for an actual call for a convention wherever possible.

Whether or not the constitutional convention issue is pending in your state legislature, the continuing campaign against a Human Life Amendment will almost certainly be underway in your state. Materials on the constitutional convention issue and such amendments, which include fact sheets, brochures, flyers, legal writings, etc., are available from pro-choice organizations such as the ACLU's Reproductive Freedom Project, the Planned Parenthood Federation of America, and the National Abortion Rights Action League, among others.

2 / WOMEN'S RIGHTS
by Barbara Shack

31 March, 1777: . . . in the new code of laws which I suppose it will be necessary for you to make, I desire you would remember the ladies and be more generous and favorable to them than your ancestors. . . . If particular care and attention is not paid to the ladies, we are determined to foment a rebellion, and will not hold ourselves bound by any laws in which we have no voice or representation.
—Abigail Adams to her husband John

Some two hundred years have passed since John Adams was urged by his wife Abigail to include women within the protection of the law governing the new American nation, which he was helping to draft. Although Adams and his colleagues ignored the request, the following two centuries witnessed a revolutionary change in the legal status of women in this country. Hundreds, probably thousands, of legal barriers to women's full participation in society—barriers created largely by tradition and habit—have toppled when legislatures and courts were forced to recognize their injustice. The progress made has been so enormous that it sometimes obscures how far there is yet to go.

On June 30, 1982, on the threshold of full citizenship, women lost their campaign to obtain the ultimate legal recognition of their equality when the proposed Equal Rights Amendment to the United States Constitution died. Approval by thirty-eight states was required, but only thirty-five states had ratified the Amendment by the deadline for such votes. This great loss will lead women to the various state legislatures, where the struggle for true equality and justice will continue.

This chapter will discuss three important state legislative issues that are ripe for major lobbying efforts, and why it is important for women to continue lobbying for freedom. These three issues are: the addition of Equal Rights Amendments to state constitutions; the inclusion of husbands in statutes that criminalize rape; and remedies for insurance discrimination. There are obviously many other women's issues which require state legislative remedies. The three presented here were selected because they are ripe for lobbying in many states and because they portray the broad range of women's concerns. Before we turn to these three issues, however, it is useful to review briefly the history of women's fight for legal recognition and justice.

THE LEGAL BACKGROUND

Alfred Lord Tennyson described the relationship of a woman to her man in nineteenth-century England as "something better than his dog, a little dearer than his horse." In fact, this view of women accurately reflected the traditional and legal status of women at that time. English law treated women as the property of their husbands and fathers. Like children, they had no legal rights of their own.

That legal view was exported to the American colonies and then became part of the law of each of the states. Until the middle of the nineteenth century a woman in this country had no legal right to keep any salary she earned, being compelled on demand to turn it over to her husband; to own property in her own name; to sign a contract or to sue or be sued; to attend school without her spouse's permission; to obtain legal custody of her own children; or to leave her husband's or father's home, regardless of her age. Moreover, if she misbehaved, her husband was legally entitled to administer physical punishment.

By the second half of the nineteenth century, women began to secure some legal rights when the states gradually enacted "Married

Women's Property Acts." But it was not until 1920—fifty years after the black man was granted the right to vote—that women could vote or participate in the political process.

One of the most notorious relics of the then prevailing attitude toward women is contained in an 1873 United States Supreme Court decision which upheld the constitutionality of an Illinois statute that prohibited women from practicing law in that state. Speaking for the Court in *Bradwell v. Illinois*, Justice Bradley wrote:

> The harmony, not to say identity, of interests and views which belong, or should belong, to the family institution is repugnant to the idea of a woman adopting a distinct and independent career from that of her husband . . .
>
> The paramount destiny and mission of woman are to fulfill the noble and benign offices of wife and mother. This is the law of the Creator. And the rules of civil society must be adopted to the general constitution of things and cannot be based upon exceptional cases.

Indeed, as recently as 1948, the Supreme Court, interpreting the Fourteenth Amendment, upheld a Michigan statute that barred women from employment as bartenders unless they were the wives or daughters of the tavern owners. Women were permitted to serve as waitresses in these establishments but prohibited from the better paying jobs as bartenders. In *Goesaert v. Cleary*, the state argued, and the Court agreed, that the provision was not discriminatory but a benign preference for the protection of women.

It was not until 1971, more than one hundred years after the adoption of the Fourteenth Amendment, that the Supreme Court recognized that the equal protection guarantee of that Amendment should also apply to women. In the landmark case *Reed v. Reed*, the Court struck down an Idaho statute which explicitly preferred men over women as estate administrators. The statute was based on the assumption that men are better in business matters. *Reed* signaled a fundamental change in the Court's view of sex discrimination. However, a majority of the Court did not then—and has not yet—ruled that sex, like race, is entitled to the full measure of that guarantee of equal protection.

Coinciding with the development of constitutional law concerning the permissible boundaries of sex discrimination, another monumental legal upheaval was taking place: the legal battle to permit women to control their own reproductive functions. The principal victory came in 1973, when the Supreme Court declared that a woman's right to terminate a pregnancy by having an abortion is a constitutional right that may not be prohibited by any branch of government. The recognition of reproductive freedom for women, which this decision largely accomplished, is probably the most liberating phenomenon of the century. The subject of reproductive freedom is discussed at length in the preceding chapter. However, no discussion of women's rights would be complete without mention of this fundamental right.

Professor Alfred Conrad, a former President of the Association of American Law Schools, put it aptly when he said that the "Motherhood Draft" has ended:

> We ought to realize that for the past two million years women have been subjected to a twenty-five-year draft lottery—the motherhood draft. If they did not choose to be nuns—in or out of habit—they had very little control over the duration and frequency of their years of motherhood.
> This aspect of women's lives has changed dramatically . . .
> As a result of women's emancipation, we are going to have women play more important roles in the public and commercial life of our country and of the world.

During the 1960s and 1970s Congress and the states moved swiftly—especially when compared with Professor Conrad's reference to two million years—to enact new laws to protect women from discrimination in jobs, housing, credit, public accommodations, education, and insurance. Women's lobby groups during the past twenty years have worked effectively to translate the spirit of the equal rights movement into concrete laws and have generally found state legislatures receptive to their cause. The "women's movement" created the impression that women are generally united in their goals and that there are concerns which women share almost universally. A sense of political sorority was conveyed to politicians and legislators which they perceived as a new political force. Women had finally reached the point where, as 53 percent of the voting population, it was no longer safe to ignore them. That political power is still a potent force.

But in spite of all these gains, women are still second-class citizens in several important respects. They are still grossly underrepresented in the halls of government, still poor when compared with men, and, in many ways, still the victims of entrenched discrimination.

More women have been elected to public office than ever before; yet, although they are 53 percent of the population, they constitute a minute fraction of all elected officials. Much of this progress has occurred in the last ten years. For example, in 1971 there were 11 women in Congress, which was 2 percent of that body. In 1981 there were 21, or 4 percent. The increase of women in state legislatures is threefold: In 1971, 362, or 5 percent, of state legislators were women, while in 1981 there were 901 women, or 12 percent, in the state-houses. In early 1982, 71 women served as mayors of cities with populations over 30,000. At that time, however, there was no female governor. Three of the states have never had a woman serve in their state senates.

Women in this country are still far poorer than men. Ninety-three percent of welfare recipients are women and children. Women represent 69 percent of food stamp recipients, use 67 percent of federally funded legal services programs, 66 percent of subsidized housing, 61 percent of Medicaid, and 67 percent of Medicare. In short, twice as many women as men qualify for, and depend on, government subsidy.

The median income for women who worked full-time in 1979 was $10,168, while for men it was $17,062. Women are earning 59 cents for every dollar paid to men. This gap has widened since 1955, when the median earnings of women were $2,179 compared with $4,252 for men, which translates to 65 cents to the dollar.

Some of the more interesting comparisons can be seen from 1979 Census data which showed that women in clerical jobs averaged $9,855 a year while male clerical workers averaged $16,503, or 40 percent more. Other data from the Census Bureau compiled by NOW in a publication, *E.R.A. and the 59¢ Wage Gap*, illustrate the pattern of salary differentials:

Male-Female Wage Gap by Full-Time Occupations and Job Titles

Occupation	Men	Women	Women's Pay to Men's Dollar
Clerical Workers	$16,503	$9,855	60¢
Typists	12,122	9,248	76¢
Cashiers	11,244	7,645	68¢
Service Workers	11,925	7,319	61¢
Private Household	12,991	3,618	28¢
Health Services	11,238	8,346	74¢
Professionals	21,310	13,701	64¢
Teachers	18,158	13,431	74¢
Grade & High School	16,905	13,107	78¢
College	22,958	16,219	71¢
Computer Specialists	21,774	18,342	84¢
Operatives	14,921	8,562	57¢
Manufacturing	15,109	8,725	58¢
Sales Workers	17,084	8,880	52¢
Sales Clerks	10,994	7,208	66¢
Retail Trade	12,245	7,297	60¢
Managers	21,835	11,705	54¢
Finance/Insurance	24,127	12,044	50¢
Public Administration	20,401	14,753	72¢
Laborers (except from	11,974	8,985	75¢
Manufacturing)	13,457	9,217	68¢
Construction	10,916	7,821	72¢
Craft Workers	17,106	10,585	62¢

Before turning to a discussion of three separate legislative issues that affect women, it should be emphasized that this selection should be seen merely as a sampler. There are numerous other areas for legislative change that women require and will be working for. Many groups in Washington and in every state are lobbying for such changes. They would all welcome additions to the lobbying ranks.

THE LEGISLATIVE ISSUES FOR THE 1980s

Equal Rights Amendments to State Constitutions

"Equality of rights under the law shall not be denied or abridged by the United States or by any state on account of sex."

This was the language of the proposed federal ERA that died on June 30, 1982, because it was not ratified by the requisite thirty-eight states. For such an Amendment to be adopted now, it would again have to pass each house of Congress by a two-thirds vote and then be ratified by thirty-eight states. There is very little likelihood that this will happen in the near future. As a result, the political campaign to achieve equal rights for women will shift to the states, where advocates will be lobbying to add Equal Rights Amendments to state constitutions.

The need for a state ERA is the same as for the federal ERA—to change the fundamental law of the state in order to ensure an end to sex discrimination. The subordinate status of women is ingrained in our legal system. Laws and policies of each state are permeated with a double standard that provides different rights for men and women. Some laws exclude women from rights and opportunities; some were designed to protect women and have now become barriers to full opportunity; and others create a separate legal status for women.

As long as the law permits different treatment for the sexes, women will occupy an inferior status. As one commentary in the April 1971 Yale Law Journal put it:

> History and experience have taught us that in such a dual system one group is always dominant and the other subordinate. As long as women's place is defined as separate, male-dominated society will define her place as inferior.

A state ERA could prevent many common practices that discriminate against women, including:

—sex-based legal presumptions about the ownership and control of marital property, such as presumptions that all the household goods belong to the husband;
—differences in juvenile offender laws which punish noncriminal behavior of girls until they are eighteen but boys only until they are sixteen;
—discrimination in public employment which causes women to be in the lowest paid jobs;
—discrimination in public schools, especially vocational schools, and the exclusion of women from athletic programs;

—different treatment of women prisoners, such as denial of education and recreation benefits, use of law libraries, and job training.

An ERA will bar a state from categorizing people solely on the basis of their sex. It will require government to remain neutral with respect to the roles men and women play in society. This will mean that men and women will be *equal* before the law, not the *same*. It will foster a legal system in which each person will be judged on individual merit and ability. An ERA regulates what the government can do; it does not affect private individuals or groups.

An Equal Rights Amendment is our highest form of lawmaking—a way of changing our fundamental, enduring law. It provides a general principle to govern the people and their lawmakers through the ages.

Without an Equal Rights Amendment, the federal Constitution does not expressly prohibit discrimination based on sex. The principle that women and men have equal rights under the law is not stated in the Constitution. That is because the equal protection guarantee that is contained in the Fourteenth Amendment was adopted after the Civil War to prohibit discrimination based on race. Since that time, the Supreme Court has never found that the Fourteenth Amendment prohibits sex discrimination to the same extent that it prohibits racial, religious, or ethnic discrimination.

Thomas Jefferson, one of the principal authors of the Constitution, once stated as follows:

> Were our state a pure democracy there would still be excluded from our deliberations women, who, to prevent deprivation of morals and ambiguity of issues, should not mix promiscuously in gatherings of men.

The idea that men and women might be equal in the law was never even considered by the framers of the Constitution, which was drafted at a time when women had no legal status at all. The Declaration of Independence, signed in 1776, proclaimed that "all men are created equal." The Constitution of 1787 was inspired at least in part by English common law, which did not recognize women as citizens with any rights of their own.

Following the Civil War, early feminists who fought in the abolition movement looked to Congress to provide a guarantee of sexual equality in the Constitutional amendments that were being adopted to free the slaves and grant them full legal rights. But the Fourteenth Amendment was written in a way that repudiated those early champions of sex equality. It introduced the word "male" for the first time in the Constitution, and made clear to all that the "due process" and "equal protection" guarantees of that long awaited Amendment would not apply to women. Women were also excluded from the Fifteenth Amendment, which gave the vote to the freed male slaves.

In 1872, after asserting her right to vote, Susan B. Anthony was charged with a federal offense because she voted in that year's presidential election. In finding her guilty, the trial judge said:

> I have decided as a question of law . . . that under the Fourteenth Amendment, which Miss Anthony claims protects her, she was not protected in a right to vote.

It took another fifty years, and the adoption of the Nineteenth Amendment in 1920, before women won the right to vote. Three years later, in 1923, the National Women's Party was successful in having an ERA introduced in Congress. It has been reintroduced every year since then. It is indeed a bitter footnote to the history created by those brave women that, fifty-nine years after it was first introduced, the ERA came so close to national ratification but ultimately fell three states short.

It was not until one hundred years after the Fourteenth Amendment was adopted that the Supreme Court, in *Reed v. Reed*, construed the Amendment's equal protection clause to protect women against at least some forms of sex discrimination.

Sally Reed, an Idaho woman whose twenty-year-old son died, applied to be the administrator of his estate. Cecil Reed, the boy's father, also applied, and was appointed in accordance with a state law which required that between persons "equally entitled" to administer a decedent's estate, "males must be preferred to females." It was this statute that the Supreme Court struck down in its landmark decision in 1971. And although the decision was based on the Fourteenth Amendment, the Court did not apply the same standard that it does when considering race discrimination.

With this decision, the Supreme Court devised a dual approach to analyzing discrimination cases. When confronted with government-created discrimination on the basis of race, religion, or alienage—what the Supreme Court calls "suspect classifications"—the Court will require the government to show that the discrimination is justified by a "compelling state interest," which as a practical matter is a burden that can almost never be satisfied. In contrast, however, when confronted with sex discrimination, the Court will only require the government to show that its discriminatory actions are supported by some rational explanation.

Since the *Reed* case, the Supreme Court, using this double standard, has upheld sex discrimination in some cases and overturned it in others. However, no majority opinion of the Court has ever found sex to be a "suspect" classification. If the Court had applied to sex classifications the same constitutional test that it applies to race classification, there would be no need for an equal rights amendment for women.

Justice Lewis Powell, in a recent sex discrimination case, *Frontiero v. Richardson*, gave his explanation as to why the Court has not chosen to apply that stricter standard to sex discrimination cases:

> The Equal Rights Amendment . . . will resolve the substance of this precise question. . . . If this Amendment is duly adopted, it will represent the will of the people accomplished in a manner prescribed by the Constitution. . . . [R]eaching out to pre-empt by judicial action a major political decision which is currently in process of resolution does not reflect appropriate respect for duly prescribed legislative processes.

Ruth Bader Ginsburg, one of the most prominent and skilled legal advocates for gender equality in this century and now a Judge of the United States Court of Appeals for the District of Columbia, summarized the current status of this issue as follows:

> Constitutional law in this area, like the public debate on the roles of men and women, is in mid-passage state. Ratification of the Equal Rights Amendment would give the Supreme Court a clear signal—a more secure handle for its rulings than the Fifth

and Fourteenth Amendments. In the meantime, doctrine is evolving, but the Court is sharply divided and its future course is uncertain. As one district judge put it: lower court judges searching for guidance in 1970's Supreme Court sex discrimination precedents have an "uncomfortable feeling"—like players at a shell game who are "not absolutely sure there is a pea."

Now that the campaign for the federal ERA has failed, it has become necessary to accomplish that goal on a state-by-state basis by adding Equal Rights Amendments to state constitutions.

A state constitution provides the same kinds of guarantees for residents of the state that the federal Constitution does for every person in the country. The state courts in each state interpret its constitution, and the highest court in the state ultimately decides what the ERA means in that state. The United States Supreme Court cannot reverse a state court decision that interprets a state constitution.

State ERAs, then, can set the standards for government conduct and provide the legal basis for individuals to challenge discriminatory government action against them in the state's court system. Courts in states with an ERA will be encouraged to develop more stringent protection for women than the standards adopted by the United States Supreme Court for sex discrimination cases. A clear statement of such a test was made by the Pennsylvania Supreme Court in *Henderson v. Henderson*:

> The thrust of the Equal Rights Amendment is to insure equality of rights under the law to eliminate sex as a basis for distinction. The sex of citizens of the Commonwealth is no longer a permissible factor in the determination of their legal rights and legal responsibilities.

Sixteen states have added ERAs to their state constitutions: Alaska, Colorado, Connecticut, Hawaii, Illinois, Maryland, Massachusetts, Montana, New Hampshire, New Mexico, Pennsylvania, Texas, Utah, Virginia, Washington, and Wyoming. Nine of these states have language which is very similar to the defeated federal ERA. Colorado's provision is a good example:

Equality of rights under the law shall not be denied or abridged by the state of Colorado or any of its political subdivisions on account of sex.

Although the federal ERA was lost, thirty-five state legislatures voted for it. Taking into account that three states tried to rescind their ratification votes, thirty-two states are clearly on record as supporting an ERA. Of those thirty-two, thirteen already have ERAs. This leaves nineteen states that have already supported a federal amendment but do not have ERAs of their own. These nineteen states are ripe targets for serious lobbying efforts and will undoubtedly see such efforts in the years to come. These states are: California, Delaware, Indiana, Iowa, Kansas, Kentucky, Maine, Michigan, Minnesota, New Jersey, New York, North Dakota, Ohio, Oregon, Rhode Island, South Dakota, Vermont, West Virginia, and Wisconsin.

Curiously, three states that failed to ratify the federal ERA nevertheless have state ERAs of their own. They are Utah, Virginia, and Illinois, the home state of Phyllis Schlafly, who led the national campaign against the federal ERA.

The nineteen target states will almost certainly become the newest battlegrounds for ERAs as women recover from the defeat of the federal ERA and resume their historic struggle for legal equality.

As a result of excellent research by the ERA Impact Project, a project of the NOW Legal Defense and Education Fund and the Women's Law Project, it is clear that state ERAs have resulted in the expansion of rights for women in those states. Court decisions and statutory revisions caused by these amendments have helped both women and men. Probably the single most important effect of the adoption of a state ERA is the impetus it creates for a comprehensive reform of state laws.

Those who lobby to improve the status of women have learned how difficult it is to repeal or change existing discriminatory statutes, no matter how archaic they are. Most states have hundreds of sex-based laws embedded in their statute books. There is clear evidence from ERA states that those states experienced significant—and long overdue—law reform as a result of the adoption of the ERA. Indeed, it is also clear that even where they are unsuccessful, the federal and state ERA drives have provided an impetus for law reform. For example, the New York legislature, preparing for a state referendum on an ERA, requested its Law Revision Commission to examine all state statutes and recommend legislative changes to conform with the equality principle. More than two hundred recommendations were made.

Unfortunately, the sad part of the New York story is that the state's voters failed to ratify the amendment. But a happier side effect was that the legislature enacted most of the recommended revisions.

One specific area in which ERA drives have had a demonstrable impact is employment. Legislatures eliminated restrictions on women's employment rights and extended to both sexes rights that previously were reserved for only one. According to the ERA Impact Project:

—In Connecticut and Illinois, limits on the number of hours women (but not men) could work have been repealed, thereby increasing employment opportunities for women.

—In Hawaii, pregnancy may no longer disqualify women from eligibility for unemployment benefits.

—The Illinois Attorney General found that the state's sex-based accidental death benefits law violated the ERA. Consequently the Illinois legislature broadened the law to provide employment-related benefits to both male and female surviving spouses of covered workers.

Another major area that has been and will be shaped by state ERAs is education. The experience of states with ERAs indicates that they have been used successfully to challenge sex discrimination in education and to remove arbitrary limits on opportunities for women and girls in athletics. The ERA Impact Project has reported several such cases brought and won under state ERAs:

—In Massachusetts, female law students won the right to apply for a scholarship previously awarded only to male students.

—In Texas, a court held that a university must provide both male and female students with equivalent on-campus housing. It also ruled that it was a violation of the state ERA to permit males to live off campus while denying such choice to female students.

—In New Mexico, the Attorney General ruled that under the state's ERA girls could not be excluded from a special high school program in a state-operated school.

Another area where state ERAs have had a significant impact involves family law, particularly with respect to marital property, alimony, and child support. State courts in ERA states are beginning to see marriage as an economic partnership and, as a result, married women, and especially those who are dependent homemakers, are beginning to acquire new rights.

But probably the most important long-term effect of state ERAs is that they create substantial barriers against regressive legislation. During the past decade, the ERA movement has provided an impetus to most of the states to repeal voluntarily the worst of their sex-biased laws. However, without an ERA in the Constitution, there is no guarantee that future legislatures could not reverse those gains. An Equal Rights Amendment is a lifetime guarantee.

Those who successfully campaigned against the federal ERA did so by fearmongering—by raising doubts and even hysteria with claims that the ERA will compel unfortunate and ridiculous legal results. We will now review some of the most notorious of these myths.

First, there is the "potty excuse," a phrase coined by United States Senator Marlow Cook in response to the claim that the federal ERA would lead to coed toilet facilities. Senator Sam Ervin, in making that claim, stated as follows:

[I]f the ERA is to be construed absolutely, as its proponents say, then there can be no exception for elements of publicly imposed sexual segregation on the basis of privacy between men and women.

The short response to this ridiculous suggestion is that we currently provide separate toilet facilities for men and women not because of any constitution or statute but because it is a traditional recognition of the right to privacy of both sexes. An ERA would merely require equal facilities for men and women. Again, the equal rights principle means that men and women have to be treated equally, not the same. Indeed, this conclusion has been confirmed by a ruling of a New Mexico court which rejected a claim that that state's ERA required coed dorm visits in state schools.

State ERAs will not affect women's obligations to participate in a federal draft. Such a draft is entirely a federal matter which the state has no power to affect.

State ERAs will also not compel women to go outside the home to support their husbands. No state can force any person to work to support a family. The Thirteenth Amendment to the United States Constitution prohibits involuntary servitude. No person in this country can be forced to work for any reason.

State ERAs will not affect the practices of any religious institution or private club.

The ERA has been supported by the last six presidents of the United States prior to Ronald Reagan, who does not support it, and it was passed by a vote of 354 to 23 in the House of Representatives in 1971 and a vote of 84 to 8 in the Senate in 1972. More than two hundred organizations have also supported the ERA, including: American Association of University Women; American Baptist Women; American Bar Association; the AFL-CIO and twenty-six affiliated unions; American Home Economics Association; American Jewish Congress; American Veterans Committee; B'nai B'rith Women; Board of Church and Society of the United Methodist Church; Catholic Women for the ERA; Child Welfare League of America; Christian Church (Disciples of Christ); Coalition of Labor Union Women; Common Cause; General Federation of Women's Clubs; Girl Scouts of the USA; League of Women Voters; Lutheran Church; NAACP; National Catholic Coalition for the ERA; National Coalition of American Nuns; National Council of Churches (of Christ); National Council of Jewish Women; National Council of Negro Women; National Federation of Business and Professional Women's Clubs; National Organization for Women; National Secretaries Association; National Women's Political Caucus; United Auto Workers; United Presbyterian Church, USA; and Young Women's Christian Association.

The foregoing discussion is not intended as a complete guide for those who will conduct ERA campaigns. Instead, it is presented with the hope that it will provide encouragement and a general background for individuals who wish to become involved in a lobbying effort in their states.

Those who seek to organize such campaigns will have to develop their strategies. Difficult questions concerning the political climate in the state will have to be raised and answered. For instance, is it better to have an ERA referendum in the same year as a general election, or in an off-year? Experience in New York demonstrated that although polls showed that a majority of the state's population supported a state ERA, it was a disaster for the amendment to be on the ballot in 1975, a year when there were no statewide or legislative elections. Postmortem analyses revealed that off-years attract voters who are disgruntled and come out to vote "no" on various state appropriation issues. Many supporters of the ERA were so confident of victory that they simply stayed home, especially since it was the only item on the ballot that concerned them.

Coalitions will have to be formed and campaign materials prepared. The experience of other states will be valuable.

There is also a major resource for information and materials on state ERAs at the ERA Impact Project of the NOW Legal Defense and Education Fund and the Women's Law Project, 132 West 43rd Street, New York, New York 10036.

Marital Rape Exemption

In thirty-six states it is not a crime for a man to rape his wife. Only nine states specifically outlaw marital rape. Five states' laws are silent on the subject. The remaining states, either by statute or judicial decision, have adopted the English rule which since the seventeenth century has immunized husbands against prosecution for rape.

The first formal recognition of a rape exemption for husbands was set forth by Lord Matthew Hale, a seventeenth-century English scholar, who wrote:

[T]he husband cannot be guilty of rape committed by himself upon his lawful wife, for by their mutual matrimonial consent and contract, the wife hath given up herself in this kind unto her husband, which she cannot retract.

Relying on that statement, a Massachusetts court in 1857 gave the first judicial recognition in the United States to the Hale rule. Lord Hale is still the most cited authority in England and in the United States for the legal justification for a husband's immunity for rape.

From 1857 to 1980 the courts in this country accepted the exemption without question, and there had been little if any serious analysis of its justification. In three cases in 1980 and 1981—in New Jersey, Massachusetts, and Florida—courts for the first time in this country seriously questioned the marital exemption. However, Hale's ancient notion that a wife gives lifelong consent to sexual intercourse when she agrees to the marriage contract still prevails in our courts and legislatures. This is in dramatic contrast to the remarkable changes in other areas of the law which have been inspired in recent decades by emerging egalitarian values and a new respect for the worth of woman.

The idea that a husband cannot be prosecuted for rape is rooted in the principle that a married woman's identity is merged with her husband's and, according to Blackstone's *Commentaries*, "the very being or legal existence of the woman is suspended during the marriage, or at least is incorporated and consolidated into that of the husband; under whose wing, protection, and cover she performs every thing." This "unity of person" notion was the same rationale that justified giving the husband sole power over the wife's property and civil rights earlier in our history.

The rape exemption derives from rules that governed ancient societies and were recorded thousands of years before the English bequeathed it to the Western world. Those old rules made a woman the property of her husband or father, and rape laws developed to protect her value as a sexual object to her husband or future spouse. A man who raped his wife was simply using his own property.

Susan Brownmiller, in her 1975 landmark examination of the history of rape, *Against Our Will: Men, Women and Rape*, put it this way:

Slavery, private property and the subjugation of women were facts of life, and the earliest written law that has come down to us reflects this stratified life. Written law in its origin was a solemn compact among men of property, designed to protect their own male interests by a civilized exchange of goods or silver in *place of force* wherever possible. The capture of females by force remained perfectly acceptable *outside* the tribe or city as one of the ready fruits of warfare, but clearly *within* the social order such a happenstance would lead to chaos. A payment of money to the father of the house was a much more civilized and less dangerous way of acquiring a wife. And so the bride prize was codified at fifty pieces of silver. By this circuitous route the first concept of criminal rape sneaked its tortuous way into man's definition of law. Criminal rape, as a patriarch father saw it, was a violation of the new way of doing business. It was, in a phrase, the theft of virginity, an embezzlement of his daughter's fair price on the market.

In the 1980s, the notion of women as property continues to haunt our legal system. Although women now have independent legal status in most respects, about half of the states still do not allow husbands and wives to sue each other for negligence, assault, and other personal torts. The husband's rape immunity, however, is the most obnoxious of the remaining legal impediments to the physical safety of wives.

Because the laws on rape are changing in every jurisdiction, it is not possible to provide an up-to-date listing. The most comprehensive catalogue of rape statutes by state was published in 1977 and updated in 1981 by the Women's Rights Law Reporter; it is updated periodically by the excellent research of the National Center on Women and Family Law (NCOWFL), which publishes a newsletter containing a column on statutory and case law developments on the marital rape exemption. This organization will also provide a state-by-state summary of the marital rape exemption in each state's criminal laws, including citations. In addition, the National Clearing House on Marital Rape provides research and legislative information on the subject.

As of the early 1980s, a few states have completely eliminated the exemption; some allow women to charge their husbands with rape only if they can prove that they were living apart at the time of the crime; some states require a legal separation or court order; and one state, New York, even requires that the legal separation agreement or court order give notice to the husband that his wife will be able to charge rape if she is assaulted. A few states have classified rape in two degrees, distinguishing between persons who are married or have had previous sexual contact and total strangers, with different proof requirements for each category. Several states have even extended the exemption to unmarried people.

The obvious and persistent obstacle to reform of the rape exemption may be due, in part, to the fact that legislatures and courts are overwhelmingly male. The staunch resistance of legislatures to lobbying by women's groups on this issue is eloquent testimony to the passion with which the battle lines have been drawn. One can only wonder whether California State Senator Bob Wilson was speaking for most state legislatures when he declared to a group of women lobbyists: "But if you can't rape your wife, who can you rape?"

Although the progress has been slow, there is an emerging sensitivity to the view that married women are entitled to the full protection of the law against rape. It is possible that during the 1980s women and men working together can lobby successfully to change the attitudes that underlie this relic of a different age, and then, perhaps, to change the law itself.

Insurance Discrimination

The insurance industry has always treated men and women differently, which has resulted in less insurance coverage and generally higher rates for women.

Sex discrimination by the insurance industry results primarily from the assumption that women are dependents who do not require protection from the economic risks of illness, disability, death, and old age. The 1973 underwriting manual of the North America Re-Assurance Company illustrates this in its advice to employers:

> . . . women's role in the commercial world [is] a provisional one . . . they work not from financial need, but for personal convenience. The subjective circumstances which create "convenience" tend to change, and if a woman has disability coverage, the temptation exists to replace her earnings with an insurance income once work loses its attractiveness.

The Metropolitan Life Insurance Company's manual of that year contained this instruction:

Hiring procedures for female employees deserve special attention . . . married women are, under certain circumstances, responsible for above-average claim costs and other serious problems connected with excessive absenteeism. Very often these problems are related to home responsibilities which were not looked into at the time of hiring. Family relations, the number of children in the family, provision for care of the children while the mother is at work, and transportation arrangements for getting to and from work are important considerations which may directly affect both the employee's attendance record and job performance. Because of income tax advantages, Weekly Indemnity benefits may be very close to normal take-home pay. Some employees who must arrange for the care of their children during working hours may actually be better off financially if they can collect insurance benefits. Some married women are willing to accept a loss of income periodically rather than face up to the hardships of working full time and caring for their homes and families.

Since 1973 there have been many changes in insurance practices in response to pressure from women's groups and the rising percentage of women in the work force. Some states have passed laws restricting certain of the more blatant practices and the industry itself has discarded some of its archaic rules. However, the assumption that women are bad insurance risks still permeates the industry. It will take a great deal of education and lobbying to challenge these underlying assumptions and then to enact laws which prohibit the resulting discriminatory practices.

Until very recently, discriminatory practices and policies were so pervasive in the insurance industry that women could not buy the same insurance as men at any price. During the past ten years there have been many reforms in the industry's manner of doing business. Because of the reform movement and because insurance laws and practices vary from state to state, it is not possible to index the current problems.

The listing below is presented to illustrate the nature and extent of the recent problems. Many of these problems still exist in some states.

It should also be understood that state and federal laws against sex discrimination in employment prohibit discrimination in *all employment-related insurance plans.* Many of the practices listed below are clearly illegal if they are contained in employee insurance plans.

Disability Income Policies

—Males are offered coverage to age sixty-five while females are offered policies that provide one, two, or five years of benefits.

—The definition of disability is different for men and women. For women, it is the inability to perform the duties of any occupation; for men, it is the inability to perform the duties of his own occupation.

—Premiums are as much as 150 percent higher for women, even where the coverage and benefits are lower.

—Coverage is not available to women in the lowest occupational classifications where it is available to men in these jobs.

—Women's policies often have longer waiting periods than do men's before benefits begin.

—Guaranteed renewable policies are limited to females in "permanent, career-type occupations."

—Females, but not males, who are gainfully employed in their own home at commencement of disability receive reduced monthly benefits, as much as 60 percent less than they would have gotten if they had been working outside of the home.

—Women cannot obtain coverage if they work part-time, work at home, or are employed by relatives, while similarly situated males can.

—Limits on the amount of insurance a woman may buy are lower than for men of similar age and occupation.

—Many special riders are not available to females, such as guaranteed increase options, options to increase length of own occupation period, partial disability riders, lifetime accident insurance, and hospital indemnity on the husband.

Health Insurance

Group

—Females may be restricted from including husbands as dependents even though males are permitted to include wives.

—Married women are unable to enroll as individuals in group coverage even though men may do so.

—Women who are covered by their husbands' policies are dropped when there is a divorce, with no right to obtain a comparable policy.

—Medical, surgical, and hospitalization coverage for legal abortions may be excluded entirely or limited to family contracts or to those having maternity coverage.

Nongroup

—Maternity coverage is unavailable to single women or single parents unless they enroll in higher cost "family" coverage in which premiums are based on coverage for two adults and children.

—A woman who is eligible for group coverage through her own or her husband's group may not enroll in nongroup plans, even where she finds her group coverage to be inadequate or inappropriate for her needs.

—A simple procedure performed several years earlier may result in a rider excluding coverage for "all female reproductive organs."

Maternity-related coverage

—Prenatal and postpartum maternity care is usually not covered by insurance.

—Waiting periods before maternity coverage goes into effect are longer than waiting periods for non-maternity care.

—Maternity coverage may be subject to a flat maximum benefit unrelated to true expenses, while other conditions are covered on an indemnity basis related to actual claims.

—There is no coverage, generally, for pregnancy-related expenses of dependent female children.

—Major Medical will not cover expenses related to normal pregnancy.

Homeowner's and Property Insurance

—Single persons, especially women, who work away from home may have difficulty purchasing homeowner's or renter's insurance.

—Agents' attitudes toward working women may affect whether or not a married couple has difficulty purchasing insurance.

—A married woman may have difficulty obtaining insurance in her name only, leading to interruption of coverage in the case of divorce.

Annuities and Pensions

—Individual annuity programs are sex-segregated, leading to lower monthly benefits for women based on the longer life expectancy of the female group, even when they have made contributions equal to those made by men.

—Group pension plans often have vesting requirements which women workers are less able to meet, due to higher turnover among women workers.

—Group pension plans often have a two-tier program based on salary levels. Since women are concentrated among lower paid workers, employers contribute less to their pension programs in these situations.

Life Insurance

—Guaranteed insurability riders are not available to females.

—Agents are reluctant to insure women with illegitimate children, or write policies on such children.

—The waiver of premium option is available only to selected women, and at rates much higher than male rates. The waiver may be available for a shorter time period, or may be available for a limited amount of the premium.

—Coverage for a married woman may depend upon the extent of her husband's coverage, which must be as much or more than hers. Some companies specify a percentage of the husband's amount as the top available to the woman.

—Companies prescribe special criteria for female insurability, such as the requirement that a woman be self-supporting, leave home to work, or be employed in a "responsible" position.

Automobile Insurance

—Divorced and separated women are treated as undesirable risks. They find their rates go up so that they can't buy in the regular insurance market.

—Women may be dropped from their husband's policies at the time of separation or divorce and then have difficulty obtaining insurance on their own.

—Agents treat females, particularly unmarried, divorced, and widowed women, more cautiously than men.

—Women living with men outside of marriage are refused insurance, have their insurance cancelled, or are refused renewal altogether.

There are no federal laws that specifically prohibit sex discrimination in insurance outside of the employment context. The McCarran-Ferguson Act of 1945 exempts the insurance industry from virtually all federal regulation, leaving this subject entirely up to the state legislatures. State insurance departments have been lax in requiring fair insurance practices and have been handicapped by the lack of legislative authority.

Some states have prohibited the most obvious discriminatory practices by amending state laws to prohibit discrimination based on sex and marital status in the sale of insurance. A 1975 New York law is a good example:

No association, corporation, firm, fund, individual, group, order, organization, society or trust shall refuse to issue any policy of insurance, or shall cancel or decline to renew such policy, because of the sex or marital status of the applicant or policyholder.

To overcome the exclusion of pregnancy-related and gynecological coverage for hospital and doctors' fees, some state laws now mandate that all health insurance policies cover pregnancy-related care to the same extent as other conditions are covered by that policy. Some states require a minimum coverage of three days' hospitalization for a normal childbirth and full coverage for complications of childbirth. Coverage for abortion is always a more controversial issue, and whether pregnancy-related insurance coverage includes abortion often depends on the political climate in each state. Sometimes abortion is specifically excluded and in some instances it is not mentioned in the statute, leaving interpretation to the regulatory agency and ultimately the courts.

Insurance discrimination is a fertile area for state legislative reform.

Women's rights activists in each state should consult with their state insurance regulatory authorities and their state women's rights commissions for further information.

No discussion of insurance would be complete without mention of the problem of discrimination in insurance rates. This discrimination results from the universal insurance industry practice of classifying customers by sex in order to predict how long they will live, how sick they will be, or how many automobile accidents they will have. The insurance industry has always classified people by sex in order to predict their risk and has constructed its rate scales according to sex. Differences between the races are no longer used to justify different insurance rates for blacks and whites, but sex differentials continue in effect.

Women's rights advocates believe that the overriding social and legal policy in this country that prohibits all classifications based on race should also apply to sex classifications. Most individuals do not conform to the "averages" for their sex or race, and to treat them as if they do is to penalize some of them. For instance, women live longer than men on the average—but not most women. About 84 percent of women and men match in death ages; 8 percent of the women will live longer and 8 percent of the men will live shorter than the remaining 84 percent.

Insurance companies translate this statistic either to charge all women higher premiums or to pay all women lower monthly benefits because as a group they will be more expensive to the company. This assumes that all women can be predicted to live longer. Of course this is not the case, and if a woman is one of the 84 percent who do not live longer than the average male she will receive less return for her money simply because she is a woman.

Women generally pay more for annuities, pensions, health insurance, and disability plans. Men pay more for life and automobile insurance.

It may be that only federal insurance regulation will uniformly prohibit the pervasive problems that flow from sex classifications in insurance. House Resolution 100, introduced in 1980, is such a bill, and women's rights advocates all over the country are working for its passage.

3 / GAY RIGHTS
by Thomas B. Stoddard

If any man lyeth with mankinde, as a man lyeth with a woman, both of them have committed abomination, they both shall surely be put to death. . . . And if any woman change the naturall use into that which is against nature, . . . she shall be liable to the same sentence. . . .

—Laws of the New Haven Colony, 1655

My will is to love according to my nature, and to find a place where I can be what I am.

—Christopher Isherwood, *Christopher and His Kind*, 1976

America, the self-proclaimed cradle of religious liberty, the haven for the tired, hungry and poor, that land that prides itself on its spirit of tolerance, has been remarkably intolerant of its homosexuals. Throughout American history homosexuals and homosexuality have been scorned, derided, and persecuted with regularity and vigor. America's churches have condemned homosexuality in the strongest possible terms, ranking it with the most heinous of sins. And for over three hundred and fifty years homosexual acts were serious crimes in every part of the country. Indeed, until well into the nineteenth century those acts were punishable in many states by the harshest penalty available—death. Perhaps prophetically, the first known record of homosexuality in Colonial America is an account of the murder in Saint Augustine in 1566 of a Frenchman alleged to be "a great Sodomite."

Yet the number of gay people now living in the United States is very large, and there are indications that it has always been so. A book published in 1915 contained this description of the size of the male homosexual community in American cities at that time:

> The great prevalence of sexual inversion in American cities is shown by the wide knowledge of its existence. Ninety-nine normal men out of a hundred have been accosted on the streets by inverts, or have among their acquaintances men whom they know to be sexually inverted. Everyone has seen inverts and knows what they are. The public attitude toward them is generally a negative one—indifference, amusement, contempt.

More than three decades later, in the 1940s and 1950s, Alfred Kinsey conducted his famous surveys of adult sexuality in America and reached some startling conclusions. He discovered that 37 percent of the males and 20 percent of the females in his sample had had at least one post-puberty sexual encounter with someone of the same sex. He further found that 13 percent of the males and 7 percent of the females in those samples were exclusively or predominantly homosexual (or, as the writer of the 1915 account would have put it, "sexually inverted") for at least three years of their lives between the ages of sixteen and fifty-five. If applied to the present population of the United States, those percentages would yield a raw number of more than 22 million living Americans with significant homosexual histories—or approximately one in ten. It seems reasonable to conclude that the numerous efforts over the years to suppress homosexuality, including harsh criminal sanctions, have been spectacularly unsuccessful.

Before 1965, however, few people—including gays themselves—viewed gay people as comprising a separate political community or thought that gay people should have recognized and distinct political rights as gay people. The spirit of intolerance was too strong. The sense of persecution was too deep. But the cultural and political upheaval of the 1960s and early 1970s—with its new attitudes toward sexual mores, the role of women in society, and individual rights in general—

precipitated a change in attitude toward homosexuality. For one thing, it permitted the subject to be discussed openly for the first time in American history. More importantly, by erasing some of the taint surrounding homosexuality, it allowed—and to a degree even encouraged—gay people to identify themselves. It also helped to mold a new political movement—the gay civil rights movement.

In comparison with the black civil rights struggle and the women's rights effort, the gay rights movement is still young—scarcely more than fifteen years old. This chapter will describe the advances in the law that it has so far helped to bring about. (They are not insignificant, despite the youth of the movement.) It will then review the major issues now before state and local legislatures throughout the country. Finally, it will discuss the special problems of those who lobby on gay issues.

A BRIEF HISTORICAL OVERVIEW

The Law Before 1965

Before 1965, references in American law to homosexuality were essentially limited to one subject—statutes that made certain consensual sex acts a crime.

Those laws did not originate in this country. During the reign of Henry VIII, the British Parliament enacted a statute that made it a crime to commit "the vice of buggery," by which was meant anal intercourse between two males, for which the penalty was death. This law, like most of the rest of English law, was transported to the new American colonies and, eventually, was retained by each American state, with occasional modifications. (The statute of the New Haven Colony set forth at the outset, for example, took the unusual step of including lesbian conduct within its prohibition.)

Over the years, the "buggery" or "consensual sodomy" law of each state underwent significant changes. The evolution of the North Carolina statute provides a good example. During the first half of the nineteenth century, North Carolina's statute read as follows:

Any person who shall commit the abominable and detestable crime against nature, not to be named among Christians, with either mankind or beast, shall be adjudged guilty of a felony, and shall suffer death without the benefit of clergy.

In 1854, for reasons that are unclear, the state deleted the phrases "not to be named among Christians" and "without the benefit of clergy." In 1869, during Reconstruction, North Carolina saw fit to lessen the penalty—to a maximum of sixty years' imprisonment. That penalty remained in the law until 1965, when the state legislature reduced the crime to a felony punishable "in the discretion of the court." Here is the statute as it now reads:

> If any person shall commit the abominable and detestable crime against nature with mankind or beast, he shall be subject to imprisonment for up to ten years, or a fine, or both.

In 1975, and again in 1980, the Supreme Court of North Carolina was asked to declare the statute unconstitutional, but it declined the opportunity to do so.

Until the 1960s, every state in the Union made it a crime for two men, and ordinarily for two women as well, to engage in certain consensual sex acts, usually oral and anal intercourse. These statutes differed in scope (some, for instance, also applied to certain heterosexual acts); in penalty (some, like New York's, had lowered the crime to a misdemeanor); and in specificity of language (some were quite graphic in their description of the proscribed conduct while others relied on coy euphemisms like "unnatural and lascivious act" or "crime against nature"). But in every state such conduct was a crime.

Apart from these criminal consensual sodomy statutes, the law in virtually every state had little to say about homosexuals or homosexuality. But, of course, even in not speaking, the law had its effect. Since it offered gay people no specific affirmative protection, the law left employers, landlords, shopkeepers, and others free to discriminate against gays on the basis of their homosexuality—a "freedom" that was fully exploited.

The Spirit of Reform and Redefinition

The political and social upheaval of the 1960s brought a new awareness of homosexuality and a new spirit of reform. It also gave rise to the gay civil rights movement.

The 1960s and 1970s saw at least the beginnings of three major reforms in the law as it related to gay people, together with a number of lesser improvements.

The Repeal or Invalidation of Consensual Sodomy Statutes

In 1955, the American Law Institute, a highly respected private association of legal scholars that provides "model" bills for the consideration of state legislatures, issued a version of its Model Penal Code that for the first time did not contain the crime of consensual sodomy. The Institute explained that omission by stating that it now believed it was inappropriate for the states to criminalize private, consensual sexual acts between adults. Two years later, a special legislative commission in Great Britain recommended the repeal of Britain's anti-sodomy statutes in a paper that became known as the Wolfenden Report. Together, these two documents helped to create an atmosphere of reform that eventually led nearly half of the states to decriminalize consensual sodomy.

The first state to act, in 1962, was Illinois. Over the next two decades, these twenty-one states followed Illinois' lead: Connecticut (1971); Colorado (1972); Oregon (1972); Delaware (1973); Hawaii (1973); New Hampshire (1973); Ohio (1974); California (1976); Maine (1976); New Mexico (1976); Washington (1976); West Virginia (1976); Indiana (1977); South Dakota (1977); Vermont (1977); Wyoming (1977); Iowa (1978); Nebraska (1978); North Dakota (1978); New Jersey (1979); and Alaska (1980). In most of these states, the repeal took place not as a result of direct deliberation by the state legislature on the issue of consensual sodomy, but as a part of the state's revision of its entire criminal code in conformance with the American Law Institute's Model Penal Code.

The District of Columbia represents a special, and noteworthy, case. In 1981, its City Council voted to repeal its consensual sodomy ordinance, as well as rewrite a number of other ordinances on sex crimes, but the United States Congress, in a rare exercise of its power to overrule legislative acts of the District government, acted later that year to reinstate the law. As a result, the District is now in the anomalous position of having both an ordinance protecting gay people from discrimination in employment, housing, and public accommodations and a criminal law attaching severe penalties—including imprisonment for up to ten years—to certain sex acts in which two men or two women might engage.

In addition to the states listed above, three others should be added to the roster of states that no longer have consensual sodomy statutes:

The highest courts of New York and Pennsylvania have recently struck down their states' consensual sodomy statutes on the ground that they infringe the constitutional right to privacy, and a federal court in Texas has invalidated that state's prohibition for the same reason. Thus, as of the end of 1982, a total of twenty-five states—half the states in the nation—have eliminated their consensual sodomy laws, a remarkable achievement considering that every state had such a law in 1960. It is particularly significant that they include the five most populous states—California, New York, Pennsylvania, Texas, and Illinois—so that a clear majority of Americans now live in jurisdictions in which it is no longer a crime for people of the same gender to have sex with one another.

The importance of the elimination of anti-sodomy statutes cannot be overemphasized. Although the statutes are seldom enforced, largely because the proscribed conduct almost always takes place in private, they have enormous symbolic significance. They are the keystone of anti-gay oppression. For more than three centuries they have been offered up as the principal legal justification for the hatred and persecution of homosexuals, surrounding the entire subject of homosexuality with an aura of criminality. At heart, their widespread repeal thus represents a repudiation of the legacy of repression.

The issue of the constitutionality of the consensual sodomy statutes will be discussed below.

Added Protection for Government Workers

In the absence of state statutes enacted to shield particular categories of workers in specific instances, the law offers those who work in private industry little protection against arbitrary, discriminatory, or hostile acts by their employers. An employee may be fired for a foolish reason, or for no reason whatsoever, so long as the employer has not behaved in a way that violates one of those statutes. For example, laws have been enacted to provide that an employer may not discriminate on the basis of race, sex, or national origin, and that an employer may not favor a non-labor union member over a worker who does belong to a union. Otherwise, the employer is free to hire and fire employees at will.

The situation, however, is much better for government employees, whether they work for the federal, state, or local government. This is because all actions of government, including those taken in its role as employer, are subject to the restraints of both the United States Constitution and the relevant state constitution.

The Fourteenth Amendment to the U.S. Constitution, as well as most state constitutions, forbid the government to "deprive any person of life, liberty, or property, without due process of law" or to deny to any person "the equal protection of the laws." The courts have made clear that these two guarantees are, in effect, general assurances of rational conduct on the part of the government in its dealings with individual citizens. The government must act rationally when it makes a decision that directly disfavors one citizen as against others, at least when an important property or liberty interest is involved. Thus, unlike a private employer, the government may not "arbitrarily or capriciously" fire a tenured employee. If it does make such an attempt, it must have a valid explanation for its decision.

The Fourteenth Amendment guarantee of equal protection has been in existence since 1868, but before 1969 it had little meaning for government employees who happened to be gay. Before 1969, the government often dismissed employees on a mere suspicion of homosexuality. Typically, the worker would simply acquiesce in the dismissal, fearing that a challenge might increase his or her embarrassment or disgrace and believing (usually correctly) that there was no recourse anyway. When a gay employee did question his or her dismissal, the government's standard response was that the employee's continued employment would be a source of embarrassment or scandal for the agency or would impair the agency's moral climate or efficiency. In the few court decisions before 1969, the courts almost invariably found such excuses sufficient to justify the dismissal.

Two cases decided in 1969 changed this state of the law, giving new force and effect to the Fourteenth Amendment's "equal protection" guarantees for gay government employees. The first case, *Norton v. Macy*, involved the dismissal of an employee of the National Aeronautics and Space Administration (NASA) who had been stopped—allegedly on a traffic offense—by members of the District of Columbia's Morals Squad who suspected that he had made a "homosexual advance" to another man. The employee, who was never accused of any crime, challenged the dismissal. At trial, a NASA administrator admitted that the man had been a "competent employee" doing "very good work." However, the administrator also testified that the agency had concluded that the employee had made an advance to another man,

that that action amounted to "immoral, indecent, and disgraceful conduct," and that his continued employment might "turn out to be em-
barrassing to the agency."

The trial court upheld the dismissal, but the federal appellate court
in the District of Columbia—one of the most influential federal courts
in the country—reversed that decision in a stirring and far-reaching
opinion by Chief Judge David Bazelon. The Court rejected totally the
use of "immorality" as a standard by which to judge the plaintiff's
conduct, noting that "[a] pronouncement of 'immorality' tends to discourage careful analysis." The Court explained:

> We are not prepared to say that the Commission could not reason-
> ably find appellant's homosexual advance to be "immoral," "inde-
> cent," or "notoriously disgraceful" under dominant conventional
> norms. But the notion that it could be an appropriate function of
> the federal bureaucracy to enforce the majority's conventional
> codes of conduct in the private lives of its employees is at war with
> elementary concepts of liberty, privacy, and diversity.

The Court also rejected the agency's "embarrassment" rationale:

> A claim of possible embarrassment might, of course, be a vague
> way of referring to some specific potential interference with an
> agency's performance; but it might also be a smokescreen hiding
> personal antipathies or moral judgments which are excluded by
> statute as grounds for dismissal. A reviewing court must at least be
> able to discern some reasonably foreseeable, specific connection
> between an employee's potentially embarrassing conduct and the
> efficiency of the service.

In short, the Court required more than speculation and suspicion; it
demanded concrete proof of harm, or, as the Court put it, "some
reasonably foreseeable, specific connection" between the conduct
complained of and job efficiency.

This requirement of proof to support a dismissal has become known
as the "rational nexus" test, and *Norton v. Macy* has been cited again
and again by other courts in support of the principle that mere speculation of harm is not enough to warrant dismissal.

The second case, *Morrison v. State Board of Education*, involved that most volatile of contexts—the classroom. In that case, a California teacher of "exceptional children" lost his teaching licenses because he had once engaged in "a limited, non-criminal physical relationship" with another man. The State Board of Education asserted that Morrison's behavior constituted "immoral and unprofessional conduct" and was evidence of "moral turpitude." The California Supreme Court, following the example of the *Norton* court, ordered his licenses reinstated. In explaining its decision, the Court stated as follows:

> Terms such as "immoral or unprofessional conduct" or "moral turpitude" stretch over so wide a range that they embrace an unlimited area of conduct. In using them the Legislature surely did not mean to endow the employing agency with the power to dismiss any employee whose personal, private conduct incurred its disapproval. Hence the courts have consistently related the terms to the issue of whether, when applied to the performance of the employee on the job, the employee has disqualified himself.

This is, at heart, the *Norton* "rational nexus" requirement stated slightly differently.

The decisions in *Norton* and *Morrison* indicate that gay employees who happen to work for the government (regardless of whether it is the federal government, a state government, or a local government) are entitled to at least a degree of protection against discrimination, protection that is as yet unavailable to their counterparts who work for private employers. Indeed, the United States Civil Service Commission has explicitly adopted the *Norton* standard for all of the agencies under its jurisdiction, which is virtually the entire federal bureaucracy, excluding only the armed services, the foreign service, the Federal Bureau of Investigation, and the Central Intelligence Agency (all of which still can—and mostly do—discriminate against gays). Here is an excerpt from the Civil Service Commission's Bulletin of December 21, 1973, directed to job supervisors:

> [Y]ou may not find a person unsuitable for Federal employment merely because that person is a homosexual or has engaged in homosexual acts, nor may such exclusion be based on a conclusion that a homosexual person might bring the public service into public contempt. You are, however, permitted to dismiss a person

or find him or her unsuitable for Federal employment when the evidence establishes that such person's homosexual conduct affects job fitness—excluding from such consideration, however, unsubstantiated conclusions concerning possible embarrassment to the Federal Service.

Norton and *Morrison* do not guarantee job security for gay government employees—sad to say, there have been a significant number of cases after 1969 that pay homage to one or both and then uphold the firing of gay workers—but together they do represent a major advance in the legal protection available to gays in this country.

The Enactment of Anti-Discrimination Ordinances

Since the mid-1960s, and the beginning of the gay rights movement, scores of cities across the country—including Los Angeles, San Francisco, Washington, D.C., Minneapolis, and Seattle—have enacted anti-discrimination ordinances for the protection of their gay residents. Typically, these ordinances are broad in scope, prohibiting discrimination on the basis of "sexual preference or orientation" in employment, housing, public accommodations, and sometimes educational facilities as well. They usually take a very simple form, merely adding a new category—"sexual preference or orientation"—to an already established list of discriminatory classifications that are prohibited in those cities. (Virtually every city already prohibits discrimination based on race, religion, color, creed, national origin, and sex, and some have added physical disability, mental disability, age, marital status, and similar categories.)

Only one state, however, has so far chosen to enact gay anti-discrimination legislation: Wisconsin, whose law has just taken effect. Many other states have considered bills to this effect, but none has yet to act.

A similar anti-discrimination bill has been pending in Congress for several years, but the likelihood of passage is remote in the present political climate.

Other Developments

Since the early 1970s there have been a number of less important but still noteworthy developments in the law's treatment of gays.

• Several courts have ruled that state universities must give formal recognition to gay student organizations that otherwise qualify for official status and must permit those organizations to hold events on campus.

• The Supreme Court of California has declared that privately owned corporations that are quasi-public in character, such as utility and telephone companies, are subject to the restrictions of the State Constitution and may not discriminate against gay people. Unfortunately, this decision is based largely on special legal precedent in California law, and it is therefore unlikely that other states will follow this decision in the near future.

• Although all three branches of the military continue to exclude gay people and to expel persons already serving who are found to be gay, they no longer automatically taint those who are expelled with less than honorable discharges. Instead, a person who is discharged merely on the ground of homosexuality is ordinarily entitled to an honorable discharge and to veterans' benefits.

• Although the Immigration and Naturalization Service still denies entry to the United States to anyone it knows to be gay because it believes that federal law requires such an exclusion, under regulations promulgated during the last years of the Carter Administration it will not pry into a visitor's sexual life unless the visitor makes "an unsolicited, unambiguous oral or written admission of homosexuality."

Potential Problems

These positive legal developments over the past fifteen years demonstrate a clear trend toward full civil rights for gay people. This trend, however, is not without challenge or danger.

Two developments are particularly ominous. The first is the recent rise to power of various evangelical and self-righteous political groups that strongly oppose civil rights for gay people. These groups, the most prominent of which is the Moral Majority headed by Reverend Jerry Falwell, advocate the adoption of laws that promote what they call "family values." And "family values," by their definition, include a virulent hostility to homosexuals and homosexuality. By the early 1980s these groups had acquired considerable influence in the Reagan Administration and the Congress. Indeed, it was largely because of lobbying by the Moral Majority that Congress overruled the District of

Columbia City Council and reinstated the District's criminal consensual sodomy statute in 1981.

The second ominous development, which is obviously related to the rise of these groups, is the introduction of a spate of anti-gay bills in legislative chambers throughout the country. The most prominent example on the federal level is the proposed Family Protection Act, which, among other things, would bar the dissemination of federal funds to any individual or group that openly supported civil rights for gays.

There are many recent examples on the state level. An amusing (but very real) bill introduced in the Louisiana legislature in 1981 would have required every teacher in the state to file with his or her local school board a "statement of sexual preference" indicating that the teacher was "heterosexual," "homosexual," or "both." If the teacher answered "both," the school board would have to hold a public hearing to determine whether he or she was really "heterosexual" or "homosexual." The bill would then have given parents the right to demand that their child be taught by a heterosexual teacher. The bill did not pass the Louisiana legislature, but it is enough to know that it was the subject of serious debate and consideration.

A more disturbing example concerns a statute actually enacted by the Oklahoma legislature in 1978. That law permits local school boards to fire any teacher "advocating, soliciting, imposing, encouraging, or promoting public or private homosexual activity in a manner that creates a substantial risk that such conduct will come to the attention of school children or school employees." The statute is now under challenge in the federal courts, where it has already been upheld on the district court level.

In 1981, the Florida legislature added to a general appropriations bill a rider denying state funds to any college that had given official recognition or assistance to a group "that recommends or advocates sexual relations between persons not married to one another." The history of the rider made clear that the sponsors' true intent was to stop schools from recognizing gay student groups. The State Supreme Court invalidated the law shortly after it took effect, ruling that it violated free speech guarantees.

As the Florida decision indicates, many of these anti-gay measures are so crudely drawn that they cannot withstand constitutional scrutiny. But the law in this area is not entirely clear, and these bills do pose real threats to the gay civil rights movement. If adopted, they would not merely represent a return to the unenlightened age before 1965; they would affirmatively engraft anti-gay discrimination into the law, actually encouraging and in some cases (as with the Florida statute) mandating it.

THE LEGISLATIVE ISSUES FOR THE 1980s

Consensual Sodomy Statutes

In twenty-five states, consensual sodomy is no longer a crime. But in the remaining twenty-five, it remains a crime that can be—and sometimes is—enforced (usually for public sex acts).

Are consensual sodomy laws constitutional? Probably not, but the court decisions thus far have been contradictory.

At the outset, it is important to emphasize that homosexuality *per se* has never been a crime in the United States. Only certain acts that are identified with gay people, often incorrectly, are criminal, and only in those states that still outlaw consensual sodomy. Under the Anglo-American legal system, a crime must involve the commission of a forbidden *act*, and must generally involve an intent to commit that act as well. Being a certain type of person or being someone with a certain disposition or orientation cannot be a crime. Indeed, the Supreme Court has said that any attempt to criminalize a person's status—as opposed to an act—would violate the Eighth Amendment's prohibition against cruel and unusual punishment.

It is also important to understand the derivation of the constitutional "right of privacy" (which is discussed at length in the chapter on Reproductive Freedom). The United States Constitution contains no explicit guarantee of a general right to privacy, although it does establish rights that relate to privacy, such as the prohibition on unreasonable searches and seizures. Nevertheless, in 1965, in *Griswold v. Connecticut*, the Supreme Court found that a general right to privacy was included in the Constitution. The Court concluded that certain rights set forth specifically in the Bill of Rights, such as the ban on unreasonable searches and seizures, have "penumbras" that together create a generalized right of the people to "privacy and repose."

The issue in *Griswold* was the constitutionality of a Connecticut statute making it a crime to use contraceptives. In the light of the constitutional right to privacy that it found in the Constitution, the Court nullified the law, ruling that it invaded "the sacred precincts of marital bedrooms." In subsequent cases, the Court expanded the right of privacy still further. In 1972, the Court found that the right of privacy included the right of unmarried people to use contraceptives. And in 1973, in one of the Court's most controversial—and momentous—decisions, it declared that the right to privacy "was broad enough to encompass a woman's decision whether or not to terminate her pregnancy."

Against this background, it remains to be determined definitively whether consensual sodomy statutes are unconstitutional as a violation of the right to privacy. As of late 1982, the Supreme Court has not yet addressed the issue directly, and the lower courts have reached differing conclusions.

In 1975, in a case called *Doe v. Commonwealth's Attorney*, a federal district court in Virginia rejected a challenge by two gay male adults to that state's consensual sodomy statute. The court said that the privacy right established in *Griswold* was limited to "the privacy of the incidents of marriage . . . the sanctity of the home . . . [and] the nurture of family life." It then went on to conclude that Virginia's ban on consensual sodomy was rationally supportable because the state could reasonably determine that certain sexual acts, including consensual sodomy, were likely to result in a "contribution to moral delinquency."

That decision in *Doe* is almost certainly wrong. The Supreme Court's cases after *Griswold* make clear that the right to privacy does not exist only for married couples and for traditional families. However, the plaintiffs appealed the decision to the Supreme Court, and the Supreme Court, without writing any opinion, summarily affirmed the lower court's decision. Some observers insist that the Supreme Court's summary affirmance amounts to a determination that consensual sodomy statutes are fully constitutional. Others, however, assert that the decision cannot be construed as a ruling on that issue because there were other bases for upholding the lower court's decision, including the possibility that the Court found that there were procedural defects in the plaintiffs' challenge. Indeed, subsequent comments by members of the Supreme Court and lower courts have taken this position. But the Supreme Court's decision in *Doe* is extremely troubling and will continue to be cited in support of the claim that consensual sodomy statutes are constitutional—at least until the Court reaches a contrary result in a future case.

There are, however, recent judicial developments that counteract to some extent the grim implications of the *Doe* case. As already stated, since *Doe*, the highest courts of two states, New York and Pennsylvania, have reached conclusions directly contradictory to *Doe*, as has another federal district court.

The New York case, *People v. Onofre*, which was decided in 1980, is particularly important. In that case, the New York Court of Appeals declared unequivocally that consensual sodomy statutes violate the *Griswold* right to privacy. The Court first concluded that notwithstanding the lower court's statements in *Doe*, the right to privacy did cover the unmarried. It also concluded that the right extended to "noncommercial, cloistered" sexual behavior in general, regardless of whether procreation was the aim and regardless of the distastefulness of that behavior under prevailing community standards. It then stated:

> In light of [the relevant Supreme Court] decisions, protecting under the cloak of the right to privacy individual decisions as to indulgence in acts of sexual intimacy by unmarried persons and as to satisfaction of sexual desires by resort to material condemned as obscene by community standards when done in a cloistered setting, no rational basis appears for excluding from the same protection decisions—such as those made by defendants before us—to seek sexual gratification from what at least once was commonly regarded as "deviant" conduct, so long as the decisions are voluntarily made by adults in a noncommercial, private setting.

The Court also declared that there was no evidence indicating that the prohibition of consensual sodomy furthered a legitimate state interest, like protecting health. General distaste for the conduct in question is not enough to support a statute that infringes upon basic constitutional rights, the Court explained.

In addition, the New York court found a second reason to invalidate the statute, apart from privacy. The New York consensual sodomy statute, like that in some other states, prohibited all anal and oral intercourse, both homosexual and heterosexual, with one exception:

two married persons with one another. The Court found this distinction to be irrational and therefore a violation of the constitutional guarantee of equal protection. As the Court put it:

> [T]he only justifications suggested are a societal interest in protecting and nurturing the institution of marriage and what are termed "rights accorded married persons." As has been indicated, however, no showing has been made as to how, or even that, the statute banning consensual sodomy between persons not married to each other preserves or fosters marriage. Nor is there any suggestion how consensual sodomy relates to rights accorded married persons; certainly it is not evident how it adversely affects any such rights.

People v. Onofre stands now as the most authoritative statement to date on the issue of the constitutionality of consensual sodomy statutes and will probably remain so until the Supreme Court speaks directly on the issue. Lobbyists working for the repeal of consensual sodomy laws in those states that still have them should emphasize the reasons—and the humanity—that so clearly motivated the New York Court of Appeals in that case.

Other Criminal Statutes

Many states have other kinds of criminal statutes that relate to private, consensual sexual conduct by adults, and those statutes may also be used to harass or oppress gay people. Generally, they fall into three categories: lewdness statutes, solicitation statutes, and loitering statutes.

Lewdness statutes are laws that outlaw "lewd," "indecent," "disorderly," "lascivious," or "obscene" acts without specifying precisely what they might be. Michigan, for example, has two "gross indecency" statutes. One prohibits a man from engaging in an "act of gross indecency" (a term nowhere defined) in public or private with another man. The other prohibits a woman from engaging in such conduct (again, nowhere defined or explained) with another woman. The penalty for both is the same: up to five years in prison. California, which repealed its consensual sodomy statute in 1976, still has on its books a statute that outlaws the commission of any act that "openly outrages public decency," without any explanation of what activities such an offense might entail. In most states, lewdness statutes apply only to acts in a public place, or within the view of non-participants, but in some states, like Michigan, they extend to purely private conduct.

Solicitation statutes are laws that prohibit inviting, offering or suggesting the commission of a crime. In this general form, they exist in every state of the union; every state makes it a crime to entice or induce another to take part in a criminal act. Many states, however, have in addition statutes that specifically outlaw inviting someone else to engage in a sex act, even though the sex act itself might not be a crime. For example, Ohio rescinded its consensual sodomy statute in 1974, but it is still a crime in Ohio to solicit another person of the same sex to engage in consensual sodomy, although the Ohio courts have now narrowed the scope of the statute a bit by judicial interpretation.

Loitering statutes are those that make it a crime to remain or wander in a public place, either for a specifically forbidden purpose (to solicit "deviate sexual intercourse," for example) or without good reason. Of all three kinds of statutes, they are the most objectionable and pernicious, for they require little in the way of an overt act. In some states, merely being in the wrong place at the wrong time with an explanation deemed insufficient by the police may subject one to arrest for loitering.

Lewdness, solicitation and loitering statutes are often of dubious constitutionality, and in recent years the courts have begun to strike them down or to limit their scope. In 1979, the Supreme Court of California severely restricted that state's disorderly conduct statute, which on its face prohibits, among other things, soliciting in public any "lewd or dissolute conduct." The court in essence nullified that particular provision of the statute, saying that it could not, within the bounds of the Constitution, bar solicitations of sexual conduct that the speaker intended to take place in private. The high courts of Colorado, Maryland, Massachusetts, Oregon, and Virginia have reached similar conclusions.

These criminal statutes vary from state to state in both language and type of conduct prohibited. However, in general they may be vulnerable on three constitutional grounds. First, insofar as they reach acts committed behind closed doors, they may infringe upon the constitu-

tional right of privacy enunciated by the U.S. Supreme Court in
Griswold v. Connecticut. Second, they may offend basic First Amendment principles; asking someone to engage in an act that is not illegal,
for example, has been repeatedly held to be a form of speech within
the purview of the First Amendment. Third, statutes of this kind are
often absurdly vague, in violation of the constitutional principle that
criminal statutes must be explicit enough to give would-be offenders
fair warning of their scope.

These are also the arguments most likely to convince state legislators
to vote to repeal these statutes.

Anti-Discrimination Statutes

Government workers, as we discussed above, enjoy a degree of protection against discrimination on the job by virtue of the special
constitutional limitations on the government as an employer. In addition, certain other categories of workers may also have certain protections against anti-gay discrimination. For example, some labor unions
have begun to insist on clauses in their agreements with employers
that bar discrimination on the basis of sexual orientation.

In general, however, gay people who work for private employers
may be fired or demoted or denied advancement merely because they
are gay. Gay people in most localities may also be refused housing or
public accommodations because they are gay.

Private employers, landlords, and shopkeepers in the United States
have enormous latitude in deciding with whom to deal or not. They
may, in general, do whatever they like, unless they violate specific
statutory requirements. A recent case in New York demonstrates in a
dramatic way the significance of this rule of law. A black woman who
was divorced applied for an apartment in New York City, and the
landlord turned her down. She then sued him, claiming discrimination
on three grounds: race, sex, and marital status. (New York, like some
other states, has a statute prohibiting discrimination in housing on the
basis of all three of those classifications.) The landlord responded by
asserting that he had an entirely different reason for rejecting her: she
was a lawyer, and he did not want to have a lawyer as a tenant. The
Court accepted his explanation and permitted him to reject the plaintiff's application, stating:

Absent a supervening statutory proscription, a landlord is free to
do what he wishes with his property, and to rent or not to rent to
any given person at his whim. The only restraints which the law
has imposed upon free exercise of his discretion is that he may not
use race, creed, color, national origin, sex, or marital status as
criteria. . . . He may decide not to rent to singles because they are
too noisy, or not to rent to bald-headed men because he has been
told they give wild parties.

Lawyers, like bald-headed men, enjoy no special protection in New
York, and so the woman lost the apartment.

It is by now well settled that Congress and the state legislatures have
the power to enact anti-discrimination statutes limiting the discretion
of private employers, landlords, and shopkeepers. Most local legislative bodies also have this authority. The only question, then, is
whether they will choose to act.

Why should gay people be given the special recognition of an ordinance banning discrimination on the basis of sexual preference? What
makes them different from other classes of people—such as lawyers or
bald-headed men?

The answer lies in the historical treatment of homosexuals and homosexuality in the United States. Gay people have been traditional
objects of hatred and persecution in this society throughout its history.
They have been condemned and persecuted by the church, by the
state, by employers and landlords, and by the medical profession.
They have lost jobs, homes, friends, family, and some even their lives
on account of their homosexuality. Those gay people who have escaped
censure have been able to do so only through disguise and deception,
until the gay civil rights movement started to open minds. Any group
so abused needs special protection and redress to overcome the barriers of the past and present.

Moreover, discrimination on account of sexual orientation, like discrimination on the basis of race and sex is, at bottom, irrational. There
is no evidence of any kind that indicates that gay people are less
responsible or less hard-working than anyone else. There is no sociological data that suggests that they are, as a class, less intelligent or
loyal.

Nor is there any data that gives substance to the fear of many parents that gay teachers pose a threat to the health or well-being of students under their control, an issue that has haunted the gay rights movement since its inception. For one thing, all studies on the subject show that child molestation is almost exclusively a heterosexual phenomenon. For another, if the worry is that exposure to gay teachers will influence a student's sexual development, recent studies indicate that a child's sexual preference is either based in biology or determined at such an early age that exposure to gay teachers in school can have little effect on it.

Some opponents of protective legislation for gay people have asserted that homosexuals are not entitled to special classification because, unlike women or racial minorities, their status is not an accident of birth. Gay people, the argument goes, are gay people by choice. These opponents seem to say that if one chooses to be a homosexual, one must accept the inevitable penalties.

This argument, like the fear surrounding gay teachers, betrays a misunderstanding of the origins of homosexuality. As already stated, most recent research indicates that one's sexual preference is rarely if ever a matter of personal choice.

But even if it were a simple matter of choice, that fact alone should not mean that gay people are not entitled to fair treatment.

Ours is a system of government designed specifically to permit as much individual liberty as feasible within an organized society. Our highest political values have always been individual liberty and tolerance. Anti-discrimination ordinances simply seek to give force and effect to those principles for all members of society by assuring equal opportunities in those areas that are essential to personal survival—employment, housing, and public accommodations. As H.L.A. Hart, the distinguished English jurisprudential scholar, has said:

> Recognition of individual liberty as a value involves, as a minimum, acceptance of the principle that the individual may do what he wants, even if others are distressed when they learn what it is that he does—unless, of course, there are other good grounds for forbidding it. No social order which accords to individual liberty any value could also accord the right to be protected from distress thus occasioned.

Protective legislation for gay people thus represents simply a further development of basic American ideals, and that is the principal justification for their enactment.

Domestic Issues

Same-Sex Marriages

Very few states specifically require that the partners to a marriage be of opposite sexes. But appellate courts in three states—Minnesota, Kentucky, and Washington—have nonetheless held that the marriage statutes in those states imply a male partner and a female partner. As the Supreme Court of Minnesota stated in 1971:

> [The Minnesota law], which governs "marriage," employs that term as one of common usage, meaning the state of union between persons of the opposite sex. It is unrealistic to think that the original draftsmen of our marriage statutes, which date from territorial days, would have used the term in any different sense. The term is of contemporary significance as well, for the present statute is replete with words of heterosexual import such as "husband and wife" and "bride and groom." . . .

All three courts, as well as at least one other, have also ruled that there is no constitutional basis for overturning this limitation. As the Minnesota Supreme Court put it:

> The institution of marriage as a union of man and woman, uniquely involving the procreation and rearing of children within a family, is as old as the book of Genesis. [In *Skinner v. Oklahoma*, the U.S. Supreme Court] stated in part: "Marriage and procreation are fundamental to the very existence and survival of the race." This historic institution manifestly is more deeply founded than the asserted contemporary concept of marriage and societal interests for which petitioners contend. The due process clause of the Fourteenth Amendment is not a charter for restructuring it by judicial legislation.

The Minnesota court's views may be antediluvian, but they indicate that the prospects for a judicial change in the law are gloomy, at least in the near future. The only real hope for reform is probably the state legislatures, which unquestionably have the authority to expand the statutory definition of marriage to include same-sex couples.

The arguments in favor of such a change are that it is a matter of simple equity, that it would promote the interests of the entire society by helping to stabilize relationships, and that it would conform the law to modern concepts of marriage. Worth particular emphasis is this last point. The day is long past when marriages were viewed principally as procreative units. The contemporary notion of marriage is that it is essentially a formal coupling of two people who have pledged a special bond of care and trust. The union may, but need not, produce children. It may, but need not, involve formalized roles of breadwinner and homemaker.

Same-sex marriage may seem a radical notion to some legislators, but it is fully consonant with this modern view.

Cohabitation Agreements

Traditionally, the courts have refused to enforce property agreements between two people—heterosexual or homosexual—who live together and have a sexual relationship but who are not married. Cohabitation agreements were thought to undermine the institution of marriage by formalizing in some sense an "illicit" or "immoral" arrangement. They were also viewed as akin to prostitution—the exchange of money or something else of value in return for sexual services.

This notion has now been discarded in many states, thanks in part to a far-reaching 1976 decision by the California Supreme Court. In that case, a woman who had lived with actor Lee Marvin for six years sued him for alimony and a division of property. The California court declared, in forthright language, that nonmarital partners did have the legal right to enter into property agreements, with one important proviso:

The fact that a man and woman live together without marriage, and engage in a sexual relationship, does not in itself invalidate agreements between them relating to their earnings, property, or expenses. Neither is such an agreement invalid merely because the parties may have contemplated the creation or continuation of a nonmarital relationship when they entered into it. Agreements between nonmarital partners fail only to the extent that they rest upon a consideration of meretricious sexual services.

When does an agreement rest on "meretricious sexual services"? Only when the pooling of property and earnings is "explicitly and inseparably based upon services as a paramour"—i.e., an agreement for prostitution. Moreover, the property agreement, under the *Marvin* decision, need not even be in writing; it may be oral. It need not be an express agreement at all. Under some circumstances, in the interest of fairness, the courts will infer such an agreement from the facts surrounding the relationship.

The *Marvin* decision makes no outright reference to homosexual couples. But the principles of *Marvin* would seem to extend logically to gay relationships as well. One court in California, in fact, has already applied the *Marvin* principles to a gay relationship. The Court refused to recognize the plaintiff's claim in that case, but not (at least by the face of the opinion) because the couple was homosexual.

Courts in a number of other states have embraced the *Marvin* teachings, although usually with less sweep than the California Supreme Court. The New York courts, for instance, will enforce cohabitation agreements only if they are express. Thus, in at least some states, unmarried couples may now enter into agreements by which they transfer certain property from one to the other, or pool their assets, or enter into arrangements for financial support, without worrying that the courts will later refuse to enforce them. This would seem to include gay couples.

In the other states, unless the courts choose to overthrow the common-law rule, cohabitation agreements will be valid only if the state legislature sees fit to enact new rules by statute.

This is not so much an issue of gay civil rights, of course, as it is an issue of the rights of the unmarried. Before *Marvin*, couples who, for whatever reason, chose not to marry were punished for their choice with archaic limitations on their ordinary legal right to enter into agreements involving their property in accordance with their own wishes and needs. However, for gay people, the matter is of particular importance because gay couples are legally incapable of marriage. For them, the old rule is nothing short of cruel. Lobbyists for gay civil rights should work toward the introduction, and passage, of such legislation wherever possible.

Child Custody and Visitation

The courts of every state have very wide latitude in deciding child custody and visitation questions. Almost without exception, the only explicit statutory standard for resolving such issues is the "best interests" of the child, and the courts are generally free to determine in each case precisely what those "best interests" are. Every custody case involves its own set of facts, with different personalities and different needs, and each case requires thoughtful independent analysis. Thus, judges probably need all the discretionary powers with which they have been invested. But discretion, for some judges, can be a temptation to indulge personal prejudices, particularly when a gay parent is involved.

In one notorious New York case, for example, an eleven-year-old girl was removed from her mother's care largely because the mother lived with her female lover. The judge declared:

> From the testimony elicited in these hearings, it appears that [the mother] takes care of the physical needs of the child in a satisfactory manner, but it also appears that the home environment with her homosexual partner in residence is not a proper atmosphere in which to bring up this child or in the best interest of this child.

The Court then awarded custody to the father, even though the child had lived with her mother for the entire seven-year period since the couple's separation. The Court also severely limited the mother's visitation rights, forbidding her to keep the child overnight or to see her at all "while . . . other homosexuals are present."

Is there a way to draft a statute that would curb this kind of abuse without unnecessarily limiting the court's discretion? A bill recently introduced in the New York State Assembly attempted to do so, proposing as an addition to the statute setting forth the "best interests" standard the following sentence: "No presumption as to fitness or unfitness for custody or visitation rights shall arise based on the sexual orientation of either parent." Another, more general approach has been suggested by the National Conference on Uniform State Laws. That proposal would add the sentence: "The court shall not consider conduct of a proposed custodian that does not affect his relationship to the child."

The painful truth is that neither bill—if enacted—would necessarily restrain an obviously hostile or homophobic judge. The principal value of such a law would be precautionary; judges would be forewarned against allowing unfounded assumptions about homosexuality to influence them, and the more responsible and open-minded judges on the bench would probably take special care to avoid such assumptions.

LOBBYING FOR GAY RIGHTS

Fighting Anti-Gay Legislation

The radical right is not only persistent, but inventive as well. It has shown extraordinary ingenuity in its drafting of anti-gay legislation. The Louisiana bill that would require teachers to file "statements of sexual preference" with their boards of education, the Oklahoma statute that would authorize the dismissal of any teacher, gay or not, who "advocated homosexual activity," and the Florida rider that would have cut off state funds to any college that gave formal recognition to a gay student group, all described above, are just samples of the countless punitive proposals offered for legislative consideration over the past two years.

Many, like the Louisiana bill, are both laughable and patently unconstitutional. But the question of constitutionality is less clear with respect to many others. Moreover, constitutional law is now in a state of flux and it is increasingly difficult to predict with assurance what the courts will do.

Some generalizations are, however, possible. Many of the anti-gay bills that have already been proposed implicate the constitutional right to privacy as articulated by the Supreme Court and are vulnerable to attack on that basis. For example, the most obvious flaw of the Louisiana bill is its requirement that teachers disclose the nature of their sexual activity to the government. A more intrusive, offensive assault on individual privacy rights is scarcely imaginable.

Many other bills are constitutionally suspect on First Amendment grounds. Any proposal that expressly punishes advocacy or expression of political beliefs, like the Oklahoma statute, almost certainly violates the First Amendment.

So too may any bill that penalizes someone for "coming out"— publicly declaring to others that he or she is gay. In the political and social context of America in the 1980s, "coming out" is inevitably more than a mere statement of identity. Explicitly or implicitly, it amounts to an assertion that gay people exist, that they have historically been repressed, and that it is time to emerge. "Coming out" is thus inherently political and, as such, should be entitled to the historic protection of the First Amendment. Some lower courts have already accepted this idea, and one court has actually held that attending a high school prom with a partner of the same sex is an act protected by the First Amendment.

On the other hand, there are also recent legal developments that can only be viewed as lending support to those who favor anti-gay legislation. For example, the Supreme Court's 1973 obscenity decisions (which are discussed in the chapter on Censorship)—as well as some of the Court's more recent abortion decisions (discussed in the chapter on Reproductive Freedom)—can and will be cited as precedents for the proposition that it is permissible for the government to promote its own notions of "morality," "decency," and "family values."

The law in this area is still largely unsettled. However, the citizen-lobbyist can take encouragement in this simple fact of political life: it is much easier to defeat a bill than to enact one. To defeat a bill, a lobbyist often need only raise sufficient doubts about its wisdom—or constitutionality—to frighten or discourage its legislative supporters.

Special Advice to Lobbyists on Gay Issues

There is no political issue that is more volatile or more controversial than civil rights for gay people. Lobbying is never an easy job, requiring seemingly limitless reserves of persistence, patience, and wit, but lobbying on gay issues is particularly demanding. In recognition of the special problems of the gay rights lobbyist, we offer the following suggestions:

1. *Seek allies.* The gay civil rights movement cannot succeed alone. The numbers are against it. Seek help from logical allies: civil liberties

organizations, feminist organizations, labor unions, family planning groups. The different issues they address are all, in essence, the same—the right of each person, regardless of birth, background, or private life, to live peaceably and productively without interference from the government.

2. *Be informed.* Most people know very little about gay people, or about homosexuality, and will look to you for information. You should be familiar enough with the writings on the subject to provide them with essential data and recommend certain helpful works. At the very least, you should read the two most recent publications of the Kinsey Institute on the subject of homosexuality: *Homosexualities: A Study of Diversity Among Men and Women* (1978) and *Sexual Preference: Its Development in Men and Women* (1981). A list of other useful works appears in Part III of this book.

3. *Avoid discussions of morality.* Once the debate moves toward questions of morality or of religious views of homosexuality, you are in trouble. Try to keep the discussion on a political plane. The only truly relevant issue is whether gay people are to be granted the same civil rights that have been accorded to other minorities. Commitment to the basic American values of tolerance, diversity, and equality would seem to compel the conclusion that gay people deserve equivalent legal recognition and protection.

4. *Above all, be reasonable in your expectations.* The black civil rights struggle is centuries old, but only in the past twenty years have the legislatures of this country enacted statutes outlawing racial discrimination. The gay civil rights struggle is barely fifteen years old. Quick victories are unlikely. Be reasonable about what you can accomplish. Do not be discouraged if you fail to achieve even one new piece of legislation after only one or two years of effort. Indeed, your most valuable task may be in simply educating the legislature and the public that gay people exist and deserve equal treatment.

4 / MARIJUANA AND OTHER DRUG LAWS
by George L. Farnham

At least 65 million Americans—more than 30 percent of the adult population—have tried marijuana.

By 1982, there were estimated to be more than 30 million regular marijuana smokers in the United States.

Retail sales from the illicit marijuana market are estimated to be over $25 billion each year, all of which goes untaxed by any level of government.

The domestic cultivation of marijuana has emerged as a central source of supply to the American market, with an annual retail value surpassing $10 billion in 1982, all of which also goes completely untaxed.

A recent study conducted by the National Academy of Sciences found that there is no conclusive evidence that experimental or intermittent use of marijuana causes physical or psychological harm. A further study on policy by the Academy supported the decriminalization of marijuana.

Nevertheless, in at least thirty-nine states in this country, the personal use of small amounts of marijuana in private can still result in a criminal conviction for the user and a fine or prison sentence. In fact, federal, state, and local law enforcement officials spend over $4 billion each year attempting to enforce marijuana and other drug laws.

Clearly, the production and use of marijuana in the United States today has become a major social, economic, and legal phenomenon that directly involves countless individuals. Yet the issue of marijuana remains shrouded in confusion, misinformation, and fear, with the result that our government's approach to it—on the local, state, and federal levels—remains essentially unchanged from the approach that was first adopted more than fifty years ago and that has proved utterly futile and tragic.

To many people, the continuation of the kinds of punitive drug laws that exist today throughout the country constitute a misguided and unnecessary infringement of personal privacy and individual freedom as well as a terrible waste of precious governmental and human resources. In every state, people who share that view are lobbying to modify—if not repeal—those laws. This chapter will discuss the history, background, and current issues involved in such efforts. (Although primarily concerned with marijuana, much of what it contains is equally applicable to cocaine and other illicit drugs as well.)

Contrary to what many people believe, it was not until this century that state legislatures began to limit the right of Americans to use or experiment with recreational drugs. Similarly, it was not until 1937, several years after the end of Prohibition, that the federal government for the first time outlawed the possession of marijuana.

The decade of the 1960s saw an explosion not only in the number of people using drugs but also in the variety of drugs that were available to them. At the same time, harsh drug laws that had swept through state legislatures in earlier decades in an atmosphere of ignorance and racism were suddenly being enforced with equal vehemence against middle- and upper-class whites as well as against poor minorities. Drug arrests, previously totaling in the thousands each year throughout the country, rapidly escalated to the hundreds of thousands.

As the political turbulence of this era began to subside, more and more state legislatures were confronted with a fundamental question: Should a person be prosecuted and incarcerated for the possession of a small amount of marijuana or other drugs for personal use? Although today it is relatively rare for a person actually to be sentenced to jail for marijuana possession, that was not the case a mere ten years ago. In Texas, in 1970, more than seven hundred persons were in state prisons or county jails for possession of marijuana. Their sentences ranged from ten to forty years, in some instances for the possession of a single marijuana cigarette.

To best understand the drug issue as it exists today, it is important to know the history of drug laws in the United States. The bulk of the discussion to follow deals with the state legislatures and how they have responded to the recreational drug issue over the last decade or so.

Confusion has always existed as to the precise definition of what constitutes a "drug." The word "drug" itself has taken on a negative connotation when used in any context other than medicine. There has been a general resistance on the part of society to accept the concept of a legal drug being used for recreational purposes. Therefore, it is common to see statements concerning "alcohol *and* drugs" when it is obvious that alcohol itself is a drug. To give it its proper definition, a "drug" is any substance that exists, either in an organic state or in a chemically synthetic state, which when introduced into the body alters the consciousness or emotional level of the individual. Only illegal drugs, and primarily marijuana, will be discussed in this chapter.

THE HISTORY OF DRUG LAWS IN THE UNITED STATES

Early Marijuana Laws

Recreational drug use was more prevalent in the United States during the late nineteenth century than at any other time, with the possible exception of the present. Marijuana use was widespread among blacks and Mexican Americans in the South and Southwest. Coca-Cola, originally invented as a tonic ("the pause that refreshes"), contained cocaine until the early 1900s. Opium use was commonplace in many cities. Tens of thousands of people routinely consumed cough syrup and other "medicines" that contained narcotics or other addictive drugs. Alcohol use was then, as now, the most widespread recreational drug of choice among Americans.

Marijuana has a colorful history in the United States. In Colonial America, hemp—the plant from which marijuana is derived—was the number two cash crop, second only to tobacco. But, during this era, hemp was grown as a commercial crop for its fiber, which is more durable than either cotton or wool. If there was a recreational use of hemp as an intoxicant in Colonial America, the record has been lost to history. Although George Washington grew acres of hemp at his Mt. Vernon residence, reports of his having smoked marijuana have no apparent basis in fact.

The use of hemp, which is also referred to as cannabis, as a recreational drug in the United States began nearly a century ago. It is believed that Mexican workers introduced marijuana to the United States around the turn of the century in numerous areas throughout the southwestern and southern states. Texas and Louisiana had the largest concentration of marijuana smokers at that time.

New Orleans was the central distribution point for marijuana entering the United States from Mexico or Cuba. Sailors who used the Mississippi River became the nation's first marijuana smugglers. By the early 1930s there were an estimated 50,000 marijuana users throughout the country, and every major American city had a distribution system, albeit on a far smaller scale than exists today.

Little attention was paid to marijuana by the news media or legislative bodies, chiefly because marijuana smoking was restricted almost exclusively to minority groups. But, as "Prohibition fever" swept across much of America, so did a sense of "reefer madness." Because of a mistaken belief that branding recreational drug users as criminals would rid society of drug use, a growing demand developed for laws to prohibit such drugs.

In 1925, Louisiana became the first state to classify the use of marijuana as a felony. Many other states in the region quickly followed suit. These actions were primarily racial in nature. Legislators were routinely told horror stories at hearings to encourage the passage of strict penalties for drug-related offenses. These stories concerned black men who smoked marijuana and who purportedly turned into raving lunatics of superhuman strength with tendencies toward violent crimes and possessed by uncontrollable sexual desires. By 1930, sixteen states had enacted legislation against the possession or sale of marijuana.

One man more than any other was responsible for creating the sense of hysteria surrounding marijuana use—Harry J. Anslinger, the head of the Federal Bureau of Narcotics and a contemporary and rival of J. Edgar Hoover. During the 1930s, Anslinger became obsessed by the notion that it was essential for federal legislation prohibiting marijuana to be enacted. His successful propagandizing, which resulted in passage of the federal Marijuana Tax Act of 1937, was based upon his reports of hundreds of bloodcurdling crimes allegedly committed by persons under the influence of marijuana.

The following is a typical story from Anslinger's "files"—stories that never used real names and could never be substantiated by the few journalists who tried to do so instead of simply reporting them verbatim:

> Del Rio, Texas. 1940. One Eleutero G., while allegedly under the influence of marihuana, shot to death two women and then committed suicide by literally slicing himself to bits about the abdomen, heart, and throat, in a manner which indicated that he was bereft of all reasoning. Law enforcement officers believed that G. was under the influence of marihuana at the time of the double murder and suicide and that he had previously used marihuana. It was the opinion of the doctor who saw G. just before he died that no one could so mutilate himself unless he was unable to feel "shock" and the only thing he knew that would produce such a condition, to such a degree, is marihuana. G. had wandered around in the fields for hours after the killing and after his self-mutilation. (H.J. Anslinger and W.F. Tompkins, *The Traffic in Narcotics*, New York, 1953, pp. 23–24.)

The most notorious piece of propaganda that Anslinger created was the now famous "dope" film of 1937, *Reefer Madness*. That movie predicted dire consequences for anyone who took even a single "puff" from a marijuana cigarette.

In certain circles, however, particularly among black musicians, marijuana was an accepted part of the culture. In his later years, Louis Armstrong sadly recalled:

> One reason we appreciated pot was the warmth it always brought forth. . . . Mary Warner, honey, you sure was good. I enjoyed you "heep much!" But the price got a little too high, law wise. At first you was a misdemeanor. But as the years rolled by you lost your misdo and got meanor and meanor. (Quoted by Patrick Anderson in *High in America*, New York, Viking Press, 1981, p. 49.)

Armstrong himself spent ten days in jail in 1931 after being arrested for marijuana possession in Los Angeles.

Early Cocaine History

The history of cocaine use and its prohibition is strikingly similar to that of marijuana. Cocaine is a naturally occurring stimulant extracted from the leaves of the South American coca plant. Coca leaves have been chewed by Bolivian and Peruvian Indians for thousands of years. The leading authority in the nineteenth century on the effects of cocaine was Sigmund Freud. He published five works, known as the "Cocaine Papers," which are still used for reference today.

The legislative history of cocaine began earlier than that of marijuana. Congress outlawed possession and distribution of cocaine with the Harrison Act of 1914, and it increased penalties with amendments to the Act in 1922. Cocaine, like marijuana, was misunderstood as a drug and was also mistakenly classified by the federal government as a narcotic.

The following comments made in an article that appeared in the May 1914 *Hampton's Magazine* illustrate the racist nature of the attitudes that led to the prohibition of cocaine:

> Such crimes require a certain kind of courage that cocaine gives; it may be a fictitious temporary courage, but it is very real while it lasts. It is a matter of common knowledge that yegg men, pickpockets, sneak thieves and sometimes safeblowers are habitual users of cocaine, nerving themselves up with a "sniff of the flake" before attempting their coups.
>
> Even greater crimes than these may be laid at the door of cocaine. Only a few weeks ago the slayer of little Marie Smith at Asbury Park, New Jersey, confessed himself a victim of the cocaine habit, and no less a person than the assistant chief of the Chicago police force told me of an unsolved murder mystery (the Cleghorn case, January, 1910) where suspicion pointed to cocaine.
>
> "It was a Whitechapel case in our red light district," he said, "head missing, body mutilated, evidently the work of a maniac and some of us thought, a dope fiend. Judging by the skillful dissection we came to the conclusion that the murderer was a medical student or a doctor."

In writing of the evils of the cocaine habit, it is impossible to avoid mention of one that is of grave importance; I mean the stimulation of negroes, who are as a race largely addicted to this drug, to a certain class of crimes. "Most attacks upon white women of the South," declares Christopher Koch, "are the direct result of a coke-crazed negro brain."

In the face of such ludicrous but readily believed statements about cocaine, most states outlawed the possession and sale of cocaine by the 1930s.

The Spread of Marijuana Use

Such was the situation with marijuana and cocaine laws by the mid-1930s. Both drugs were viewed as "evil," capable of causing the user to undergo dangerous and violent reactions. Almost no one questioned the Anslinger "body counts" that increased in much the same way as the lists of "Communists" that Joe McCarthy always claimed to carry. In that atmosphere, there was only one person who can be remembered for his attempt to bring a sense of objectivity to the hysteria that dominated the issue. During 1937 Congressional hearings, Dr. W.C. Woodward, Legislative Counsel for the American Medical Association, made the following statement:

The newspapers have called attention to it [marijuana] so prominently that there must be some grounds for their statements. It has surprised me, however, that the facts on which these statements have been based have not been brought before this committee by competent primary evidence. We are referred to newspaper publications concerning the prevalence of marihuana addiction. We are told that the use of marihuana causes crime.

But as yet no one has been produced from the Bureau of Prisons to show the number of prisoners who have been found addicted to the marihuana habit. An informal inquiry shows that the Bureau of Prisons has no evidence on that point.

You have been told that school children are great users of marihuana cigarettes. No one has been summoned from the Children's Bureau to show the nature and extent of the habit among children. Inquiry of the Children's Bureau shows that they have had no occasion to investigate it and know nothing particularly of it.

Inquiry of the Office of Education—and they certainly should know something of the prevalence of the habit among school children of the country, if there is a prevalence of the habit—indicates that they have had no occasion to investigate and know nothing of it.

Dr. Woodward's questioning of marijuana's tendency to cause crime and violence brought nothing but ridicule from the committee. Woodward's testimony ended with a condemnation from the chairman of the committee holding the hearings, who addressed Woodward as follows:

You are not cooperative in this. If you want to advise us on legislation you ought to come here with some constructive proposals rather than criticisms, rather than trying to throw obstacles in the way of something that the Federal Government is trying to do.

The intention of the Marijuana Tax Act, enacted in 1937, was to eliminate the use of marijuana in the United States through harsh criminal sanctions. However, despite those sanctions, the number of marijuana users has never fallen below the number that existed at the time marijuana was prohibited. Marijuana use remained fairly constant through the 1940s. During this period, little was heard about the issue or about those who were arrested for marijuana offenses. Once Anslinger accomplished his goal of having marijuana legislatively banned, for the most part he discontinued his crusade against the "devil's weed." Literature on marijuana became almost nonexistent. Anslinger was so successful in the creation of his marijuana mythology that it became impossible to conduct a rational debate on the subject.

The use of marijuana increased somewhat during the 1950s. Anslinger made one final attempt to eliminate marijuana through scare tactics. In 1957, he participated in a second movie, *Marijuana: Assassin of Youth*, which was the story of teenagers who brutally butchered their families after smoking marijuana. The movie, along with the Boggs Act of 1956, which further increased federal penalties for marijuana possession and sale, was presented from only one perspective, which again had little to do with the facts about marijuana.

In the 1960s, the use of marijuana reemerged as a public issue.

Marijuana arrests increased from 18,000 in 1965 to over 400,000 in 1973. Since 1970, there have been more than five million marijuana-related arrests in the United States. Nearly 90 percent of these arrests were for the possession of small amounts of marijuana.

The colossal increase in marijuana arrests obviously parallels the explosion in the number of marijuana users in the United States. This increase occurred on two entirely different sociological levels. First, marijuana smoking became commonplace among middle- and upper-class college students for whom it became a symbol of rebellion that generally represented an antiestablishment point of view. Secondly, millions of young American servicemen, mostly from lower economic levels and minority groups, began smoking marijuana in Vietnam, where it grew wild and was sold for a fraction of its cost on college campuses. When these men returned from the war, most continued to smoke marijuana, many bringing home hundreds of pounds in hollowed-out stereo speakers or other containers which were not required to pass through customs.

As a result, for the first time in the United States, marijuana smoking became predominantly accepted within an entire age group. Its use cut across all sociological and economic barriers. Marijuana was smoked at least once by a majority of American adults who were under the age of thirty during the 1970s. It became a common link—the largest classification of criminals in America.

Suddenly it became apparent to many legislators, who had previously unthinkingly voted to classify marijuana as a narcotic and to make its possession a felony, that thousands of people were being convicted and imprisoned for minor marijuana offenses. What was most disconcerting to those legislators was the obvious fact that those people were not raving lunatics, hell-bent on destruction, depravity, and debauchery, but were, for the most part, otherwise law-abiding citizens who were different from their non-criminal counterparts only in that they smoked marijuana.

DRUG LAWS AS A VIOLATION OF
INDIVIDUAL FREEDOM

A Movement is Born

The escalating number of marijuana arrests during the 1960s and 1970s led to the creation of a political movement dedicated to alleviating the harshness and injustice of the laws that made those arrests possible. Groups such as the American Civil Liberties Union began to speak out against such laws, and one called the National Organization for the Reform of Marijuana Laws (NORML) became a leading force in the reform movement. Its founder was Keith Stroup, a graduate of the Georgetown University Law School and a young lawyer in Washington, D.C. In Stroup's first criminal case as a lawyer, he won the acquittal of a friend who had been arrested for marijuana possession. In preparing his defense in that case, Stroup realized that no organization existed that could provide accurate information to assist in the defense of individuals arrested for marijuana offenses.

NORML opened its doors in the fall of 1970. Its principal purposes then, and now, are, first, to remove the marijuana consumer from the criminal justice system and, second, to serve as a clearinghouse for all types of information on the marijuana issue. In addition, NORML serves as a nationwide source of legal advice for people arrested for marijuana offenses, and its legal committee is composed of over two hundred criminal defense attorneys from across the country who specialize in the defense of people arrested for drug-related offenses. To accomplish its goals, NORML acts as a lobbying organization and has, over the past twelve years, lobbied before state legislatures throughout the country. NORML's principal source of income derives from its membership; at present the organization has approximately 10,000 members representing all fifty states as well as numerous foreign countries.

Coinciding with these first public stirrings in favor of reform of harsh marijuana laws was a campaign by the Nixon Administration for the arrest of an even greater number of people in an effort to "crack down" on drug use. In 1970, President Nixon and Attorney General John Mitchell declared their ill-fated and much publicized "war on drugs," highlighted by "Operation Intercept" which caused logjams of cars for miles at the Mexican border. This "war" did succeed, however, in dramatically increasing the number of arrests for marijuana offenses, nearly doubling the number between 1970, when slightly more than 200,000 arrests occurred, and 1973, when more than 400,000 arrests were recorded. As with every other effort to eliminate marijuana use, including the recent attempts by President Reagan, the Nixon crackdown failed not only to eliminate such use, it did not even decrease the number of users. By the early 1970s, the num-

ber of marijuana users in the country was rapidly approaching ten
million.

The Marijuana Commission

In 1969, Congress passed, and in 1970 President Nixon signed into
law, the Narcotics Control Act of 1970, the first overhaul of the nation's
drug policy since the early 1950s, when penalties were increased for
individuals arrested for possession or distribution of drugs. Under the
1970 Act, penalties for possession of marijuana and other drugs were
reduced to misdemeanors, but penalties for its distribution, sale, and
cultivation were increased. In the ensuing five years, a majority of the
states adopted at least some of the provisions of that Act.

Included in the Act, but little noticed at the time, was a provision
that established a national Marijuana Commission. This provision was
added to the original bill by then Representative Edward Koch of New
York, a longtime supporter of marijuana reform. Under that provision,
the Commission was to study all aspects of marijuana use and then
make suggestions concerning the proper role of the government with
respect to such use. President Nixon appointed nine of the thirteen
members of the Commission, including its chairman, Raymond Shafer,
the Republican governor of Pennsylvania. As a result, many observers
expected the Commission to closely reflect Nixon's strong anti-marijuana views.

At the same time, those groups that were committed to reforming
marijuana laws realized that the Commission represented an extraordinary opportunity for their cause, since it was at least possible that the
Commission would recognize the futility and tragedy of current laws
and policies toward drug use and recommend changes. Although the
Commission did not have the power to issue binding laws or regulations, it did seem clear that its findings and recommendations could
have enormous influence throughout the country.

The Commission held hearings in several different cities, during
which it heard various perspectives on marijuana. Groups such as
NORML made sure that witnesses in favor of reform, including several
nationally known medical authorities, testified at each hearing. Public
attention to the hearings was generated in each city. NORML and
others followed up the hearings with personal contact and lobbying of
the members of the Commission. As the hearings progressed, it became obvious that those efforts were succeeding. The tone of the

questions asked by the Commission members and their staff gradually shifted from hostility to curiosity to clear, open-minded interest.

In the spring of 1972, the Shafer Commission issued its final report. That report represented the most exhaustive investigation of marijuana ever conducted in the United States. Among the members of the Commission were two United States Senators, two Congressmen, various public health officials, research scientists, and law enforcement officials. The findings and recommendations of the Commission stunned many, infuriated others, and evoked immediate rejection from the very man who had appointed the majority of the Commission's members—Richard Nixon.

Among the Commission's most significant findings were these:

> There is no evidence that experimental or intermittent use of marihuana causes physical or psychological harm. The risk lies instead in the heavy, long-term use of the drug, particularly of the most potent preparations.
>
> Marihuana does not lead to physical dependency. No torturous withdrawal symptoms follow the sudden cessation of chronic, heavy use. Some evidence indicates that heavy, long-term users may develop a psychological dependence on the drug.
>
> The immediate effects of marihuana intoxication on the individual's organs or bodily functions are transient and have little or no permanent effect. However, there is a definite loss of some psychomotor control and a temporary impairment of time and space perceptions.
>
> No brain damage has been documented relating to marihuana use, in contrast with the well-established damage of chronic alcoholism.
>
> A careful search of literature and testimony by health officials has not revealed a single human fatality in the United States proven to have resulted solely from the use of marihuana.

Based on those findings, the Commission recommended the following changes in laws and policies concerning marijuana:

> —Possession or use of marijuana in private would "no longer be an offense," which in effect meant it would be legal.

—The private distribution of small amounts of marijuana for no profit or "insignificant remuneration" would be legal.

—Possession of up to an ounce of marijuana in public would be legal, although the marijuana could be confiscated.

—The possession of more than an ounce of marijuana in public would be punishable by a fine of up to $100, as would its public use.

—Public distribution of small amounts for no profit would also be punishable by a fine of up to $100.

—To grow or sell marijuana for profit would remain criminal, felony offenses.

In brief, the Commission recommended that most personal use of marijuana be "decriminalized"—that is, removed from the reach of state and federal criminal laws—while it also recommended that the cultivation and distribution of marijuana remain serious crimes. As a result, the Commission created a curious dilemma for the marijuana user: Under decriminalization, he or she could use marijuana in private legally and without fear of criminal arrest and conviction, but in order to obtain marijuana he or she would still have to resort to the same underground economy—and commit a criminal offense—from which the Commission sought to remove that user. Put another way, decriminalization addressed only half of the marijuana issue.

For that reason, even then, some proponents of reform believed that only complete "legalization"—where marijuana would be treated in essentially the same way as is alcohol—was the best possible approach to the marijuana issue. Nevertheless, the recommendations of the Shafer Commission—in large part because of the stature and prominence of the Commission—were quickly adopted by most proponents of reform, including NORML, as the most realistic objective for their lobbying efforts.

The Response to the Commission

By 1973, NORML had established itself as a nationally recognized and respected organization with active chapters in over forty states. In part because of lobbying by NORML members, by the mid-1970s decriminalization bills along the lines suggested by the Shafer Commission were introduced in nearly every state legislature, and hearings in support of marijuana law reform were held throughout the country. However, opposition to marijuana reform remained strong in many areas of the country, and meaningful reform in the various legislatures remained difficult to achieve.

In 1973, Oregon became the first state to adopt a decriminalization statute. That law made possession of one ounce of marijuana a civil (instead of criminal) infraction punishable by a fine of not more than $100. However, the new law did not remove all criminal penalties for private use, and its one-ounce limitation was quite low, but it was still an impressive accomplishment for a state to enact decriminalization legislation so soon after the Shafer Commission released its report. Indeed, the Oregon law was to become the model for the ten other states that enacted decriminalization laws between 1973 and 1978. (Those states are: Ohio, California, Alaska, Maine, Colorado, Minnesota, New York, Mississippi, North Carolina, and Nebraska.)

In some states, even Oregon's limited decriminalization approach was not feasible because of the harshness of the state's existing penalties. In those states, the main thrust of legislative efforts toward reform was to reduce the penalty for the possession of marijuana from a felony to a misdemeanor. In Texas, for example, persons could be and were sentenced to as many as forty years in prison for possession of small amounts of marijuana. However, in 1972 in that state a bill to reduce those penalties was defeated.

Using strenuous lobbying techniques, NORML and other groups made Texas a prime target for their reform efforts. Among other things, a press conference was held at the Huntsville prison in central Texas, during which the press was allowed to interview several prisoners who were serving extremely harsh sentences for relatively minor marijuana offenses. In addition, individual citizens from across the state were encouraged to write their state representatives to encourage a change in the laws. More press conferences were held and more newspaper articles appeared in the weeks that followed. Representatives from NORML and other groups testified before the state legislature on behalf of a reform of marijuana laws that would make possession of marijuana a misdemeanor instead of a felony.

In 1973, in large part because of this lobbying effort, the Texas state legislature enacted those reforms. Moreover, that new law also included a provision whereby persons imprisoned for marijuana offenses under the old law could petition for resentencing under the more lenient provisions of the new law. At first, however, Governor Dolph Briscoe refused to follow the procedures in the resentencing act, but further lobbying pressure eventually led to the pardon of many who had been jailed as felons for possession of as little as a single joint.

Although eleven states enacted decriminalization laws between 1973 and 1978, the momentum toward similar reform in other states slowed down considerably by the end of that decade. In fact, Nebraska, in 1978, was the last state to decriminalize marijuana possession.

There were several reasons for this slowdown. The number of marijuana users continued to increase at a rate of approximately three million people a year. Many of these new consumers were adolescents. In 1977, there were an estimated sixteen million marijuana consumers in the United States, and one in four, or approximately four million, were between the ages of twelve and seventeen. Perhaps predictably, the parents of those teenagers, who themselves may never have been directly exposed to marijuana, became increasingly concerned about the implications and consequences of their children's possible use of marijuana.

In December 1978, NBC broadcast a one-hour show called "Reading, 'Riting, and Reefer," which was a modern version of *Reefer Madness*. Similarly, *Reader's Digest* published a series of articles employing the same scare tactics that Harry Anslinger had used in the 1930s in an attempt to frighten people away from marijuana use. Instead, however, of making marijuana seem the cause of violent and destructive behavior, the modern hysteria was based on the belief that marijuana produced "amotivational syndrome," brain damage, or other imagined and exaggerated results. In this same vein, one Congressman placed "evidence" in the *Congressional Record* that smoking marijuana caused "wrinkled fingernails" and a desire to urinate in public.

Distorted health claims about the dangers of using marijuana were sensationalized even further. Once again, marijuana was portrayed as "the most dangerous drug in America," an idea that was perpetuated by Ronald Reagan and a number of others. Beginning in the late 1970s, it was once again politically popular for state legislators to sponsor anti-marijuana legislation—legislation which included bills to outlaw drug paraphernalia, to provide harsh and mandatory prison sentences for drug offenders, and to increase penalties for possession or cultivation of marijuana.

As a result, by the time of Ronald Reagan's election in 1980, the prospects for significant progress in the area of drug use were not encouraging. Nevertheless, by 1982 such groups as NORML, the ACLU, and others were as determined as ever to work toward the reform of the harshest aspects of state drug laws.

THE LEGISLATIVE ISSUES FOR THE 1980s

Decriminalization

As discussed earlier, during the 1970s bills to decriminalize the private use of marijuana were introduced in virtually every legislature and were actually enacted in eleven states. Similar or more progressive bills will continue to be introduced in every state where a user can still be convicted for the mere possession and use of marijuana.

The principal arguments in support of such bills remain the findings and recommendations of the Shafer Commission. In addition, in 1980 and 1982 two other highly respected agencies largely reinforced those findings and recommendations. The first, the Liaison Task Panel on Psychoactive Drug Use/Misuse, issued a report in 1980 to the President's Commission on Mental Health that contained the following conclusions concerning marijuana and its use:

Enough is now known about marijuana decriminalization to offer an assessment of its effects and how the public has responded to it. The evidence would indicate that the use of marijuana, other than experimental, has not significantly increased in those states adopting the decriminalization approach, that the public has approved of lessened penalties, and that law enforcement resources have been diverted to serious criminal activity. Recent national surveys would indicate that the public is ready to eliminate criminal penalties completely for personal possession and use of marijuana and that public opinion is moving in the direction of approval of regulation and control schemes for distribution.

Marijuana usage is accepted behavior by large segments of our younger population and its general acceptance into the culture appears to be only a matter of time.

If the dichotomy between licit and illicit drugs is discarded in favor of the view that all psychoactive drug policy, including that for alcohol and tobacco, should be founded on the same general principles, then drug use can be viewed as representing common

behavior, though society through legal and other restraints has
defined any use of some drugs as deviant. These societal and legal
definitions of the permissible parameters of drug use can have
profound and lasting effects upon the individual user.

The highly respected National Academy of Sciences set a positive
tone for future marijuana reform with two reports in 1982. One report,
"An Analysis of Marijuana Policy," created immediate controversy by
endorsing marijuana decriminalization. The uproar was similar to what
occurred after the Shafer Commission report a decade earlier. The
president of the Academy instantly rejected the findings of the report,
as did the Reagan Administration.

The conclusions of the report were:

For the last decade, concern with health hazards attributable to
marijuana has been rising. The hearts, lungs, reproductive functions, and mental abilities of children have been reported to be
threatened by marijuana, and such threats are not to be taken
lightly. Heavy use by anyone or any use by growing children
should be discouraged. Although conclusive evidence is lacking of
major, long-term public health problems caused by marijuana,
they are worrisome possibilities, and both the reports and the a
priori likelihood of developmental damage to some young users
makes marijuana use a cause for extreme concern.

At the same time, the effectiveness of the present federal policy of
complete prohibition falls far short of its goal—preventing use. An
estimated 55 million Americans have tried marijuana, federal enforcement of prohibition of use is virtually nonexistent, and eleven
states have repealed criminal penalties for private possession of small
amounts and for private use. It can no longer be argued that use
would be much more widespread and the problematic effects greater
today if the policy of complete prohibition did not exist: The existing
evidence on policies of partial prohibition indicates that partial prohibition has been as effective in controlling consumption as complete
prohibition and has entailed considerably smaller social, legal, and
economic costs. On balance, therefore, we believe that a policy of
partial prohibition is clearly preferable to a policy of complete prohibition of supply and use.

We believe, further, that current policies directed at controlling the supply of marijuana should be seriously reconsidered. The demonstrated ineffectiveness of control of use through prohibition of supply and the high costs of implementing such a policy make it very unlikely that any kind of partial prohibition policy will be effective in reducing marijuana use significantly below present levels. Moreover, it seems likely to us that removal of criminal sanctions will be given serious consideration by the federal government and by the states in the foreseeable future. Hence, a variety of alternative policies should be considered.

At this time, the form of specific alternatives to current policies and their probable effect on patterns of use cannot be determined with confidence. It is possible that, after careful study, all alternatives will turn out to have so many disadvantages that none could command public consensus. To maximize the likelihood of sound policy for the long run, however, further research should be conducted on the biological, behavioral, developmental, and social consequences of marijuana use, on the structure and operation of drug markets, and on the relations of various conditions of availability to patterns of use.

The most comprehensive study on marijuana and health in the last decade was also released by the National Academy of Sciences in 1982. The NAS study was prepared by twenty-two respected members of the medical and scientific communities who conducted an objective and unbiased investigation into the issue of marijuana and health. The study successfully debunked many of the "reefer madness" hysteria stories that were re-popularized in the late 1970s. The following is a summary of the report prepared by the NAS.

Psychomotor and Behavioral Effects

Marijuana significantly impairs motor coordination and the abilities to follow a moving object and to detect a flash of light. These functions are essential for safe driving and the operation of other machines, and their impairment "may suggest a substantial risk for users who are operating machines." Moreover, these effects may last four to eight hours after the time the user felt "high."

Marijuana also hampers short-term memory, impairs oral communication, slows learning, and may produce a gamut of mental phenomena ranging from euphoria to confusion and delirium. These are of special concern, the committee emphasized, because much of the heavy use of marijuana is by adolescents during school hours.

Tolerance to many of marijuana's psychological and physical effects develops readily, said the committee, along with relatively mild temporary symptoms on withdrawal, indicating that the drug can lead to physical dependence. However, the committee stressed, there is no evidence that marijuana causes addiction to the extent that narcotics do, or that physical dependence plays a significant role in persistent use of the drug.

The committee found no conclusive evidence that prolonged use of marijuana causes changes in the brain or in human behavior that are not reversible once drug use is discontinued.

Based on available research, the committee found it "difficult to sort out the relationship" between the use of marijuana and the complex symptoms known as the amotivational syndrome. "Self-selection and effects of the drug," suggested the committee, "are probably both contributing to the amotivational problem seen in some chronic users of marijuana."

Respiratory and Cardiovascular Systems

The committee found that marijuana's long-term effects on physical health are probably similar to those of tobacco smoking. Chronic heavy smoking of marijuana causes inflammation and other changes in the lungs, some of which may be reversible when use is stopped. Also, there is a "strong possibility" that prolonged, heavy marijuana smoking will lead to cancer of the respiratory tract or to serious lung impairment. In fact, experimental studies suggest that a combination of tobacco and marijuana may have greater carcinogenic potential than either substance alone.

Smoking marijuana increases the work of the heart, much as stress does, by raising the heart rate and sometimes the blood pressure. These effects, noted the committee, do not appear to be harmful in healthy people, but do pose a threat to those with hypertension, cerebrovascular disease, and coronary atherosclerosis, as well as limit the drug's potential therapeutic value.

Reproductive and Immune Systems

Human sperm number and movement are decreased during chronic marijuana use, but the committee said that it is not known whether the decrease has any effect on male fertility. The picture is even less clear for women, but evidence does "raise concerns for young girls using the drug," because animal studies show effects on ovulation and levels of reproductive hormones.

Although there is widespread use of marijuana in young women of childbearing age, there is "no evidence yet" of any birth defects that might be associated with the drug. Nor do marijuana and delta-9-THC, its most active ingredient, appear to break chromosomes. And while the drug may affect chromosome segregation during cell division and result in cells with fewer than normal chromosomes, the "risk for abnormalities in offspring or possible disease is not known," the committee said.

Evidence is conflicting, said the committee, on whether marijuana suppresses the human body's immune system, which protects it against infection.

Therapeutic Potential

The committee found that marijuana and its derivatives or analogues might be useful in the treatment of glaucoma, of nausea and vomiting brought on by cancer chemotherapy, and of asthma. The committee recommended seeking derivatives that would increase marijuana's therapeutic actions while decreasing its psychotropic and cardiovascular side effects.

Research Recommendations

The committee found marijuana research to be "particularly inadequate when viewed in light of the extent of marijuana use in this country, especially by young people." Among a host of research recommendations, the committee called for increased emphasis on studies in human beings and other primates, more information on the metabolic and biological effects of the various marijuana chemical compounds, and long-term studies on the behavioral and biological consequences of using the drug. The committee also pointed out an "urgent need" for more comprehensive endocrine and gynecologic investigations of women who use marijuana.

In addition to the facts that disprove most of the assumptions underlying most criminal marijuana laws, another argument in support of decriminalization is that laws that make the private consumption of marijuana a crime violate our right of privacy. One of the best statements of that position may be found in a decision of the Supreme Court of Alaska, in which it declared unconstitutional a state law that criminalized the possession of marijuana by adults in private. As part of its unanimous 54-page ruling, the court stated:

> Privacy in the home is a fundamental right under both the federal and Alaskan constitutions. We do not mean by this that a person may do anything at any time as long as the activity takes place within a person's home. . . . No one has an absolute right to do things in the privacy of his own home which will affect himself and others adversely. Indeed, one aspect of a private matter is that it is private, that is, that it does not adversely affect persons beyond the actor, and hence is none of their business. When a matter does affect the public, directly or indirectly, it loses its wholly private character, and can be made to yield when an appropriate public need is demonstrated.
>
> Thus, we conclude that citizens of the state of Alaska have a basic right to privacy in their homes under Alaska's constitution. This right to privacy would encompass the possession and ingestion of substances such as marijuana in a purely personal noncommercial context in the home unless the state can meet its substantial burden and show that proscription of possession of marijuana in the home is supportable by achievement of a legitimate state interest.

Significantly, even though the Alaska court decision did not mention the cultivation of marijuana, the state's Attorney General subsequently ruled that cultivation for personal use was implicitly covered by it.

Decriminalization is the most moderate approach to drug law reform, especially since it leaves unaffected existing laws relating to production and distribution, and whenever such bills are pending concerned citizens should work toward their adoption.

Legalization

In contrast to decriminalization, the "legalization" of marijuana is a much more ambitious proposal, since it entails an entirely different governmental approach to the marijuana phenomenon. Essentially, legalization of marijuana would result in its being treated in much the same way as alcohol is treated today, with government regulations of quality and quantity and with some form of taxation as well.

As indicated at the beginning of this chapter, marijuana production and use has become a multi-billion-dollar business involving tens of millions of Americans as regular consumers. Indeed, it is estimated that the primary source of income for several hundred thousand people in this country today is illicit drug sales.

Thus, for the first time in our history, the marijuana issue has become an economic one. Fifteen years ago, with only a million users in the country, a smuggler who brought several hundred pounds of marijuana across the Mexican border would be classified as a large-scale supplier and be pursued as a top priority by the federal government. Today, the federal government has an informal policy not to prosecute marijuana cases unless the amount involved is more than two thousand pounds. The large-scale smuggler of yesterday would be a mere amateur today, not even worthy of federal scrutiny.

This phenomenon in turn leads to an ever increasing burden on state and local governments. Ninety-nine percent of all drug arrests and prosecutions occur on the state or local level. Many states, particularly those in which marijuana importation is most intense, have increased their penalties for felony drug cases. As sentences have increased, so have the number of felony arrests for drug offenses. As a result, the economic burden to enforce drug laws—which includes the costs of arrest, prosecution, and incarceration—have fallen primarily on state and local governments. At a time of severe prison overcrowding, many states, often by judicial decree, have been forced to release prisoners to alleviate overcrowded conditions. Often, many of those released are drug offenders who are discharged on the premise that they tend to be nonviolent criminals.

This "revolving door" situation, which has caused the destruction of tens of thousands of lives of otherwise law-abiding citizens and has accomplished little else, is increasingly coming under attack. More and more people are beginning to consider whether the government should regulate and control marijuana rather than continue an obviously futile and increasingly costly effort at prohibition.

Under all proposals for legalization, it is certain that there will still be restrictions on marijuana when the government removes criminal sanctions. Moreover, there will almost certainly be sales taxes on marijuana, just as there are presently on alcohol and tobacco. Even high-quality marijuana can be produced at very low cost, especially in comparison to the inflated prices paid on the illicit market. Marijuana generally sells on the illicit market for $20 to $150 an ounce. Present estimates are that Americans consume more than 25,000 tons of marijuana each year. If there were an average tax of $10 per ounce, $8 billion dollars in revenues a year could be raised from the sale of marijuana.

To date, legalization legislation has been introduced into only a few state legislatures. In 1971, the first marijuana legalization bill was introduced by a member of the New York State Assembly, Franz Leichter. That bill would have permitted the legal sale of marijuana in liquor stores under the control of a state regulatory agency. The bill, however, went nowhere. Since 1971, legalization bills have been introduced in several other state legislatures. The Massachusetts state legislature held hearings on a marijuana legalization bill in 1981, thus becoming the first state to hold legislative hearings on the subject.

The marijuana issue in the 1980s is vastly different from what it was in the 1970s. Economics is one of the most important reasons. The emergence of the domestic marijuana market is another crucial difference. Prior to 1978, almost all of the marijuana smoked in the United States was imported from Mexico, Colombia, and Jamaica. In March 1978, the United States government admitted that it had been working in conjunction with the Mexican government to spray paraquat, a lethal herbicide, on marijuana crops grown in Mexico. The purpose of the program was to destroy the marijuana crop. The program was ultimately unsuccessful because paraquat must be left in direct sunlight after spraying for three days to be effective. Mexican farmers, for whom marijuana was usually the sole source of income, immediately harvested the marijuana after the helicopters left. It would then be shipped to the United States where it was indistinguishable from uncontaminated marijuana.

The United States government was then forced to admit the possibility that smoking the contaminated marijuana could lead to permanent lung damage. The result of this admission was the "paraquat panic" which created an instant demand among marijuana consumers for an uncontaminated product. As most imported marijuana is not easily differentiated, consumers looked to the small domestic marijuana market as a source. Domestic marijuana was of a higher quality, much greener in color and easily distinguishable from the imported variety.

The "paraquat panic" started in March 1978. Within months, thousands of people began to cultivate their first crop of marijuana. The first billion-dollar domestic marijuana crop was harvested that same year. Since that time the value of the domestic crop has doubled each year. NORML estimated that the domestic marijuana market in 1982 had a "street value" of $10.4 billion. Thirty states now generate crops valued at $100 million or more. In California, the largest agricultural state in the country, marijuana is the number one cash crop, estimated by NORML at $1.7 billion for 1981. Hawaii's crop was valued at $750 million, Kentucky's at $600 million, Oregon's at $400 million, and Arkansas's at $350 million.

The continuing escalation in the growth of domestic marijuana production has led to a large increase in the number of persons arrested for the cultivation of marijuana. Nearly all states treat cultivation with the same severity as the sale of large amounts of marijuana. Few of the eleven states which have decriminalized marijuana possession include cultivated marijuana under their provisions. Only Alaska permits the cultivation of marijuana by adults in private without criminal penalty. In 1981, there were 20,000 cultivation arrests—more than double the number from previous years.

More and more legislative attempts have been and will be made to decriminalize domestic cultivation. California has come very close in recent years to legislating a cultivation decriminalization law. The removal of criminal penalties for cultivation will remove one of the problems of decriminalization laws. Cultivation decriminalization offers the consumer an alternative source of marijuana, so that he or she would not be forced to buy from the illicit market.

Any serious move toward marijuana legalization in the United States must include provisions that establish guidelines for the domestic production of marijuana. It is doubtful that American consumers will import marijuana once it has been legalized because of the economic advantages of keeping the industry in the country. And since the

American marijuana market has already proven that it can compete with foreign markets on the basis of quality, importation would be limited if it existed at all.

Paraphernalia Laws

A new marijuana issue that emerged during the latter part of the 1970s was whether state and local legislatures should attempt to ban the sale of drug paraphernalia. Legislators, frustrated by their inability to prohibit the recreational use of drugs, began to outlaw the sale of drug paraphernalia, using the inverted logic that persons who used drugs only did so after buying paraphernalia. Dozens of municipalities and at least three dozen states enacted statutes prohibiting the sale of implements that could be used for marijuana, cocaine, or other drugs. The major problem that this issue presents is how drug paraphernalia are defined. So far, the lack of clarity of definition has led to numerous lawsuits challenging the constitutional validity of these laws, beginning with NORML's challenge to the 1975 Indiana drug paraphernalia law, the first such law in the country.

Since then there has been a proliferation of laws prohibiting paraphernalia. Most early paraphernalia laws were enacted by county legislatures, banning sale in municipal areas. Later, after the federal Drug Enforcement Administration prepared a model bill that removed some of the more glaring constitutional problems of earlier laws, state legislatures began to ban such sales statewide. A variety of methods have been used to outlaw the sale of drug paraphernalia in these states.

The majority of these laws, particularly those based on the DEA Model Act, make it difficult to distribute drug law reform literature. Prosecutors have used such literature as evidence to prove that a pipe was sold to be used for the smoking of marijuana, which is illegal, and not for smoking tobacco, which is not illegal. Many stores now refuse to distribute literature on drugs or drug reform, NORML T-shirts, and even marijuana leaf lapel pins due to the fear of arrest. Important avenues of free speech have been closed by the drug paraphernalia laws now in effect in more than thirty states.

A good example of early paraphernalia legislation is Indiana's. The law was challenged by NORML's Indiana chapter and was enjoined. One year later, the state legislature reenacted exactly the same law.

Again it was challenged by NORML, and again it was found by the court to be unconstitutional. The court stated:

> The statute includes in its definition of paraphernalia instruments "used" or "intended for use." This means that a person could be deemed a dealer in paraphernalia because the buyer of his product intends to use the item to administer drugs. For example, a maker of corncob pipes or tie bars could be brought under the provisions' sanctions because a customer of his has devious designs for the otherwise legitimate item. A maker of pipes, spoons, or hand mirrors could be found to be in violation of the statute because his legitimate products are bought by a middleman who intends to advertise and sell the products as drug devices or who sells them simply as pipes or spoons but to someone who later uses the items to ingest drugs. Thus, someone can be considered to be dealing in paraphernalia because of the intent of someone once, twice, or even several times removed. The same problem of lack of notice faces a seller who may sell items such as pipes or spoons or paper clips to someone who intends to use the items for the ingestion of drugs rather than for their legitimate functions.

After the failure of these early laws, the United States Department of Justice prepared a model Drug Paraphernalia Act in 1979. This law was designed to be enacted at local and state levels. The Model Act, unlike earlier paraphernalia laws, required proving an intent that the item for sale was to be used with drugs. Rather than saying that a certain type of pipe is by itself a part of drug paraphernalia, the Model Act states that the pipe, when coupled with certain extenuating circumstances, comes under the heading of drug paraphernalia.

The courts have been divided on the constitutionality of state and local laws based on the Model Act. The leading case on the issue is *Record Revolution v. City of Parma,* where the United States Court of Appeals for the Sixth Circuit in 1980 found that the Model Act's use of the term "designed for use" was unconstitutionally vague. Other courts have upheld the statute in part or in its entirety. However, because of the difficulty of proving "intent," as the Act requires, there have been few prosecutions under these laws.

These laws also raise a number of free speech issues. Under them, extenuating circumstances, including the distribution of literature, may be used as evidence of criminal intent. This has led to challenges to the laws based upon the First Amendment. One such challenge in Virginia resulted in a decision that recognized NORML's free speech was being violated, but found that society's need to prohibit drug use overrode the free speech considerations involved.

Paraphernalia laws present difficult choices for drug law reformers. Any legislative attack on drug paraphernalia laws must begin with the realization that legislators find it difficult to vote against these laws, since such a vote is often perceived as a vote in favor of drug use. Therefore, many paraphernalia laws have been altered after NORML, the ACLU, and other groups challenged their constitutionality and then offered more sensible alternatives. For example, the City of Chicago passed a bill outlawing the sale of paraphernalia to minors rather than banning the sale outright.

Nearly every paraphernalia law passed in the country has been challenged in court, and those legislatures that may be considering such a law should forcefully be reminded of the litigation and uncertainty that will inevitably follow any such enactment.

In March 1982, the United States Supreme Court issued its first decision in a drug paraphernalia case. The statute involved was not based on the DEA Model Act that has been enacted by most of the states which have acted on this issue. The case, *Village of Hoffman Estates v. The Flipside*, involved a local ordinance which licensed and regulated drug paraphernalia businesses and made it a civil offense, punishable by up to a $500 fine, for violations of its provisions. In an 8 to 0 decision, the Court upheld the ordinance, stating:

> Many American communities have recently enacted laws regulating or prohibiting the sale of drug paraphernalia. Whether these laws are wise or effective is not, of course, the province of this Court. We hold only that such legislation is not facially overbroad or vague if it does not reach constitutionally protected conduct and is reasonably clear in its application to the complainant.

Broad language distinctions between this case and other paraphernalia cases can be made. These include differences between criminal and civil fines, licensing and prohibiting paraphernalia, and pre-enforcement and post-enforcement challenges. Because of these differences, this case does not settle the issue. Future cases will determine that.

Mandatory Sentences

In 1973, at the urging of its then governor, Nelson Rockefeller, the State of New York enacted a sweeping program of mandatory minimum sentences for a wide variety of drug offenses, including a mandatory life sentence without possibility of parole for certain drug sales. Unquestionably, these "Rockefeller drug laws" represented the most severe approach to the drug phenomenon in this country's history.

Almost immediately, however, it became apparent that that approach was a dismal failure. Not only did it not serve its intended purpose, which was presumably to substantially reduce drug traffic in the state, but it also wreaked havoc with the state's criminal justice system and led to outrageously unfair sentences in particular cases. Indeed, within five years after those laws were enacted they were substantially modified if not repealed outright.

Nevertheless, the notion that severe mandatory sentences serve as an effective deterrent is a convenient and appealing one to many legislators otherwise frustrated by a seemingly insoluble problem, and more and more states in the 1980s may be expected to consider such laws. In fact, some states have already enacted laws under which a person selling specific amounts of marijuana must receive a longer sentence than persons convicted of assault, rape, and other violent crimes.

One of those laws, enacted in Michigan, has already been declared unconstitutional by the courts as a violation of the Constitution's prohibition against "cruel and unusual punishment." The defendant in the case, a man in his late twenties who had no previous criminal record, was convicted of possessing four pounds of cocaine for sale. Under the Michigan law, the judge was required to impose a sentence of life imprisonment. The judge decided, however, that such a sentence would be intolerable and struck down the law instead. The state has appealed that decision, and a decision on the appeal was expected in early 1983.

Wherever such mandatory sentences are proposed, the citizen-lobbyist should emphasize as strongly as possible the proven futility and injustice of such an approach to the drug phenomenon.

Therapeutic Use of Marijuana

Marijuana's therapeutic potential has been known for more than 5,000 years. The Chinese Emperor Shen-Nung is thought to have prescribed hemp preparation for a variety of ailments as early as the 28th century B.C.

Marijuana is classified under federal law as a Schedule I drug. Legally, that means that the federal government believes marijuana has "no accepted medical use in the United States."

NORML first sued the federal government to reschedule marijuana into a lower classification and to recognize its medical value in 1972. The lawsuit is still pending, with four separate orders from the Federal Court of Appeals for the District of Columbia to hold hearings on the subject.

In the meantime, at least thirty-three states have enacted laws recognizing the therapeutic value of marijuana or its synthetic derivatives in at least two medical areas. The first is in the treatment of glaucoma, an eye disorder that increases interocular pressure and leads to eventual blindness if left untreated. Marijuana reduces the eye pressure and, when used in conjunction with other medicines, can stabilize the pressure and prevent further deterioration of eyesight.

The second condition covered by these therapeutic laws is in the treatment of patients undergoing cancer chemotherapy. Marijuana has proven effective in alleviating the violent nausea brought on by this treatment and in increasing the appetite of patients undergoing chemotherapy.

Federal bureaucracy has delayed effective implementation of most of these state laws. In September 1981, a bill was introduced into Congress to reschedule marijuana. That bill, H.R. 4498, had more than sixty co-sponsors. A new bill will be introduced into the 98th Congress. Its introduction was the result of efforts by the Alliance for Cannabis Therapeutics (ACT), a Washington, D.C.–based lobbying organization devoted to removing legal restrictions on the availability of marijuana for medical treatment.

Wherever possible, lobbyists in the state legislatures should seek the enactment of appropriate bills recognizing and authorizing the therapeutic use of marijuana.

CONCLUSIONS

Marijuana is not a harmless drug, particularly if used chronically over a long period of time. Yet thousands of studies have failed to establish conclusive evidence that moderate marijuana use poses any serious medical problems to healthy adults. Marijuana does contain large amounts of tar and carcinogens; as a result, a person who smokes large amounts of marijuana over a lengthy period of time faces a serious risk of pulmonary disorders and potentially even lung cancer. In addition, persons under the influence of many drugs, including marijuana, may pose certain dangers to others, as for example when driving under that influence, although the risks presented by marijuana are much less serious than those posed by the use of alcohol.

Thus, state legislators have legitimate reasons to be concerned about the use of marijuana, and especially its use by adolescents. At the same time, however, they also have an obligation to protect the right of privacy of adults, including the freedom to consume recreational drugs so long as their actions do not endanger others.

Plainly, the criminal approach to the marijuana phenomenon has proved to be a dismal and tragic failure, and one that has literally cost Americans many billions of dollars in actual governmental expenditures and lost tax revenues. Sooner or later, it seems inevitable that our legislatures will have to attempt a different approach, including the legalization of marijuana use under appropriate regulations and safeguards. Such an approach will best serve the interests of individual freedom and should be supported.

5 / CENSORSHIP
by Kenneth P. Norwick

"Congress shall make no law . . . abridging the freedom of speech, or
of the press."

With these few immortal words, in the First Amendment to the
Constitution, this nation's founding fathers established what the Supreme Court has called "the matrix, the indispensable condition, of
nearly every other form of freedom." Of all the rights and freedoms
guaranteed us in the Constitution, it is generally agreed that those set
forth in the First Amendment are among the most precious and vital.

But what do these few words really mean? What did the framers of
the First Amendment have in mind by "freedom of speech" and "of the
press"? Do those words prohibit all governmental censorship? If not,
what kinds of speech and publication can be censored? And if there can
be censorship, what standards apply, and who can do the censoring?

Even today—almost two hundred years after the First Amendment
was adopted—the answers to these questions are far from clear. Under
our constitutional system of government, the ultimate responsibility
for answering these questions lies with the Supreme Court, and that
Court—especially during the last two decades—has repeatedly tried
to provide answers, most often in the context of so-called obscene or

pornographic works. In 1973, and again in 1974, the Court set forth its most recent attempts to provide those answers. Those answers have become the law of the land, and every other branch of government—including all state legislatures—must comply with them. These decisions have had and will continue to have a direct and immediate impact on the censorship laws of every state and on every state legislature that will be considering those laws. Before we examine those decisions, we will first review briefly the history that led up to them, for it is only with that perspective that the significance of those decisions can be fully appreciated.

STRUGGLING WITH CENSORSHIP: AN HISTORICAL PERSPECTIVE

The Old World

In light of this country's contemporary concern with obscenity and pornography, it may be surprising to many that the likelihood of explicit sexual materials being suppressed as obscene is little more than a hundred years old. Even though governmental censorship has existed throughout recorded history, for the most part such censorship has been concerned with political and religious heresy rather than sexual materials. During Greek and Roman times, and indeed until just a few centuries ago, sexual explicitness was widely accepted in popular literature, drama, and ballads. Bawdy stories often became vehicles for the presentation of religious themes. Governmental and religious censors during these ages—who plainly had no qualms about suppressing material that displeased them—apparently saw no need to bother with even the most licentious matter.

In sixteenth-century England, with the advent of the printing press, the first system of book licensing was established. Here too, however, licensing was directed toward books dealing with sedition and heresy rather than those dealing with sex. Indeed, the principal purpose of the licensing system had less to do with censorship than with the protection of English printers and bookbinders from foreign competition.

During the latter part of the sixteenth century, Puritanism as a mode of living became increasingly widespread, and the Puritans, who rejected all pleasure as "sinful and immoral," sought to purge England of everything they considered obscene. At this time, the tolerant attitude toward sexual materials that marked almost every earlier age began to change. And, except for a brief period following the Restoration in 1660, the Puritan influence has continued to be felt.

But even the newly emergent Puritan concern for the "intollerable corruption of common lyfe and manners, which pestilently invadeth the myndes of many that delight to heare or read the said wantone woorkes," failed to specify precisely what ought to be condemned. Indeed, books and pamphlets that would be considered hard-core pornography today circulated freely in England during this time, reinforcing the conclusion that if they lacked anti-religious content they apparently violated no law.

Significantly, no obscenity legislation was enacted in England until 1824, and those laws only prohibited exposing an obscene book or print in public places. By 1857, however, the so-called Lord Campbell's Act generally prohibited the dissemination of all obscene materials in England.

Early America

Although explicit sexual materials were very much in circulation throughout the American colonies, only Massachusetts had any law addressed to them. Enacted in 1711, that law recited that "evil communication, wicked, profane, impure, filthy and obscene songs, composures, writings or prints do corrupt the mind and are incentives to all manner of impieties and debaucheries, more especially when digested, composed or uttered in imitation or in mimicking of preaching, or any other part of divine worship," and prohibited the "composing, writing, printing or publishing of any filthy, obscene or profane song, pamphlet, libel or mock sermon, in imitation of preaching, or any other part of divine worship." Nevertheless, not until 1821—over one hundred years later—was anyone prosecuted for violating that statute.

But this does not mean that there was no censorship during these times. The American colonies were closely governed by the British sovereign and his appointees, and the British law of libel and slander, which made it a crime to criticize the government, was very much in force, and enforced.

Against this background of governmental suppression of speech and press, the American colonies won their independence, and in 1789, adopted its Constitution. That Constitution, however, was not ratified until the framers added to it the Bill of Rights, which made it clear that certain precious individual freedoms—of press, speech, religion, and assembly—could not be abridged by the newly created government.

In the view of some, including the late Supreme Court Justices Hugo L. Black and William O. Douglas, the words of the First Amendment—"Congress shall make no law"—were to be construed literally to prohibit absolutely any governmental censorship or restriction of speech or press. However, that view has not prevailed, and the Supreme Court, particularly with respect to obscenity, continues to struggle with the boundaries of the First Amendment.

In 1821, Vermont became the first state in the new Union to pass an anti-obscenity statute, and many other states soon followed its lead. The first federal anti-obscenity statute, passed in 1842, was directed toward importation, and in 1865 Congress passed a statute prohibiting the sending of obscene materials through the mails.

Notwithstanding the apparently growing concern with obscenity, there was actually very little enforcement of either state or federal obscenity laws during the first seventy years of the nineteenth century. In 1868, however, the situation changed dramatically when the New York legislature enacted a law prohibiting the dissemination of obscene literature. Shortly thereafter a grocery store clerk named Anthony Comstock began a one-man crusade to ensure that the law was vigorously enforced, and, joined by the YMCA, formed a national organization called the Committee for the Suppression of Vice. In 1873, largely in response to this crusade, Congress broadened the federal mail act and named Comstock a special agent of the Post Office in charge of enforcing the federal law. Many states that had no obscenity legislation passed such statutes following the 1873 federal enactment, and by 1900 at least thirty states had some form of general prohibition against the dissemination of obscene materials.

The response to obscenity sparked by Comstock in the late 1800s continued through the first sixty years of the twentieth century. During those years many books, plays, films, and works of art were actually suppressed as obscene, while countless others had to be obtained and kept with the utmost secrecy on the assumption they would be suppressed if discovered.

Throughout this period the prevailing definition of obscenity was the

one set forth in an 1868 English case called *Queen v. Hicklin*. There
the court declared that material was obscene if it tended "to deprave
and corrupt those whose minds are open to such immoral influences,
and into whose hands a publication of this sort may fall." This decision
made clear for the first time that materials could be prohibited solely
because of their sexual content, and not just because of their attack
upon the government or upon religious institutions. It also made clear
that an entire work could be suppressed as obscene on the basis of only
a few of its passages, or if it tended to "deprave and corrupt" only the
most immature and susceptible of people. This definition prevailed
throughout the United States during the early part of the twentieth
century.

The Development of the Law

The first seven decades of the twentieth century saw an ever-increas-
ing number of obscenity cases. But confusion as to the legal definition
of obscenity seemed to increase with every case. More and more courts
came to be troubled by the shortcomings of the prevailing *Hicklin*
formulation and the distorted results it gave rise to. In one famous
case, for example, where the federal courts ruled that James Joyce's
classic *Ulysses* was not obscene and therefore could be admitted into
the United States, the word "obscene" was defined as "tending to stir
the sex impulses or to lead to sexually impure and lustful thoughts."
Also in that case, the courts rejected the *Hicklin* definition and ruled
that a finding of obscenity had to be based on a reading of the entire
book, not just of isolated passages, and on the effect of the entire book
on the "normal person."

During this same period the Supreme Court was frequently asked to
interpret the extent of First Amendment guarantees in connection
with expression that was politically (but not sexually) offensive. Rejecting the "absolutist" interpretation later espoused by Justices Black and
Douglas, the Court declared that some political speech under some
circumstances could be suppressed, although such suppression should
rarely be necessary or appropriate. In one famous case (*Schenk v.
United States*) involving antidraft materials circulated during World
War I, the Court declared: "The most stringent protection of free
speech would not protect a man in falsely shouting fire in a theater, and
causing a panic. . . . The question in every case is whether the words
used are used in such circumstances and are of such a nature as to

create a clear and present danger that they will bring about the substantive evils that Congress has a right to prevent."

Although the "clear and present danger" test seemed to many to
strike an appropriate balance between First Amendment freedoms and
government's perceived need for control, that standard did not survive
as the constitutionally required test for the suppression of speech and
press. And this was especially true when it came to so-called obscene
and pornographic works.

Not until 1957—166 years after the First Amendment was
adopted—did the Supreme Court consider whether various state and
federal anti-obscenity laws were constitutional, and if so, what kinds of
materials could be suppressed as obscene. Its decision in the case of
Roth v. United States, however, did not conclusively answer those
questions.

Although some people argued that all anti-obscenity laws—at least
in the absence of proof that obscenity presented a "clear and present
danger" of antisocial conduct—were unconstitutional because they
violated the First Amendment, a majority of the Supreme Court in the
Roth case disagreed. Instead, the Court declared that obscenity was
not the kind of material protected by freedom of speech and press, and
therefore a showing of clear and present danger was unnecessary to
justify its suppression. As the Court put it, in an opinion by Justice
William J. Brennan:

> The protection given speech and press was fashioned to assure
> unfettered interchange of ideas for the bringing about of political
> and social changes desired by the people. . . . All ideas having
> even the slightest redeeming social importance . . . have the full
> protection of the guaranties, unless they encroach upon the lim-
> ited area of more important interests. But implicit in the history of
> the First Amendment is the rejection of obscenity as utterly with-
> out social importance.

A recognition of the overriding importance of First Amendment
values, however, caused the Court to limit severely the kinds of materials that could be censored. "Sex and obscenity are not synonymous,"
declared the Court. Rather, it continued, obscene material "deals with
sex in a manner appealing to the prurient interest. The portrayal of sex,
e.g., in art, literature and scientific works, is not itself sufficient reason

to deny material the constitutional protection of freedom of speech and press. Sex, a great and mysterious force in human life, has indisputably been a subject of absorbing interest to mankind throughout the ages; it is one of the vital problems of human interest and public concern." Further, the Court made clear that the "isolated passages" and "most susceptible person" doctrines were not to be applied, and that to be found obscene a work must offend "the common conscience of the community by present-day standards."

In addition, in another case decided that same year, the Court insisted that obscenity statutes be narrowly tailored to the evils they were intended to control. *Butler v. Michigan* concerned a statute that sought to forbid distribution of sexually explicit material to adults because of its potential harm to minors. Though the material in question was explicit, it was not obscene. In an opinion by Justice Frankfurter, the Court stated:

> The State insists that by thus quarantining the general reading public against books not too rugged for grown men and women in order to shield juvenile innocence, it is exercising its power to promote the general welfare. Surely, this is to burn the house to roast the pig. . . . We have before us legislation not reasonably restricted to the evil with which it is said to deal. The incidence of this enactment is to reduce the adult population of Michigan to reading only what is fit for children.

In *Roth*, the Supreme Court attempted to settle upon a constitutional definition of obscenity. But since it was not called upon to determine the status of the particular materials involved in that case, that definition remained somewhat abstract. In fact, *Roth* merely set the stage for the intense legal, philosophical, and sociological debate over obscenity that still continues. Moreover, although they were intended as further refinements, the Court's decisions in 1973 and 1974 in many ways constituted a return to the confusion that existed in 1957. Before we consider those decisions, we should first understand what has happened—legally and otherwise—in the years since *Roth* was decided.

The Legal Developments in the 1960s

Because the *Roth* decision stated that government could censor obscenity, but that only limited kinds of materials qualified as such, the question of which materials actually were obscene, and how they were to be censored, soon became a recurrent one for the courts. Literally thousands of obscenity cases came before the courts in the decade and a half following the *Roth* decision, but the lack of clear and coherent guidelines from the courts lent an arbitrariness to judicial holdings, and the confusion only mounted.

Although this period was generally marked by a trend toward narrowing the definition of obscenity, the Supreme Court continued to insist that there was such a thing, and that government could suppress it when it found it. However, no majority of the Court could agree on any one approach. Virtually every Justice had his own definition of obscenity, perhaps the most notorious being Justice Potter Stewart's "I know it when I see it." The result was that authors, publishers, and producers, among others, never really knew what could safely be published or produced.

In 1966, in *Memoirs v. Massachusetts,* a case concerning the much-litigated eighteenth-century novel *Fanny Hill,* three Justices joined in articulating a definition of obscenity. Under that definition, three separate requirements had to be met before a work could be declared obscene: "(1) that the dominant theme of the material as a whole appeals to a prurient interest in sex; (2) that the material is patently offensive because it affronts contemporary community standards relating to the description or representation of sexual matters; (3) that the material is utterly without redeeming social value." Because Justices Black and Douglas declared that the First Amendment prevented the suppression of any material by reason of obscenity, no matter how defined, most lower courts and state legislatures concluded that anti-obscenity laws had to include this *Memoirs* test before a majority of the Supreme Court would find those laws constitutional. (*Fanny Hill* was finally determined not to be obscene.)

Just a year later, in 1967, the Supreme Court confused things even more. In a brief, unsigned opinion in *Redrup v. New York,* the Court confessed that there was no single definition of obscenity but broadly hinted that so long as allegedly obscene material was not made available to children, was not thrust upon an unwilling audience, and was not pandered, it should not be suppressed. As a result of that decision, more and more people came to believe, as the title of a contemporary book put it, that "the end of obscenity" was at hand.

Significantly, however, especially in light of present-day developments, the Court had far less reluctance to deal with obscenity insofar as children were concerned. In *Ginsberg v. New York,* in 1968, the Court upheld a statute which prohibited the sale to anyone under seventeen of material that was not obscene as to adults but was defined as "harmful to minors." Writing for the majority, Justice Brennan asserted that "even where there is an invasion of protected freedoms, 'the power of the state to control the conduct of children reaches beyond the scope of its authority over adults.'" The state not only had an independent interest in the welfare of its minors, the Court found, but a responsibility to aid parents in the process of child-rearing. Justice Brennan recognized the vigorous dispute among authorities with respect to the impact of obscenity on the moral development of youth. Nevertheless, he expressly noted one psychoanalytic opinion which held that the easy availability of pornography to children implied a subtle and dangerous form of parental approval. Unlike the Court's decision in the *Butler* case, which concerned sales of sexually explicit material to adults, the *Ginsberg* decision upheld the power of government to regulate obscenity when the interests of children were involved.

The trend toward limiting government control in the area of adult rights, however, continued. In a major 1969 case, *Stanley v. Georgia,* the Supreme Court struck down a state law that made it a crime simply to possess obscene materials. "[T]he state has no business," declared the Court, "telling a man, sitting alone in his own house, what books he may read or what films he may watch. Our whole constitutional heritage rebels at the thought of giving government the power to control men's minds." The Court made clear that this privacy right applied even if the material in question was admittedly obscene. *Stanley* seemed to declare the end of legal censorship and, in fact, was so interpreted by several lower courts. If a person has the constitutional right to read and view such materials in his own home, they reasoned, then surely there must also be a right to produce and sell those materials. Nevertheless, until the Supreme Court itself either adopted or rejected that interpretation, no one could be sure of anything.

The unsettled state of the law throughout the 1960s essentially threw the onus of the obscenity issue onto authors, publishers, artists, and producers. After all, they were the people who faced the substantial fines and jail sentences that a legal finding of obscenity could incur. Many chose self-censorship as the only means of deflecting the threat of government action. However, encouraged by the judicial trend toward free expression, many did not.

The Sexual Revolution of the 1960s

Compared to the present, the sexual climate of the United States when *Roth* was decided can only be described as tame and innocent. To be sure, explicit sexual materials were available to those who wanted them, but they were obtainable only through presumably illegal, under-the-counter transactions. Motion pictures for the general public rarely dealt with sexual themes, and none depicted even partial nudity or sexual activity. Four-letter words were nonexistent in films and rare in books and plays. And even though Joyce's *Ulysses* managed to litigate its way through Customs in the 1930s, other classics such as D. H. Lawrence's *Lady Chatterley's Lover* and Henry Miller's *Tropic of Cancer* still could not be obtained openly. Sex was not considered a proper subject for either public or private discussion.

In the years since 1957, all this has changed radically. Nudity (declared by the Supreme Court not to be in itself obscene) is now common in movies, magazines, and books; there is seemingly no word that cannot be and is not used; and overt sexual activity is graphically presented in films, books, magazines, and live performances—all apparently without violating any law, at least as far as adult audiences are concerned. Topless and bottomless entertainers, waitresses, and even gas-station attendants became part of the American scene, as have specialized newspapers and clubs devoted exclusively to sex. Sexual topics—including prostitution, masturbation, homosexuality, and spouse-swapping—are discussed in print, and on radio and television; sex-education programs have been introduced into school systems at the urging of parents and educators; and sex-therapy clinics treat people with sexual problems. Indeed, it seems that sex has become this nation's major preoccupation.

But the change in sexual climate has not been universally applauded. Although its existence cannot be disputed, virtually everything else about it is. People disagree as to what gave rise to the change—many simplistically attribute it to liberal court decisions; others attribute it to European influences—and people disagree as to whether it is a lasting trend or a temporary aberration. Many believe that the proliferation of sexual materials constitutes a serious threat to the health and welfare of the American people, while others believe it represents a normal and healthy step toward the maturation of our society.

The Obscenity Commission

In 1967, the United States Congress declared that the federal government had "a responsibility to investigate the gravity of [the traffic in obscenity and pornography] and to determine whether such materials are harmful to the public," and it established an eighteen-member advisory commission which was to present its report within two years. President Johnson appointed the commission in January 1968. Among its members were judges, lawyers, psychiatrists, sociologists, law enforcement officials, clergymen, and representatives of the motion picture and publishing industries, along with two of the country's leading opponents of pornography: the Reverend Morton A. Hill, S.J., president of an organization called Morality in Media, and Charles H. Keating, Jr., founder of Citizens for Decent Literature. Professor William B. Lockhart, a leading expert on the legal aspects of the pornography phenomenon, was named chairman.

The commission's report is undoubtedly the most detailed and comprehensive review of the pornography phenomenon ever compiled. Although most of its findings produced little dispute, several generated intense controversy. In fact, the commission's ultimate recommendations proved so controversial that President Nixon felt it appropriate to formally disown them, as did the United States Senate in a roll call vote.

The commission undertook several extensive public opinion polls in an attempt to find out how the American people felt about pornography. As to whether pornography should be suppressed, the commission found that while more than half of American adults believed adults themselves should be allowed to read or see anything they wish, almost all believed that young persons should not be permitted access to certain sexual materials. At the same time, however, almost half the population believed that laws against pornography were impossible to enforce. Significantly, the commission reported that Americans had a tendency to misjudge the opinions of others in their communities, often perceiving a far more restrictive outlook on sex than actually existed.

By far the most controversial of the commission's findings involved the effects of pornography on the people who read and viewed it and, in particular, whether reading and viewing pornography led to antisocial or criminal behavior. In this connection, the commission found "a correlation between experience with erotic materials and general attitudes about sex. Those who [had] more tolerant or liberal sexual attitudes [tended] also to have greater experience with sexual materials . . . [and were] also less rejecting of sexual material." Several studies showed, in fact, that experience with erotic material led people to become less fearful of its possible detrimental effects.

With regard to the contention that reading or viewing pornography led to immorality or antisocial or criminal behavior, one study conducted by the commission revealed that such exposure had no measurable impact on moral character. The commission also cited studies in Denmark indicating that the increased availability of pornography had actually been accompanied by a decrease in sex crimes.

The commission expressed its ultimate conclusions regarding the effects of pornography as follows:

[F]or America, the relationship between the availability of erotica and changes in sex-crime rates neither proves nor disproves the possibility that availability of erotica leads to crime, but the massive overall increases in sex crimes that have been alleged do not seem to have occurred. . . . In sum, empirical research designed to clarify the question has found no evidence to date that exposure to explicit sexual materials plays a significant role in the causation of delinquent or criminal behavior among youth or adults. The commission cannot conclude that exposure to erotic materials is a factor in the causation of sex crime or sex delinquency.

On the basis of its findings, the commission set forth legislative and non-legislative recommendations for future action, many of which provoked intense and bitter debate. As to its non-legislative recommendations, the commission stated:

[M]uch of the problem regarding materials which depict explicit sexual activity stems from the inability or reluctance of people in our society to be open and direct in dealing with sexual matters. . . . The commission believes that accurate, appropriate sex information provided openly and directly through legitimate channels and from reliable sources in healthy contexts can compete successfully with potentially distorted, warped, inaccurate and unreliable information from clandestine, illegitimate sources; and it believes that the attitudes and orientations towards sex produced by the open communication of appropriate sex information from reliable sources through legitimate sources will be normal and healthy, providing a solid foundation for the basic institutions of our society.

To achieve that goal, the commission recommended a massive sex-education effort; continued open discussion, based on factual information, of the issues regarding obscenity and pornography; the collection of additional factual information; and citizens' organizations at local, regional, and national levels to help implement these recommendations.

The most controversial recommendation, however, was legislative: The commission recommended that "federal, state and local legislation should not seek to interfere with the rights of adults who wish to do so to read, obtain or view explicit sexual materials" and that "federal, state and local legislation prohibiting the sale, exhibition and distribution of sexual material to consenting adults should be repealed."

This recommendation against prohibitive obscenity legislation was endorsed by twelve of the eighteen members of the commission, and nine separate reasons were given to support it:

1. Extensive empirical investigation, both by the commission and others, provides no evidence that exposure to or use of explicit sexual materials plays a significant role in the causation of social or individual harms such as crime, delinquency, sexual or nonsexual deviancy, or severe emotional disturbances.

2. On the positive side, explicit sexual materials are sought as a source of entertainment and information by substantial numbers of American adults.

3. Society's attempts to legislate for adults in the area of obscenity have not been successful.

4. Public opinion in America does not support the imposition of legal prohibitions upon the right of adults to read or see explicit sexual materials.

5. The lack of consensus among Americans concerning whether explicit sexual materials should be available to adults in our society, and the significant number of adults who wish to have access to such materials, pose serious problems regarding the enforcement of legal prohibitions upon adults, even aside from the vagueness and subjectivity of present law.

6. The foregoing considerations take on added significance because of the fact that adult obscenity laws deal in the realm of speech and communications.

7. We do not believe that the objective of protecting youth may justifiably be achieved at the expense of denying adults materials of their choice.

8. There is no reason to suppose that elimination of governmental prohibitions upon the sexual materials that may be made available to adults would adversely affect the availability to the public of other books, magazines and films.

9. The commission has found no evidence that the lawful distribution of explicit sexual materials to adults may have a deleterious effect upon the individual morality of American citizens and upon the moral climate in America as a whole.

The commission then concluded:

The concern about the effect of obscenity upon morality is also expressed as a concern about the impact of sexual materials upon American values and standards. Such values and standards are currently in a process of complex change, in both sexual and nonsexual areas. The open availability of increasingly explicit sexual materials is only one of these changes. The current flux in sexual values is related to a number of powerful influences, among which are the ready availability of effective methods of contraception, changes of the role of women in our society, and the increased education and mobility of our citizens. The availability of explicit sexual materials is, the commission believes, not one of the important influences on sexual morality.

The commission is of the view that it is exceedingly unwise for government to attempt to legislate individual moral values and standards independent of behavior, especially by restrictions upon consensual communications. This is certainly true in the absence of a clear public mandate to do so, and our studies have revealed no such mandate in the area of obscenity.

The commission recognizes and believes that the existence of sound moral standards is of vital importance to individuals and to society. To be effective and meaningful, however, these standards must be based upon deep personal commitment flowing from values instilled in the home, in educational and religious training, and through individual resolutions of personal confrontations with human experience. Governmental regulation of moral choice can deprive the individual of the responsibility for personal decision which is essential to the formation of genuine moral standards. Such regulation would also tend to establish an official moral orthodoxy, contrary to our most fundamental constitutional traditions.

In contrast to its recommendations affecting adults, the commission did recommend "legislative regulations upon the sale of sexual materials to young persons who do not have the consent of their parents." Because of insufficient research on how exposure to sexually explicit materials affected children, the commission's conclusions in this area were expressed with only partial confidence. Further, its proposals regarding children were admittedly influenced by its finding "that a large majority of Americans *believe* that children should not be exposed to certain sexual materials." Ultimately, the commission took the view that parents should decide on the suitability of explicit sexual materials for their children, and consequently proposed legislation to help parents control children's access to such materials during their formative years. The commission believed, however, that only pictorial material should be legally withheld from children.

Other recommendations proposed legislation to prohibit displays of sexually explicit pictorial materials and to permit recipients to "turn off" unsolicited sexual mail. Both of these were based on the finding that such materials could cause considerable offense. Unwanted intrusions upon individual sensibilities, the commission felt, warranted legislative regulation. And these controls, it believed, need not significantly interfere with the rights of adults who wished to receive such materials.

Although each of these recommendations was supported by a majority of the commission, they were by no means unanimous. Two of the members, Otto N. Larsen and Marvin E. Wolfgang, both sociologists, stated that because "the First Amendment to the Constitution is abrogated by restrictions on textual and visual material that may be deemed by some as obscene or pornographic," *all* existing federal, state, and local obscenity statutes should be repealed, including limitations with respect to children.

On the other hand, six of the commission's eighteen members strongly disapproved the recommendation to repeal legal restrictions on the rights of consenting adults to read and view pornography. Three dissenting members of the panel called the majority report "a Magna Carta for the pornographer" and made clear their belief that antiobscenity laws should be strengthened and vigorously enforced.

The 1973–1974 Decisions

In 1973 and 1974, the Supreme Court announced several major decisions regarding the censorship of obscenity and pornography. The decisions constituted the first time since the 1957 *Roth* case that a Supreme Court majority—albeit by the narrowest of margins—agreed on a single approach to the definition of obscenity. Yet, although the decisions resolved many legal issues in the obscenity area, at the same time they raised at least as many new ones. The Court largely delegated to the states the responsibility for legislating and adjudicating the perennial question, "What is obscene?" For the first time, four Justices—just one short of a majority—declared that the First Amendment forbade any governmental censorship of obscene or pornographic works, at least as far as willing adults were concerned.

The most important of the 1973 decisions is *Miller v. California*. In an opinion written by Chief Justice Warren Burger for a 5–4 majority, the Court, after reiterating that state obscenity laws do not automatically violate the First Amendment, proclaimed its intention to "formulate [obscenity] standards more concrete than those in the past."

At the outset, the majority expressly rejected the three-pronged

Fanny Hill definition, noting that since the four dissenting Justices asserted that the First Amendment forbade any censorship for adults, "no member of the Court today supports [that] formulation." Acknowledging "the inherent dangers of undertaking to regulate any form of expression," the majority declared that "state statutes designed to regulate obscene materials must be carefully limited," and then set forth its new, but also three-pronged, constitutional definition:

> We now confine the permissible scope of such regulation to works which depict or describe sexual conduct. That conduct must be specifically defined by the applicable state law, as written or authoritatively construed. . . . The basic guidelines for the trier of fact must be: (a) whether 'the average person, applying contemporary community standards' would find that the work, taken as a whole, appeals to the prurient interest . . . (b) whether the work depicts or describes, in a patently offensive way, sexual conduct specifically defined by the applicable state law, and (c) whether the work, taken as a whole, lacks serious literary, artistic, political or scientific value.

Although these new guidelines seem similar to the three-pronged test of the *Fanny Hill* decision, each differs significantly from its earlier version. In the first new test, the Court eliminated the requirement that the "dominant theme" of the material taken as a whole appeal to a prurient interest in sex. Instead, it required only that "the average person, applying contemporary community standards," must find that the material, taken as a whole, "appeals to the prurient interest," even though its dominant theme may have nothing to do with sex or prurience. In the second new guideline, the Court replaced the old requirement that the material be "patently offensive because it affronts contemporary community standards relating to the description or representation of sexual matters" with the new requirement that the work "depicts or describes, in a patently offensive way, sexual conduct specifically defined by the applicable state law." While ostensibly making more specific the kinds of materials that might qualify as obscene, the new second guideline thus makes the test of patent offensiveness less specific. In its third new guideline, the Court replaced the previous requirement that the work be "utterly without redeeming social value" with a new test providing that the work, "taken as a whole, lacks serious literary, artistic, political, or scientific value," clearly a less stringent requirement.

Perhaps even more significant than its new guidelines was the majority's response to one of the most important legal questions concerning the suppression of obscenity: What is the applicable "community" for determining "contemporary community standards"? Although many lower courts and legal commentators had argued that the First Amendment required a national community standard, the 1973 Court majority emphatically disagreed:

> To require a state to structure obscenity proceedings around evidence of a *national* "community standard" would be an exercise in futility. . . . It is neither realistic nor constitutionally sound to read the First Amendment as requiring that the people of Maine or Mississippi accept public depiction of conduct found tolerable in Las Vegas or New York City. . . . People in different states vary in their tastes and attitudes, and this diversity is not to be strangled by the absolutism of imposed uniformity.

But because the opinion mentioned both entire states and individual cities, it left unclear whether the concept of an "appropriate community" applied equally to cities and towns as well as to whole states.

The second major 1973 decision came in the case of *Paris Adult Theater I v. Slaton*. In that case the State of Georgia sued two Atlanta movie theaters to enjoin them from showing allegedly obscene films. A sign outside the theaters stated, "Adult Theater—You must be 21 and able to prove it. If viewing the nude body offends you, Please Do Not Enter," and there was no evidence that minors had ever been admitted. The trial judge, relying on the Supreme Court's decision in the *Stanley* case, dismissed the state's complaints, stating: "It appears to the Court that the display of these films in a commercial theater, when surrounded by requisite notice to the public of their nature and by reasonable protection against the exposure of these films to minors, is constitutionally permissible."

After the Georgia Supreme Court reversed that ruling, the theaters appealed to the United States Supreme Court. By the same 5–4 vote, the majority, again speaking through Chief Justice Burger, upheld the

Georgia Supreme Court and expressly rejected the "consenting adults" rationale:

> We categorically disapprove the theory, apparently adopted by the trial judge, that obscene, pornographic films acquire constitutional immunity from state regulation simply because they are exhibited for consenting adults only. This holding was properly rejected by the Georgia Supreme Court. Although we have often pointedly recognized the high importance of the state interest in regulating the exposure of obscene materials to juveniles and unconsenting adults . . . this Court has never declared these to be the only legitimate state interests permitting regulation of obscene material.

In particular, the Court noted a legitimate state interest in stemming the tide of commercialized obscenity and in protecting the interest of the public in the quality of life and the total community environment.

Addressing the argument that without proof "that exposure to obscene materials adversely affects men and women or their society," any state regulation of obscenity ought to be impermissible, the majority disavowed the need for objective data. The effects of obscenity, it declared, "may be intangible and indistinct, but they are nonetheless real." Further, state legislatures could properly determine on the basis of common experience "that a sensitive, key relationship of human existence, central to family life, community welfare and the development of human personality, can be debased and distorted by crass commercial exploitation of sex. Nothing in the Constitution prohibits a state from reaching such a conclusion and acting on it legislatively simply because there is no conclusive evidence or empirical data."

The majority then expressly limited the scope of the *Stanley* decision to a person's home. Thus, the *Paris Adult* decision makes clear that even though a person has a constitutional right to read and view obscene materials in his own home, it may still be a crime to sell those materials in a store or to exhibit them in a closed theater.

In the third major 1973 decision, *Kaplan v. California*, the same 5–4 majority held that "expression by words alone can be legally 'obscene'."

In response to each of the majority's 1973 decisions, a full complement of four Justices vigorously dissented. Indeed, in the long run, these dissenting opinions may prove even more significant than the opinions of the majority.

Justice William O. Douglas strongly objected to each of the majority's decisions, reiterating his long-held view that any censorship of allegedly obscene materials violates the First Amendment. As he put it:

> The idea that the First Amendment permits government to ban publications that are "offensive" to some people puts an ominous gloss on freedom of the press. That test would make it possible to ban any paper or any journal or magazine in some benighted place. The First Amendment was designed "to invite dispute," to induce "a condition of unrest," to "create dissatisfactions with conditions as they are," and even to stir "people to anger." . . . The idea that the First Amendment permits punishment for ideas that are "offensive" to the particular judge or jury sitting in judgment is astounding. No greater leveler of speech or literature has ever been designed. To give the power to the censor, as we do today, is to make a sharp and radical break with the traditions of a free society. The First Amendment was not fashioned as a vehicle for dispensing tranquilizers to the people. Its prime function was to keep debate open to offensive as well as to staid people. The tendency throughout history has been to subdue the individual and to exalt the power of government. The use of the standard "offensive" gives authority to government that cuts the very vitals out of the First Amendment. As is intimated by the Court's opinion, the materials before us may be garbage, but so is much of what is said in political campaigns, in the daily press, on TV or over the radio. By reason of the First Amendment—and solely because of it—speakers and publishers have not been threatened or subdued because their thoughts and ideas may be offensive to some.

Perhaps even more significant than Justice Douglas's opinions are the dissenting opinions of Justice William J. Brennan, who has been the Court's leading spokesman on the obscenity issue since his majority opinion in the 1957 *Roth* case. In an exhaustive dissent to the *Paris*

Adult decision, he stated: "No other aspect of the First Amendment has, in recent years, demanded so substantial a commitment of our time, generated such disharmony of views, and remained so resistant to the formulation of stable and manageable standards."

Justice Brennan then reviewed the Supreme Court's numerous unsuccessful attempts to follow the definitional approach to obscenity set forth in the *Roth* decision, and stated:

> Our experience with the *Roth* approach has certainly taught us that the outright suppression of obscenity cannot be reconciled with the fundamental principles of the First and Fourteenth Amendments. . . . After fifteen years of experimentation and debate I am reluctantly forced to the conclusion that none of the available formulas, including the one announced today, can reduce the vagueness to a tolerable level. . . . Any effort to draw a constitutionally acceptable boundary on state power must resort to such indefinite concepts as prurient interest, patent offensiveness, serious literary value, and the like. The meaning of these concepts necessarily varies with the experience, outlook, and even idiosyncrasies of the person defining them. Although we have assumed that obscenity does exist and that we "know it when [we] see it," . . . we are manifestly unable to describe it in advance except by reference to concepts so elusive that they fail to distinguish clearly between protected and unprotected speech.

In his dissent, Justice Brennan indicated (but did not conclude) that there may well be legitimate state interests in protecting children and unconsenting adults from sexually explicit materials. But he stressed that those interests in no way applied to consenting adults:

> [T]he notion that there is a legitimate state concern in the 'control [of] the moral content of a person's thoughts' is wholly inconsistent with the philosophy of the First Amendment.

A state, he continued, "cannot constitutionally premise legislation on the desirability of controlling a person's private thoughts." The implications for freedom of expression, he felt, were dire:

If, as the Court today assumes, "a state legislature may . . . act on the . . . assumption that . . . commerce in obscene books, or public exhibitions focused on obscene conduct, have a tendency to exert a corrupting and debasing impact leading to antisocial behavior," . . . then it is hard to see how state-ordered regimentation of our minds can ever be forestalled. For if a state may, in an effort to maintain or create a particular moral tone, prescribe what its citizens cannot read or cannot see, then it would seem to follow that in pursuit of that same objective a state could decree that its citizens must read certain books or must view certain films. . . . However laudable its goals—and that is obviously a question on which reasonable minds may differ—the state cannot proceed by means that violate the Constitution.

Justice Brennan concluded by stating that, "at least in the absence of distribution to juveniles or obtrusive exposure to unconsenting adults, the First and Fourteenth Amendments prohibit the state and federal governments from attempting wholly to suppress sexually oriented materials on the basis of their allegedly obscene contents."

To many observers, Justice Brennan's dissent in the *Paris Adult* case is one of the most thorough and persuasive judicial opinions ever written on the subject of the censorship of obscenity, and it is at least possible, if not likely, that his opinion may well become the majority view in the not-too-distant future.

In 1974, the Supreme Court decided two cases involving the proper interpretation to be given its 1973 rulings. Those decisions, however, only compounded the uncertainty created just one year before. In *Jenkins v. Georgia*, the Court ruled that the film *Carnal Knowledge* was not obscene under the constitutional standards announced in the *Miller* case. An opinion by Justice William Rehnquist stated that "it would be a serious misreading of [the *Miller* decision] to conclude that juries have unbridled discretion in determining what is 'patently offensive.'" In support of its conclusion that *Carnal Knowledge* was not obscene, the Court, after viewing the film, declared:

While the subject matter of the picture is, in a broader sense, sex, and there are scenes in which sexual conduct including 'ultimate sexual acts' is to be understood to be taking place, the camera does not focus on the bodies of the actors at such times. There is no exhibition whatever of the actors' genitals, lewd or otherwise, during these scenes. There are occasional scenes of nudity, but nudity alone is not enough to make material legally obscene under the *Miller* standards.

Although agreeing with the ultimate conclusion that *Carnal Knowledge* was not obscene, the four dissenters from the 1973 decisions again rejected the majority rationale. In an opinion joined in by Justices Potter Stewart and Thurgood Marshall, Justice Brennan noted that the case simply reinforced his objections to the 1973 decisions, since under them "one cannot say with certainty that material is obscene until at least five members of this Court, applying inevitably obscure standards, have pronounced it so." Justice Douglas simply concurred in the result, stating his view that any ban on obscenity is prohibited by the First Amendment.

In the second case, *Hamling v. United States,* the Court addressed one of the thorniest questions to be raised following its 1973 decisions: Exactly what is an appropriate "community" for determining the alleged obscenity of a work?

The majority's answer to that question stated that although a state could constitutionally provide that the applicable community be the entire state, such a standard was not constitutionally required. Instead, the Court indicated, a state may provide for the use of smaller "communities," or it may make no provision at all. In such instances, the majority continued, each juror sitting in an obscenity case must be permitted to "draw on knowledge of the community or vicinage from which he comes in deciding what conclusion 'the average person, applying contemporary community standards' would reach in a given case."

Despite its obvious shortcomings and ambiguities, the *Miller* approach seems to represent, at least for the present, a relatively fixed feature of constitutional obscenity doctrine. Indeed, if anything, the reach of *Miller* may be expanding. For example, in a 1977 case, *Ward v. Illinois,* the Court upheld a conviction for the sale of sado-masochistic devices not specifically covered by the Illinois obscenity statute. Even though the second *Miller* guideline supposedly limited the kinds of materials that could be found obscene to those "specifically defined by the applicable state law," the Court nevertheless held that state laws need not provide an "exhaustive list" of materials considered "patently offensive."

Significantly, the *Ward* case, along with two other 1977 decisions, *Marks v. United States* and *Smith v. United States*, made clear that the retirement of Justice Douglas in 1975 did not necessarily cost the Court a vote and a voice against censorship. Justice John Paul Stevens, who replaced Douglas, dissented from the "Miller majority" in all three cases, stating as follows in *Marks*:

> However distasteful these materials are to some of us, they are nevertheless a form of communication and entertainment acceptable to a substantial segment of society; otherwise, they would have no value in the marketplace. . . . [T]he present constitutional standards, both substantive and procedural . . . are so intolerably vague that evenhanded enforcement of the law is a virtual impossibility. Indeed my brief experience on the Court has persuaded me that grossly disparate treatment of similar offenders is a characteristic of the criminal enforcement of obscenity law.

THE LEGISLATIVE ISSUES FOR THE 1980s

By now, most states have revised their obscenity laws to conform to the *Miller* guidelines, and it seems unlikely that they will be considering material changes to those laws in the foreseeable future. Instead, the fight for free expression and against censorship will involve very different—but equally important—legislative issues. In fact, it may well turn out that these battles will be more crucial for the future of the First Amendment than any that have been fought before.

Instead of direct attempts to achieve censorship through broadly defined obscenity laws, the forces who desire the maximum possible censorship have embarked on a much more sophisticated—and insidious—campaign to achieve those results. Some of the principal components of that campaign will now be reviewed.

Zoning

In 1972, the city of Detroit adopted certain amendments to its then ten-year-old "anti-skid-row" zoning ordinance which were designed to limit the proliferation of certain "adult" facilities, including bookstores and movie theaters, in certain areas. The facilities were defined primarily by the content of the books and movies offered in them, all of which were presumptively not obscene and thus fully protected by the First Amendment. No effort was made to displace or shut down existing facilities.

A movie theater challenged the amendments as a violation of the First Amendment, but the Supreme Court—in a sharply divided decision—upheld the "adult" zoning scheme. Speaking for a plurality of four Justices in *Young v. American Mini Theaters,* Justice Stevens declared that it was not unconstitutional for Detroit to have premised its zoning ordinances on the content of the books and movies in question:

> [E]ven though we recognize that the First Amendment will not tolerate the total suppression of erotic materials that have some arguably artistic value, it is manifest that society's interest in protecting this type of expression is of a wholly different, and lesser, magnitude than the interest in untrammeled political debate. . . . Whether political oratory or philosophical discussion moves us to applaud or to despise what is said, every schoolchild can understand why our duty to defend the right to speak remains the same. But few of us would march our sons and daughters off to war to preserve the citizen's right to see "Specified Sexual Activities" exhibited in the theaters of our choice. Even though the First Amendment protects communication in this area from total suppression, we hold that the State may legitimately use the content of these materials as the basis for placing them in a different classification from other motion pictures.

However, Justice Powell, who provided the fifth vote necessary to uphold the zoning ordinance, expressly disassociated himself from those sentiments: "I do not think we need reach, nor am I inclined to agree with, the holding . . . that nonobscene, erotic materials may be treated differently under First Amendment principles from other forms of protected expression." Since four Justices dissented precisely because the ordinances were based on the content of the material involved, the *Young* decision clearly did not represent a majority view that the First Amendment permits lesser protection for sexually explicit materials than for any other kind of speech. Nevertheless, in the wake of the *Young* decision, many municipalities have enacted pornography zoning laws. However, their interpretation of the case as indicating broad Supreme Court approval for such plans is almost certainly wrong, and most—if not all—of those laws are being challenged in the courts.

A reading of both Justice Stevens' plurality opinion and Justice Powell's concurring opinion in *Young* indicates that a pornography zoning law will have to satisfy three separate requirements in order to pass constitutional scrutiny. First, the purpose of the law cannot be to suppress sexually explicit materials. In *Young*, the Court found that Detroit's law was intended to prevent neighborhood deterioration, increased crime, and similar adverse effects believed to result from the concentration of certain kinds of businesses, and not to regulate sexually explicit expression.

Second, zoning laws may not severely restrict the exercise of First Amendment rights. In Detroit, the Court found that since the ordinance did not prevent the building of new theaters, the market for adult films remained essentially unrestrained. Significantly, had the number of outlets or the number of potential customers who could conveniently use them not remained substantially the same, the ordinance probably would have been struck down. The burdens imposed on speech by the Detroit law, noted Justice Stevens, were slight:

> The situation would be quite different if the ordinance had the effect of suppressing or greatly restricting access to lawful speech. . . . [T]he ordinances do not affect the operation of existing establishments but only the location of new ones. There are myriad locations in the City of Detroit which must be over 1,000 feet from existing regulated establishments.

Third, there must be a clear factual basis for the legislature's conclusion that the ordinance will achieve its legitimate purposes. In Detroit, the conclusion that the ordinance would prevent the deterioration of surrounding neighborhoods was supported by a substantial body of evidence. Indeed, the existence of such a factual basis was strongly relied on by Justice Powell to support his swing vote to uphold the Detroit law.

An important 1981 decision makes clear that the Supreme Court will

closely scrutinize attempts to suppress sexually oriented speech
through the use of the zoning power. In the case of *Schad v.
Borough of Mount Ephraim*, the Court had before it a local zoning ordinance
that prohibited "live entertainment (including nude dancing) in any
establishment" in the community. The Court declared the ordinance
unconstitutional, holding that entertainment merited the same First
Amendment protection as political speech and that the borough had
failed to justify its curtailment of protected expression. The Court also
stated that the simple fact of nudity was not sufficient to "place otherwise protected material outside the mantle of the First Amendment."

The lower court in *Mount Ephraim* had relied on the decision in the
Detroit case to uphold the ordinance. The Supreme Court's opinion,
however, rejected that view:

> Although [the *Young* decision] stated that a zoning ordinance is
> not invalid merely because it regulates activity protected under
> the First Amendment, it emphasized that the challenged restric-
> tion on the location of adult movie theaters imposed a minimal
> burden on protected speech. . . . The restriction did not affect the
> number of adult movie theaters that could operate in the city; it
> merely dispersed them. The Court did not imply that a munici-
> pality could ban all adult theaters—much less all live entertain-
> ment or all nude dancing—from its commercial districts citywide.
> Moreover, it was emphasized in that case that the evidence pre-
> sented to the Detroit Common Council indicated that the concen-
> tration of adult movie theaters in limited areas led to a
> deterioration in surrounding neighborhoods, and it was concluded
> that the city had justified the incidental burden on First Amend-
> ment interests resulting from merely dispersing, but not exclud-
> ing, adult theaters.

The Court's analysis of the *Mount Ephraim* situation then proceeded
along traditional First Amendment lines. "When a zoning law infringes
on a protected liberty," the Court declared, "it must be narrowly
drawn and must further a sufficiently substantial government interest."
The Court's reliance on the facts of the situation was evident. The
supporters of the *Mount Ephraim* ordinance clearly failed to justify its
restrictions on protected expression. The contention that live enter-

tainment would conflict with the borough's plan to create a commercial area "catering only to the immediate needs of its residents" was unsupported by any evidence. Nor was there evidence to support the borough's assertion that banning live entertainment was necessary to avoid parking, trash, police protection, or medical problems. Finally, the ordinance placed an excessive burden on the exercise of free expression since it neither served significant government interests nor made proper allowance for adequate alternative channels of communication.

Although the *Mount Ephraim* decision should discourage the indiscriminate use of zoning power to censor sexually oriented materials, it may nevertheless be anticipated that municipalities and states will continue to attempt just that form of censorship. Wherever such efforts are made, the citizen-lobbyist should not hesitate to point out the very serious constitutional problems any such attempt inevitably presents.

"Protecting the Kids"

As indicated earlier, the Supreme Court held in the 1968 *Ginsberg* case that the First Amendment permitted greater regulation over the dissemination of sexual materials to children than it did with respect to adults. Apparently inspired by that decision, a number of states and localities in the 1980s have begun to consider and enact laws supposedly designed to protect children from exposure to sexual materials.

These laws take various forms. Some make it a crime to offer sexually explicit materials for sale in stores open to children unless the material is somehow bagged, stapled, or otherwise sealed; others require that the same sorts of materials be kept out of children's reach. But however phrased, these laws inevitably result in the restriction of adult access to constitutionally protected materials, in the substantial impairment of the First Amendment rights of children, and in a general chill on the exercise of First Amendment rights.

The Supreme Court's most recent statement on the subject is contained in *Erznoznik v. City of Jacksonville,* decided in 1975. There, the Court struck down an ordinance making it a public nuisance for a drive-in theater to exhibit films containing nudity when the screen was visible from the street. Writing for the majority, Justice Powell first addressed the argument that the ordinance was intended to protect citizens against unwilling exposure to potentially offensive materials:

The plain, if at times disquieting, truth is that in our pluralistic society, constantly proliferating new and ingenious forms of expression, "we are inescapably captive audiences for many purposes." . . . Much that we encounter offends our esthetic, if not our political and moral, sensibilities. Nevertheless, the Constitution does not permit government to decide which types of otherwise protected speech are sufficiently offensive to require protection for the unwilling listener or viewer. Rather, absent . . . narrow circumstances . . . , the burden normally falls upon the viewer to "avoid further bombardment of [his] sensibilities simply by averting [his] eyes.

In response to the state's attempt to justify the ordinance as an exercise of its power to protect children, the Court noted that "minors are entitled to a significant measure of First Amendment protection" and in that regard stated that the scope of the law was broader than permissible:

The ordinance is not directed against sexually explicit nudity, nor is it otherwise limited. Rather, it sweepingly forbids display of all films containing *any* uncovered buttocks or breasts, irrespective of content or pervasiveness. Thus, it would bar a film containing a picture of a baby's buttocks, the nude body of a war victim, or scenes from a culture in which nudity is indigenous. The ordinance also might prohibit newsreel scenes of the opening of an art exhibit as well as shots of bathers on a beach. Clearly all nudity cannot be deemed obscene even as to minors. Nor can such a broad restriction be justified by any other governmental interest pertaining to minors.

Further, the court stated that speech that is not obscene as to minors "cannot be suppressed solely to protect the young from ideas or images that a legislative body thinks unsuitable for them." In the light of this holding, it would appear that state and local governments are limited to proscribing only materials that are "obscene" as to minors. Thus, any "sealing" or "display" statute must incorporate standards defining the term "obscene as to minors" in order to pass constitutional muster. Sealing and display ordinances ostensibly aimed at protecting children have the significant collateral effect of restricting adult access to protected material. Most people who enter bookstores like to browse before they buy, which is precisely what they cannot do if the material is sealed or out of sight. Moreover, booksellers subject to these ordinances are required either to exclude minors from their businesses or to review every book they offer for sale to determine whether it falls within the statute's proscriptions. The substantial burden these ordinances place on free expression is obvious. As one legal commentator—Professor William Lockhart—has noted:

> To prohibit dealers from exhibiting within the view of adolescents books and magazines that can be sold only to adults would raise the additional problem of undue interference with the material's primary audience. Beyond these obstacles is the disrupting effect of 'adult only' counters or shelves in bookstores and at newsstands, for the 'adult only' label would serve only to attract adolescents eager for a look at the forbidden fruit and would make it difficult for the dealer to prevent adolescent shoplifting of the books and magazines. To avoid these difficulties, cautious dealers might well decide to abandon all books and magazines claimed by anyone to be unsuitable for adolescents.

Three such "display" or "sealing" statutes have recently been struck down by lower courts. In 1981, in *American Booksellers Association, Inc. v. McAuliffe*, a Georgia display law was invalidated as unconstitutional because it prevented perusal and limited the sale of protected material to adults. Protecting minors was held to be an inadequate rationale for such severe interference with First Amendment rights. In 1982, a Colorado display statute was invalidated on similar grounds in *Tattered Cover, Inc. v. Tooley*. There the court concluded that channels for the interchange of literary, political, artistic, and scientific ideas regarding sex were effectively closed by the statute, and that its enforcement would regulate to a commercially unfeasible degree the activities of responsible members of the community.

Again in 1982, a California state court invalidated a display ordinance which required that commercial establishments seal magazines or books containing sexually explicit but nonobscene pictures, keep them out of the reach of minors, or otherwise bar minors from entering the stores altogether. The ordinance sought to control display in drug-stores, grocery stores, and newsstands, as well as stores ordinarily labeled as "adult." The court held that the ordinances denied the freedom to browse of adults because of the sealing requirements, or denied children access to material which they had "an unfettered con-stitutional right to enjoy" if the ordinances had the effect of excluding them entirely from stores. Whether accompanied by parents or not, stated the court, minors "cannot be denied access to retail establish-ments which sell a wide variety of literature, or the necessities of life, simply because such establishments also sell some materials sought to be restricted." Additionally, the court found the ordinances irrational in that they permitted the sale to minors of the very materials sought to be restricted from them.

Here again, the citizen-lobbyist should not hesitate to lobby against such sealing and display bills wherever they may be proposed.

Finally, in 1982, the Supreme Court upheld a new category of legis-lation designed to prohibit the publication and sale of certain kinds of sexual—but not obscene—materials. In *New York v. Ferber,* the Court upheld as constitutional a state "child pornography" law that made it a crime not only to produce non-obscene sexual materials that depicted children but also to sell those materials, even if the seller had nothing to do with their production. In so doing, the Court expressly acknowledged that it was creating an entirely new exception to the protections that are otherwise available for published materials under the First Amendment, but it also made clear that while the First Amendment does not prohibit such laws the states were in no sense required to enact them.

As a result of that decision, it seems likely that many states will be considering similar legislation, including bills that are virtually identi-cal to the New York law upheld in the *Ferber* case. Citizen-lobbyists who agree with the numerous publishers and booksellers who opposed the New York law should emphasize that such a prohibition of non-obscene speech is an unnecessary, inappropriate, and dangerous exer-cise of the censorship power. Further, if those bills attempt to go beyond the New York law, it should also be stressed that the Supreme Court in the *Ferber* case declared that such bills must be "limited to works that *visually* depict sexual conduct by children below a certain age," the highest almost certainly being eighteen, and that "the category of 'sexual conduct' proscribed must also be suitably limited and described."

Prior Civil Proceedings

Most of the obscenity cases that have been brought to court in the United States have been criminal cases, in which the defendant—usually the author, publisher, exhibitor, or seller of an allegedly obscene work—is charged with violating the state's law that makes dealing in obscenity a crime. If that work is ultimately found to be obscene, that defendant will be convicted of that crime and (in most cases) sentenced to prison, have to pay a substantial fine, or both. The risks in dealing with possibly obscene works are therefore great: if those works are subsequently declared obscene, drastic criminal consequences could well follow.

Such criminal actions, however, are not the only legal means available to a state for censoring obscenity. One of the most significant alternatives is for the state to bring a civil (i.e., non-criminal) action seeking a judicial determination that a particular work is obscene and an order enjoining its distribution and sale, with the possibility of a criminal action to follow if the work is thereafter exhibited or sold in violation of that injunction. Under such "prior civil proceedings," the state is still able to censor obscenity, and yet the individuals who happened to have handled such material are not confronted with the drastic consequences of a criminal prosecution.

In the 1973 *Paris Adult* case, the State of Georgia instituted such a civil suit to enjoin the further showing of certain allegedly obscene films. Significantly, in reviewing the case, the Supreme Court majority expressly approved such prior civil proceedings, stating that "Such a procedure provides an exhibitor or purveyor of materials the best possible notice, prior to any criminal indictments, as to whether the materials are unprotected by the First Amendment and subject to state regulation." Similarly, Justice Douglas, in his dissent to the majority's decision in the *Miller* case, succinctly stated his view that "until a civil proceeding has placed a tract beyond the pale, no criminal prosecution should be sustained."

Because these statements, representing the views of at least six Justices, demonstrate likely Supreme Court approval of prior civil proceedings, many states have enacted legislation requiring such proceedings before criminal prosecution for obscenity can be begun. The rationale for this policy seems eminently fair. Civil proceedings before the commencement of criminal actions fully serve the state's desire to censor obscene materials without unjustly exposing individuals to the risk of criminal sanctions, to the necessity for overly harsh self-censorship, or to the prosecutorial harassment of the more repressive forces in the community. On the whole, prior civil proceedings are a positive development in obscenity law, and every effort should be made to ensure that they are adopted wherever possible.

Nevertheless, civil proceedings are fraught with their own particular perils. A civil judgment of obscenity results both in the legal suppression of the material involved and in the exposure of anyone who thereafter sells or exhibits it to criminal penalties. Moreover, civil actions may entail prior restraints against the exercise of free expression, and may in some cases lead to the forfeiture of property. Several recent cases, in fact, make clear the necessity for stringent procedural safeguards whenever such procedures are employed.

In 1965, in *Freedman v. Maryland*, the Supreme Court addressed for the first time the issue of censorship within the setting of civil proceedings. Maryland had enacted a motion picture censorship statute requiring exhibitors to submit films to a censorship board before showing them in theaters. Declaring that "any system of prior restraints of expression comes to this Court bearing a heavy presumption against its constitutional validity," the Court struck down the statute as unconstitutional and listed the procedural safeguards that a censorship statute must contain in order to comport with the First Amendment:

> First, the burden of proving that the film is unprotected expression must rest on the censor. . . . "Wherever the transcendent value of speech is involved, due process certainly requires that the state bear the burden of persuasion to show that the appellants engaged in criminal speech. Second, while the State may require advance submission of films, in order to effectively bar all showings of all unprotected films, the requirement cannot be administered in a manner which would lend an effect of finality to the censor's determination. . . . Because only a judicial determination in an adversary proceeding ensures the necessary sensitivity to freedom of expression, only a procedure requiring a judicial deter-

mination suffices to impose a valid final restraint. To this end, the exhibitor must be assured, by statute or authoritative judicial construction, that the censor will, within a brief specified period, either issue a license or go to court to restrain the film. Any restraint imposed in advance of a final judicial determination on the merits must similarly be limited to preservation of the status quo for the shortest fixed period compatible with sound judicial resolution. . . . [T]he procedure must also assure a prompt final judicial decision, to minimize the deterrent effect of an interim and possibly erroneous denial of a license.

The procedural requirements of the *Freedman* case have had far-reaching implications for obscenity law. The absence of such procedures led to the invalidation of a federal postal statute which authorized the refusal to deliver mail based on a non-judicial determination of obscenity (*Blount v. Rizzi*, 1971), as well as various state statutes which allowed materials to be seized before judicial proceedings to determine their obscenity (*Roaden v. Kentucky*, 1973; *Lee Art Theater v. Virginia*, 1968). And in *Southeastern Promotions v. Conrad*, in 1975, a municipality was held to have unconstitutionally restrained a production of the musical *Hair* because of a procedure that lacked the *Freedman* protections.

In 1976, in *McKinney v. Alabama*, the Supreme Court had its first opportunity to consider the validity of one state's version of the kind of prior civil obscenity proceedings to which it had lent approval in the *Paris Adult* case. There, it held Alabama's civil action format to be inadequate. An Alabama civil court had determined that a particular publication was obscene, and thereafter one McKinney—who had had no notice of the earlier proceeding—was convicted for selling that publication. When McKinney tried to challenge the determination of obscenity during his criminal trial, the issue was held foreclosed on the basis of the prior civil action.

The Supreme Court overturned his conviction, stating that since McKinney had had no notice of the prior proceeding, no opportunity to participate in it or to challenge its findings, he should be allowed to relitigate the issue of obscenity at his trial. In his concurring opinion, Justice Brennan pointed out other difficulties inherent in civil obscenity proceedings, noting in particular that because of the precious First Amendment values at stake, a civil obscenity proceeding should require a stricter standard of proof than the ordinary civil "preponderance of the evidence" standard. "[T]he hazards to the First Amendment inhering in the regulation of obscenity," he stated, require that the state "comply with the more exacting standard of proof beyond a reasonable doubt." Unfortunately, however, Justice Brennan's position with respect to the applicable burden of proof was rejected by the Supreme Court in the 1981 case of *Cooper v. Mitchell Brothers,* which held that proof beyond a reasonable doubt is not required in a civil obscenity action. The Court did not specifically indicate whether an intermediate standard such as proof by "clear and convincing evidence" would be required, but it did seem strongly to suggest that the states were free to choose any burden of proof standard in a civil action, including a mere "preponderance" of the evidence, without constitutional constraint.

One of the most recent, and perhaps most frightening, developments in civil obscenity legislation has been the enactment of statutes that invoke a civil court's power to impose unique "civil" penalties on persons found to be in violation of its injunctions. Relying on traditional civil laws pertaining to "public nuisances," several states have attempted to authorize abatement injunctions that operate not only against materials adjudged obscene but against the premises where they were made or sold as well. In the case of a bookstore, for instance, a civil nuisance action could result in both the suppression of the obscene material *and* the closing of the store. Although this sort of system would seem to violate the First Amendment, the Supreme Court has thus far declined expressly to so hold. Instead, the Court has chosen to sidestep the broad constitutional issues and to review those statutes in light of the procedural requirements set forth in its *Freedman* decision.

Thus, in 1980, in *Vance v. Universal Amusement Co., Inc.,* two Texas nuisance statutes were applied to locations found to have been distributing obscene materials or showing obscene films. One statute authorized the mandatory closing of the premises for one year, and the other authorized the granting of injunctions prohibiting the future commercial manufacturing, distribution, or exhibition of obscene material. The Supreme Court held that the injunction statute violated the Constitution, but it avoided reviewing the premises-closing statute since the lower court held it inapplicable to obscenity cases. The Court was clearly concerned with the issue of procedure. With respect to the injunction statute, the Court stated

(a) that the regulation of a communicative activity such as the exhibition of motion pictures must adhere to the more narrowly drawn procedures than is necessary for the abatement of an ordinary nuisance, and (b) that the burden of supporting an injunction against a future exhibition is even heavier than the burden of justifying the imposition of a criminal sanction for a past communication.

However, the Court did provide a strong indication of its thinking on the broader First Amendment issues, stating in a significant footnote that

Any system of prior restraint . . . 'comes to this Court bearing a heavy presumption against its constitutional validity.' . . . The presumption against prior restraints is heavier—and the degree of protection broader—than that against limits on expression imposed by criminal penalties. Behind the distinction is a theory deeply etched in our law: a free society prefers to punish the few who abuse rights of speech *after* they break the law than to throttle them and all others beforehand. It is always difficult to know in advance what an individual will say, and the line between legitimate and illegitimate speech is often so finely drawn that the risks of freewheeling censorship are formidable.

As to the procedural improprieties in the Texas statute, the Court noted that it authorized prior restraints of indefinite duration on material that had not been finally adjudicated to be obscene. "Presumably," the Court declared, "an exhibitor would be required to obey such an order pending review of its merits and would be subject to contempt proceedings even if the film is ultimately found to be nonobscene. Such prior restraints would be more onerous and more objectionable than the threat of criminal sanctions after a film has been exhibited, since nonobscenity would be a defense to any criminal prosecution."

Even more recently, in 1981, the Supreme Court in *Brockett v.*

Spokane Arcades, Inc. affirmed a lower court decision that invalidated a Washington State nuisance statute similar to that involved in the *Vance* case. As the lower court put it:

> The ability of a court to close a place temporarily because obscene materials *may* have been sold, distributed, or exhibited on the premises is an impermissible prior restraint.

However, that court continued:

> We express no opinion with respect to what circumstances, if any, would justify a closure subsequent to a determination that conforms in all respects to the First Amendment.

That issue was before the Supreme Court in 1982 in *U.S. Marketing Co. v. Idaho,* but the case was settled before the Court had a chance to consider it. As a result, the ultimate constitutional guidelines in such cases remain to be determined.

Cable Television

Within the past decade, cable television has emerged as one of the most heated battlegrounds in the struggle to preserve First Amendment guarantees of free expression. Cable systems now reach more than one-fourth of America's television households and offer to their subscribers a wide variety of programming that includes first-run Hollywood movies as well as sexually explicit shows. Many cable television systems maintain "public access" channels that are available to members of the public on a first-come, first-served basis, with little or no censorship over the content of the programming provided by such "public" artists and producers.

Predictably enough, the extraordinary proliferation of cable television programming has generated a similar proliferation of self-appointed media watchdog groups. Rallying against what they call "cableporn," these groups have begun a campaign to restrict severely the kinds of programming cable systems may offer. The legal issues in this area are complex and volatile, involving not only how cable systems ought to be treated for First Amendment purposes but also the proper standards, if any, that should govern the censorship of cable television programming.

Broadcast radio and television are subject to licensing and regulation by the Federal Communications Commission, which was empowered by Congress to set programming and other guidelines in accordance with the Communications Act of 1934. Of all forms of communication, the broadcast media have received the most limited First Amendment protection, as was dramatically illustrated in the Supreme Court's 1978 "Seven Dirty Words" decision, *FCC v. Pacifica Foundation*.

In that case, the FCC imposed sanctions on a radio station that broadcast comedian George Carlin's comedic discussion of "words you couldn't say on the public airwaves." Although the routine was clearly profane, it had no sexual overtones. As the radio station put it, "Carlin [was] not mouthing obscenities, he [was] merely using words to satirize as harmless and silly our attitudes toward those words." Nevertheless, a sharply divided Supreme Court upheld the sanctions, ruling that the FCC had not violated the First Amendment in regulating "indecent" broadcast language even though that language did not qualify as obscene under the standards established in the *Miller* case. Significantly, the Court distinguished broadcast from other media on the basis of its "uniquely pervasive presence in American life," its ability to intrude into the privacy of the home, and its easy accessibility to children.

The implications of the *Pacifica* decision for cable television are unclear. Those who desire the maximum possible censorship over cable television contend that that case's less stringent First Amendment protections should also apply to cable. But others argue that while cable is superficially similar to broadcast television, it is in fact technologically distinct. Programming arrives not over the open airwaves but via coaxial cable, likened by some to an electronic newsboy. Further, those desiring cable service must actively subscribe to it, select a supplier, order installation, and pay a fee. Some systems even offer "lock boxes" to prevent access by children without parental supervision. Thus it is contended that for First Amendment purposes cable is more like newspapers than broadcast media and ought to be accorded the fullest possible First Amendment protection from governmental supervision and control.

Without reaching the question of how cable systems ought to be treated for First Amendment purposes, the Supreme Court in 1979 in *FCC v. Midwest Video Corporation* invalidated a series of federal cable regulations. In the wake of that decision, the FCC has moved steadily toward cable deregulation and cable systems currently inhabit a regulatory no-man's land. Repressive social forces like the Moral Majority and various media watchdog groups are thus turning to state and local governments to enact restrictive laws over cable television programming.

In the first major judicial review of such a statute, a lower federal court in 1982 invalidated the law because it violated the First Amendment. The case, *Home Box Office, Inc. v. Wilkinson,* involved a Utah "cableporn" law which made criminal the transmission by cable of material deemed "pornographic" or "indecent." After reviewing the history of the law of obscenity, the court indicated that "for better or worse, *Miller* establishes the analytical boundary of permissible state involvement in the decision by [Home Box Office] and others to offer, and a decision by subscribers to receive, particular cable television programming." The Utah statute, by banning programming that did not meet the *Miller* case's definition of obscenity, was thus unconstitutional. The court noted that the statute swept so broadly as to encompass movies such as *The Godfather, Being There, Annie Hall,* and *Coming Home,* and further that it made criminal the presentation by cable of material that could legally be rented or purchased for home consumption through videotape or videodisk technology.

Responding to the argument that the Utah statute was directed toward protecting children, the court noted that the law made no reference to children and applied equally to homes having no children at all. The law thus unconstitutionally restrained the First Amendment rights of adults. As to the argument that cable television could cause the intrusion of unwanted "indecent" material into the privacy of people's homes, the court stated:

> That's one of the nice things about TV—not just cable TV, but also . . . the regular broadcast channels that are allocated, licensed, and regulated by the government. There is no law that says you have to watch. There is no law that says you have to purchase a television set. There is no law that says you have to subscribe to a cable TV service any more than you have to subscribe to *The Salt Lake Tribune.* One of the greatest virtues of our system, I think, is the freedom to choose.

The Utah ruling may well become the guiding precedent for the many additional "cableporn" cases that are likely to be taken to court in the years to come. Certainly the citizen-lobbyist should bear its rationale in mind in lobbying against cable television censorship wherever it is proposed.

Even more complicated First Amendment issues are presented with respect to public access programming. Because public access channels have attracted producers of sexually explicit material, many cable companies have attempted to impose their own censorship requirements. Often taking the form of restrictive "indecency and obscenity clauses" in contracts with public access producers, these private methods of censorship are as inimical to free expression as state regulation. Some states already have enacted legislation prohibiting cable company censorship on public access channels. Nevertheless, at least some cable companies support laws that would permit them to censor nonobscene programming on public access channels. These proposals have been denounced by civil liberties groups and other organizations, and the citizen-lobbyist should vigorously oppose them wherever they arise.

PART III

Resources

For readers who are interested in pursuing further the subjects discussed in this book, the following pages provide selected materials and references. Included here are resources relating to lobbying and the legislative process; five separate resource sections corresponding to each of the five subject areas discussed in the book; and information and sample materials that might prove useful to the citizen-lobbyist.

The various sections contain citations to important court decisions. Those citations are presented in a kind of legal shorthand that is familiar to lawyers and meaningless to most other people. Suffice it to say here that the letters "U.S." in the citations refer to decisions of the United States Supreme Court; that "F.2d" and "F.Supp." refer to lower federal courts; and that references to states ("Cal." or "N.Y.") denote decisions of the state courts in those states. Persons wishing to read those decisions should call a local law library—one, for example, in a nearby law school, bar association headquarters, or local law office—to obtain access to them. (In some cities, the public library may also have some of those volumes.)

1 / LOBBYING AND THE LEGISLATIVE PROCESS

TABLE 1. Legislative Sessions

State	Years Held	Session Begins: Month	Day	Limits on Sessions*
Alabama	Annual		†	30L in 105C
Alaska	Annual	Jan.	2nd Mon.	None
Arizona	Annual	Jan.	2nd Mon.	None
Arkansas	Odd	Jan.	2nd Mon.	60C
California	Annual	Dec.	1st Mon.	None
Colorado	Annual	Jan.	Wed. after 1st Tues.	None
Connecticut	Annual	Jan.	Odd: Wed. after 1st Mon.	Not later than 1st Wed. after 1st Mon. in June
		Feb.	Even: Wed. after 1st Mon.	Not later than 1st Wed. after 1st Mon. in May
Delaware	Annual	Jan.	2nd Tues.	June 30
Florida	Annual	Apr.	Tues. after 1st Mon.	60C
Georgia	Annual	Jan.	2nd Mon.	40L
Hawaii	Annual	Jan.	3rd Wed.	60L
Idaho	Annual	Jan.	Mon. on or nearest 9th day	None
Illinois	Annual	Jan.	2nd Wed.	None
Indiana	Annual	Jan.	2nd Mon.	Odd: 61L or Apr. 30 Even: 30L or Mar. 15
Iowa	Annual	Jan.	2nd Mon.	None
Kansas	Annual	Jan.	2nd Mon.	Odd: None Even: 90C
Kentucky	Even	Jan.	Tues. after 1st Mon.	60L
Louisiana	Annual	Apr.	3rd Mon.	60L in 85C
Maine	Even	Dec.	1st Wed.	None
Maryland	Annual	Jan.	2nd Wed.	90C
Massachusetts	Annual	Jan.	1st Wed.	None
Michigan	Annual	Jan.	1st Wed.	None
Minnesota	Odd	Jan.	Tues. after 1st Mon.	120L or 1st Mon. after 3rd Sat.
Mississippi	Annual	Jan.	Tues. after 1st Mon.	90C, except first year, 120C

TABLE 1. Legislative Sessions *(continued)*

State	Years Held	Month	Day	Limits on Sessions*
			Session Begins:	
Missouri	Annual	Jan.	Wed. after 1st Mon.	Odd: June 30
				Even: May 15
Montana	Odd	Jan.	1st Mon.	90L
Nebraska	Annual	Jan.	1st Wed. after 1st Mon.	Odd: 90L
				Even: 60L
Nevada	Odd	Jan.	3rd Mon.	60C (limit only on pay; otherwise no restriction)
New Hampshire	Odd	Jan.	1st Wed. after 1st Tues.	None
New Jersey	Annual	Jan.	2nd Tues.	None
New Mexico	Annual	Jan.	3rd Tues.	Odd: 60C
				Even: 30C
New York	Annual	Jan.	Wed. after 1st Mon.	None
North Carolina	Odd	Jan.	Wed. after 2nd Mon.	None
North Dakota	Odd	Jan.	1st Mon.	80C
Ohio	Annual	Jan.	1st Mon.	None
Oklahoma	Annual	Jan.	Tues. after 1st Mon.	90L
Oregon	Odd	Jan.	2nd Mon.	None
Pennsylvania	Annual	Jan.	1st Tues.	None
Rhode Island	Annual	Jan.	1st Tues.	60L
South Carolina	Annual	Jan.	2nd Tues.	None
South Dakota	Annual	Jan.	Odd: Tues. after 3rd Mon.	45L
			Even: Tues. after 1st Mon.	30L
Tennessee	Odd	Jan.	1st Tues.	90L
Texas	Odd	Jan.	2nd Tues.	140C
Utah	Annual	Jan.	2nd Mon.	Odd: 60C
				Even: 20C
Vermont	Odd	Jan.	Wed. after 1st Mon.	None
Virginia	Annual	Jan.	2nd Wed.	Odd: 30C
				Even: 60C
Washington	Annual	Jan.	2nd Mon.	Odd: 105C
				Even: 60C
West Virginia	Annual	Jan.	2nd Wed.	60C
Wisconsin	Annual	Jan.	1st Tues. after Jan. 8th	None
Wyoming	Annual	Jan.	2nd Tues.	Odd: 40L
				Even: 20L

*"L" refers to "legislative days," which means days during which legislature is in session.
"C" refers to "calendar days."
†The first year of Alabama's four-year legislative term begins with an organizational session on the first Tuesday in January, which is followed by a regular session that begins on the third Tuesday in April. The second and third years begin on the first Tuesday in February. The fourth year begins on the second Tuesday in January.

TABLE 2. Legislators

State	Mem- bers	Senate Multi- member Districts	Term	Mem- bers	House/Assembly Multi- member Districts	Term	Total Legis- lators
Alabama	35	0	4	105	0	4	140
Alaska	20	3	4	40	10	2	60
Arizona	30	0	2	60	30	2	90
Arkansas	35	0	4	100	10	2	135
California	40	0	4	80	0	2	120
Colorado	35	0	4	65	0	2	100
Connecticut	36	0	2	151	0	2	187
Delaware	21	0	4	41	0	2	62
Florida	40	14	4	120	21	2	160
Georgia	56	0	2	180	17	2	236
Hawaii	25	7	4	51	22	2	76
Idaho	35	0	2	70	35	2	105
Illinois	59	0	2/4*	177	59	2	236
Indiana	50	0	4	100	20	2	150
Iowa	50	0	4	100	0	2	150
Kansas	40	0	4	125	0	2	165
Kentucky	38	0	4	100	0	2	138
Louisiana	39	0	4	105	0	4	144
Maine	33	0	2	151	11	2	184
Maryland	47	0	4	141	47	4	188
Massachusetts	40	0	2	160	0	2	200
Michigan	38	0	4	110	0	2	148
Minnesota	67	0	4	134	0	2	201
Mississippi	52	0	4	122	0	4	174
Missouri	34	0	4	163	0	2	197
Montana	50	0	4	100	0	2	150
Nebraska	49	0	4	(Nebraska has a unicameral legislature)			49
Nevada	20	3	4	40	0	2	60
New Hampshire	24	0	2	400	127	2	424
New Jersey	40	0	4	80	40	2	120
New Mexico	42	0	4	70	0	2	112
New York	61	0	2	150	0	2	211
North Carolina	50	18	2	120	35	2	170
North Dakota	50	1	4	100	49	2	150

TABLE 2. Legislators *(continued)*

State	Senate Members	Multi-member Districts	Term	House/Assembly Members	Multi-member Districts	Term	Total Legislators
Ohio	33	0	4	99	0	2	132
Oklahoma	48	0	4	101	0	2	149
Oregon	30	0	4	60	0	2	90
Pennsylvania	50	0	4	203	0	2	253
Rhode Island	50	0	2	100	0	2	150
South Carolina	46	13	4	124	0	2	170
South Dakota	35	3	2	70	28	2	105
Tennessee	33	0	4	99	0	2	132
Texas	31	0	4	150	0	2	181
Utah	29	0	4	75	0	2	104
Vermont	30	11	2	150	39	2	180
Virginia	40	1	4	100	28	2	140
Washington	49	0	4	98	49	2	147
West Virginia	34	17	4	100	25	2	134
Wisconsin	33	0	4	99	0	2	132
Wyoming	30	9	4	62	12	2	92

*Senate districts in Illinois have been divided into three groups, with terms of office of four, four, and two years.

Further Reading

For those who are interested in learning more about state legislatures and the legislative process, there are several sources that should prove especially useful. *The Sometime Governments: A Critical Study of 50 American Legislatures* (Bantam Books, 1971), prepared by the Citizens Conference on State Legislatures, provides an excellent review and critique of all fifty state legislatures. *The Book of the States,* published by and available from the Council of State Governments, Lexington, Kentucky, provides a wealth of up-to-date information concerning the structure, working methods, financing, and functional activities of the governments of every state. *Strengthening the States: Essays on Legislative Reform* (Anchor Books, 1972) provides a wide variety of perspectives on the functioning of the state legislatures, as well as an extensive bibliography of other materials on the subject. Finally, the United

States Supreme Court's principal decisions in the reapportionment cases also provide a valuable discussion of the state legislatures. The key decisions are *Baker v. Carr*, 369 U.S. 186 (1962) and *Reynolds v. Sims*, 377 U.S. 533 (1964).

In addition, for a work in preparation on the subject of lobbying, Professor Alan S. Chartock of the State University of New York, at Albany, has developed an exhaustive annotated bibliography on lobbying. Persons interested in obtaining that bibliography, or that entire work, should contact Professor Chartock at SUNY–Albany, Albany, New York.

2 / REPRODUCTIVE FREEDOM

Court Decisions

The following is a brief summary of major court decisions affecting reproductive rights:

Supreme Court Decisions

Skinner v. Oklahoma, 316 U.S. 535 (1942). The Court overturns an Oklahoma statute which authorized the forced sterilization of certain criminals. In this decision, for the first time, the Court recognized the importance of an individual's control over basic reproductive rights.

Griswold v. Connecticut, 381 U.S. 479 (1965). Declares unconstitutional a Connecticut statute which made it a crime either to obtain contraceptives or to counsel their use. In this decision, the Court established that the freedom of married couples to make certain basic decisions affecting the quality of their relationship, and in particular their sexual relationship, falls within the "zone of privacy created by constitutional guarantees."

Eisenstadt v. Baird, 405 U.S. 438 (1972). Expands the privacy right enunciated in *Griswold* to embrace the use of contraceptives by single persons. In this decision, which overturned a Massachusetts law forbidding the distribution of contraceptives except to married persons by prescription, the Court recognizes that an individual, married or single, possesses a right of privacy "to be free from unwarranted governmental intrusion into matters so fundamentally affecting a person as the decision whether to bear or beget a child."

Roe v. Wade, 410 U.S. 113 (1973). A landmark decision, in which the Court held that the fundamental constitutional right of privacy was "broad enough to encompass a woman's decision whether or not to terminate her pregnancy." The Court ruled that a Texas statute that outlawed all abortions except those necessary to save the life of the mother violated the constitutional right of privacy. This decision, together with the Court's decision in *Doe v. Bolton* (see below), made abortion legal in the United States and invalidated the restrictive abortion laws of most states.

Doe v. Bolton, 410 U.S. 179 (1973). In this case, which was decided together with *Roe*, the Court struck down provisions of a more liberal Georgia statute that allowed abortions in certain situations.

Planned Parenthood of Central Missouri v. Danforth, 428 U.S. 52 (1976). Overturns several provisions of a Missouri abortion statute. The Court invalidated the requirement that a married woman obtain her husband's consent prior to having an abortion, holding that since *Roe* forbids the state to prevent abortion in the first trimester, it could not give a veto power to any person to prevent an abortion. Using the same reasoning, the Court invalidated a requirement for the consent of one parent to an abortion by an unmarried minor. The Court recognized two things with respect to minors: (1) minors have the constitutional right to privacy; and (2) the state has greater authority to regulate the activities of minors than adults.

Carey v. Population Services, International, 431 U.S. 678 (1977). Holds unconstitutional a New York State law which made it a crime to distribute contraceptives to minors under sixteen, for anyone but a licensed pharmacist to distribute contraceptives to any person, and for anyone to advertise or display contraceptives. The Court, in invalidating the restriction on access to contraceptives by adults, reconfirmed that such restrictions violate an individual's privacy right. The Court rejected the argument that the restriction on minors' access to contraception is necessary to support the state's policy of discouraging childbirth. The restriction on advertising was held to violate the First Amendment.

Maher v. Roe, 432 U.S. 464 (1977) and *Beal v. Doe*, 432 U.S. 438

(1977). Uphold a Connecticut regulation and a Pennsylvania statute which limited financial assistance for abortions to those medically necessary. The Court rejected the arguments that it is a denial of equal protection for a state participating in the Medicaid program to refuse to pay the expenses incident to nontherapeutic abortion and that federal law requires that states fund the cost of all abortions. The Court held that a state has a legitimate interest in protecting potential human life throughout pregnancy and in encouraging "normal childbirth."

Poelker v. Doe, 432 U.S. 519 (1977). Upholds the refusal of a public hospital in St. Louis, Missouri, to perform abortions.

Colautti v. Franklin, 439 U.S. 379 (1979). Declares unconstitutionally vague a Pennsylvania law which subjected physicians to criminal penalties if they fail to use the abortion technique most likely to result in live birth during the stage of pregnancy when the fetus "is viable" or "may be viable."

Bellotti v. Baird, 443 U.S. 622 (1979). Invalidates a Massachusetts statute which required an unmarried minor to obtain either the consent of her parents or, if her parents refused such consent, then authority from a judge for "good cause shown," before she could obtain an abortion, holding that mature minors have a right to make their own decisions about abortion.

Harris v. McRae, 448 U.S. 297 (1981). Upholds the constitutionality of the federal Hyde Amendments which permit federal funds to be used for abortion only in very limited circumstances. The Court held that abortion restrictions in the funding context are different from other regulations and that it is legitimate for a state to promote fetal life by funding childbirth and not abortion.

H.L. v. Matheson, 450 U.S. 398 (1981). Upholds a Utah statute which requires doctors to notify a minor's parents before the minor can obtain an abortion. However, the decision was a very narrow one; the Court held that it was constitutional *only* as applied to immature, dependent minors living with their parents who have not claimed that their relationship with their parents provides a reason why notification would not be in their best interests.

Other Court Decisions

Committee to Defend Reproductive Rights v. Myers, 29 Cal.3d 252 (1981). The California Supreme Court rules that California's restrictions on abortion funding violate the privacy guarantees of the state constitution.

Moe v. Secretary of Administration and Finance, 417 N.E.2d 387 (Mass. 1981). The highest court in Massachusetts rules that the state's restrictions on Medicaid funding for abortion violate the state constitution's due process clause.

Nyberg v. The City of Virginia, 667 F.2d 754 (8th Cir. 1982). Holds that a city hospital commission in Minnesota could not prohibit staff physicians from performing abortions on paying patients.

Valley Family Planning v. North Dakota, 661 F.2d 99 (8th Cir. 1982). Overturns a North Dakota statute which prohibited any agency or person receiving public funds from referring persons for abortion, holding the statute unconstitutional because Title X of the federal Public Health Law requires that grantees make necessary abortion referrals.

Doe v. Pickett, 480 F.Supp. 1218 (S.D.W.Va. 1979). Holds that recipients of federal family planning grants cannot require parental notice or consent as a condition to the provision of family planning services.

Akron Center for Reproductive Health v. City of Akron, 651 F.2d 1198 (6th Cir. 1981). Most of the provisions of an omnibus anti-abortion ordinance enacted in Akron, Ohio, were declared unconstitutional, including (1) requiring doctors to give women biased medical information; (2) requiring doctors to give women seeking abortions detailed fetal descriptions and to tell them that a fetus is a human life from the moment the egg is fertilized; (3) requiring a mandatory twenty-four-hour waiting period between consent and performance of the abortion; and (4) requiring parental consent for minors. The ordinance's prohibition of the performance of second-trimester abortions outside of hospitals was upheld. This decision has been appealed to the Supreme Court, and its ruling is expected by the summer of 1983.

Scheinberg v. Smith, 659 F.2d 476 (5th Cir. 1981). The appellate court vacated a lower court's decision that declared unconstitutional a Florida statute requiring husbands to be notified of their wives' decisions to have an abortion. The appellate court found a compelling state interest in promoting and protecting the husband's procreative potential in the marriage and sent the case back for fact-finding. Thereafter, the lower court again held the statute unconstitutional.

In the Matter of Lee Ann Grady, 85 N.J. 235 (1981). The New Jersey Supreme Court ruled that courts have the power to authorize substituted consent for the sterilization of the mentally incompetent, although this authority is not expressly provided for by statute. The court outlined extensive standards to be followed before the courts may authorize sterilization.

Further Reading

Background of Legal Status of Abortion and Birth Control in America, and Abortion Politics

Mohr, *Abortion in America,* Oxford University Press, 1978; a thorough account of the evolution of abortion laws in the United States.

Gordon, *Birth Control in America; Woman's Body, Woman's Right,* Penguin, 1977.

Lader, *Abortion II: Making the Revolution,* Beacon Press, 1978; documents the movement to legalize abortion during the late 1960s and early 1970s.

Jaffe, Lindheim, and Lee, *Abortion Politics,* McGraw-Hill, 1981; analyzes the development of abortion policy since the Supreme Court's 1973 decisions legalizing abortion.

Crawford, *Thunder on the Right,* Pantheon Books, 1980. This book, written by a conservative, summarizes the interlocking New Right national and local organizations and describes their tactics.

Current Status of Reproductive Rights

Women's Legal Guide to Reproductive Rights. This brochure, published by the ACLU Reproductive Freedom Project, 132 West 43rd Street, New York, NY 10036, is a detailed guide to the current legal rights of women in the areas of abortion, contraception, and sterilization.

ACLU Reproductive Freedom Project Legal Docket is a compilation of all current cases involving reproductive rights. Issued twice a year, it is designed to inform interested lay people and lawyers of pending litigation and of the status of the law.

Abortion Law Reporter, published by the Antioch School of Law, Washington, D.C., contains summaries of all abortion cases, summaries of the legal issues involved, and copies of Supreme Court abortion decisions.

Speakers' Guides on Reproductive Rights

ACLU Speaker's Manual on Abortion, published by The Roger Baldwin Foundation of the ACLU, 5 South Wabash Avenue, Chicago, IL 60603 (1982), "is intended to educate the average concerned citizen to the need to speak in public on the abortion issue." This in-depth manual includes chapters on the legal status of abortion, the philosophical debate, the politics of abortion, and medical aspects of abortion.

Reproductive Freedom: Speakers Handbook on Abortion Rights and Sterilization Abuse, published by the National Lawyers Guild New York City Anti-Sexism Committee, 853 Broadway, New York, NY 10003. This handbook focuses on the issues of abortion and sterilization abuse, and how these two issues are connected.

Winning With Choice (1982), published by Voters For Choice, 1015 18th Street, N.W., Washington, D.C. 20036, is a useful guide for pro-choice candidates, staff, and activists in preparing for anti-choice attacks, responding to questions from the press and public, responding to hostile questions, and mobilizing support. This handbook describes the methods of anti-choice groups and offers advice on how to fight back. It contains an extensive appendix of valuable background information.

"Human Life" Amendments and Statutes, and the
Constitutional Convention

Copelon, "Danger—A 'Human Life' Amendment is on the Way," *Ms.* Magazine, Feb. 1981, p. 46.

Planned Parenthood Federation of America, Inc., *Outlawing Abortion: Proposed Constitutional Amendments and "Human Life" Statutes Analyzed.* New York, 1981.

Planned Parenthood Federation of America, Inc., *Anti-Abortion Measures Before Congress: A Review.* New York, 1982.

American Civil Liberties Union Foundation, *The So-Called "Human Life" Amendment: The Most Critical Threat to Our Right to Privacy.* New York, 1981.

National Organization for Women (NOW), *Stop HLA,* Washington,

D.C. 1981 (425 13th Street, N.W., Suite 1048, Washington, D.C. 20004).

The Alan Guttmacher Institute, *The Hatch Amendment: Abusing the Process, Invading Privacy*. Washington, D.C. 1982 (1220 19th Street, N.W., Washington, D.C. 20030.)

Copies of analyses of current versions of the "human life" statutes and amendments may be obtained from the Planned Parenthood Federation of America (810 Seventh Avenue, New York, NY 10019); the ACLU Reproductive Freedom Project (132 West 43rd Street, New York, NY 10036); and the ACLU Washington D.C. Office (600 Pennsylvania Ave., S.E., Washington, D.C. 20003).

Pro-choice lobbyists working against proposed resolutions for a constitutional convention can obtain information packets from the ACLU Reproductive Freedom Project and the Committee to Preserve the Constitution (225 W. 34th Street, New York, NY 10001).

Sterilization

Rosenberg, "Sterilization of Mentally Retarded Adolescents," *Clearinghouse Review*, Vol. 14, No. 5, Aug./Sept. 1980.

Gaylin, Thompson, Neville, Bayles, "Sterilization of the Retarded: In Whose Interest?" *The Hastings Center Report*, Vol. 8, No. 3 (June 1978).

Women Under Attack: Abortion, Sterilization Abuse, and Reproductive Freedom. New York: Committee for Abortion Rights and Against Sterilization Abuse, 1979 (386 Park Avenue South, New York, NY 10016).

Lottman, "Sterilization of the Mentally Retarded: Who Decides?" *Trial*, 1982.

Abortion: Medical Articles, Reports, and Studies

Many anti-abortion measures are introduced under the guise of protecting women's health. For this reason, it is extremely important for pro-choice lobbyists to present accurate statistics on the safety of abortion. It is also essential to show how proposed anti-abortion measures would burden women's access to abortion and the detrimental effect they would ultimately have on women's health. A bibliography of relevant articles, reports, and studies is available from the ACLU Reproductive Freedom Project (132 W. 43rd Street, New York, NY 10036).

Selected Pro-Choice Organizations

The following is a listing of major national pro-choice organizations and a selected listing of pamphlets, flyers, and other publications available from them. Unless otherwise indicated, the fee for this material is nominal. Many of these organizations have state chapters throughout the country.

American Civil Liberties Union
Reproductive Freedom Project
132 West 43rd Street, New York, NY 10036
(212) 944-9800

Publications: "Women's Legal Guide to Reproductive Rights" (1981)
"ABORTION: A Fundamental Right Under Attack" (revised 1981)
"The So-Called 'Human Life' Amendment: The Most Critical Threat to Our Right to Privacy" (1981)
"The Call Against a Constitutional Convention" (revised 1980)
Legal Docket (Dec. 1981)
"Denying the Right to Choose: How to Cope With Violence and Disruption at Abortion Clinics" (1978) ($1.00)

American Civil Liberties Union Washington Office
600 Pennsylvania Avenue, S.E.
Washington, D.C. 20003
(202) 544-1681

Legislative Newsletter: *Civil Liberties Alert*

National Abortion Rights Action League (NARAL)
1424 K Street, N.W.
Washington, D.C. 20005
(202) 347-7744

Publications: "Congressional Votes on Abortion" (1981)
                     "Legal Abortion: Arguments Pro and Con"
                     "Public Opinion Polls" (1980)
                     "The Abortion Prohibition Amendment" (1980)

Newsletters: *NARAL Newsletter*
                     Legislative Update ($25.00 per year)

Religious Coalition for Abortion Rights (RCAR)
  100 Maryland Avenue, N.E.
  Washington, D.C. 20002
  (202) 543-7032

Pamphlets: "We Affirm" (reprinted 1982)
                     "Abortion: Why Religious Organizations in the U.S.
                        Want to Keep it Legal" (reprinted 1982)
                     "Religious Freedom and the Abortion Controversy"
                        (reprinted 1982)
                     "To Preserve Freedom" (1982)

Newsletters: *Options*
                     Legislative Update

National Organization for Women (NOW)
  425-13th Street, N.W.
  Washington, D.C. 20009
  (202) 347-2279

Pamphlets: "Stop HLA" (revised 1981)
                     "Speakout for Abortion Rights" (1980)

Catholics For A Free Choice (CFFC)
  2008 17th Street, N.W.
  Washington, D.C. 20002
  (202) 638-1706

Publications: CFFC publishes a series of booklets on abortion
                     and the Catholic Church, including Hurst, *The*

History of Abortion in the Catholic Church, and Kohn, *The Church in a Democracy, Who Governs.* It has recently published a research study entitled *Catholic Women and Abortion.*

Newsletter: *Conscience*

Planned Parenthood Federation of
    America, Inc.
810 Seventh Avenue
New York, NY 10019
(212) 541-7800

Publications: "Anti-Abortion Measures Before Congress—A Review" (1982)
"Outlawing Abortion: Proposed Constitutional Amendments and 'Human Life' Statutes Analyzed" (1981)

3 / WOMEN'S RIGHTS

Court Decisions

The following is a brief summary of the major Supreme Court decisions affecting women:

Bradwell v. Illinois, 83 U.S. (16 Wall.) 130 (1873). The Court upholds an Illinois law that prohibited female lawyers from practicing in state courts.

Minor v. Happersett, 88 U.S. (21 Wall.) 162 (1874). Upholds as constitutional the denial of the right of women to vote, notwithstanding the "equal protection" clause of the recently adopted Fourteenth Amendment to the Constitution. Until 1920, when the Nineteenth Amendment was adopted, the right of women to vote was never protected by the Constitution.

Muller v. Oregon, 208 U.S. 412 (1908). Upholds an Oregon statute that prohibited the employment of females in factories, mechanical establishments, or laundries for more than ten hours a day. After this decision many states enacted protective laws that applied only to women. The Court explained its rationale as follows:

> That woman's physical structure and the performance of maternal functions place her at a disadvantage in the struggle for subsistence is obvious. This is especially true when the burdens of

motherhood are upon her. Even when they are not, by abundant testimony of the medical fraternity, continuance for a long time on her feet at work, repeating this from day to day, tends to injurious effects upon the body, and, as healthy mothers are essential to vigorous offspring, the physical well-being of woman becomes an object of public interest and care in order to preserve the strength and vigor of the race.

Still again, history discloses the fact that woman has always been dependent upon man. He established his control at the outset by superior physical strength, and this control in various forms, with diminishing intensity, has continued to the present . . . She is properly placed in a class by herself, and legislation designed for her protection may be sustained, even when like legislation is not necessary for men, and could not be sustained.

Goesaert v. Cleary, 335 U.S. 464 (1948). Upholds a Michigan law that provided that no woman could obtain a bartender's license unless she was "the wife or daughter of the male owner of a licensed liquor establishment."

Hoyt v. Florida, 368 U.S. 57 (1961). Upholds a Florida law which provided that no woman could be called for jury duty unless she affirmatively volunteered for it. The result of such laws was that few women ever served on juries. The Court justified this special "privilege" for women by noting that "woman is still regarded as the center of the home and family life," and that it is not unconstitutional for a state to promote the general welfare by relieving women from jury obligations.

Reed v. Reed, 404 U.S. 71 (1971). A landmark decision, in which the Court, for the first time, held that a law which treated men and women differently solely because of their sex violated the equal protection clause of the Fourteenth Amendment. An Idaho law provided that between persons "equally entitled" to administer a decedent's estate, "males must be preferred to females." The Court overturned the law on the ground that the sex preference did not bear any rational relationship to the law's purpose.

Frontiero v. Richardson, 411 U.S. 677 (1973). The Court applied the *Reed* principle (see above) and declared unconstitutional a fringe benefit scheme that provided male members of the military with housing allowances and medical care for their wives but authorized these benefits for female members only if they actually supported their husbands.

Geduldig v. Aiello, 412 U.S. 484 (1974). The Court rejects the claim that discrimination because of pregnancy is sex discrimination. A California state disability program provided benefits to virtually all disabled workers except workers who had been disabled by pregnancy or childbirth. The Court found this scheme did not violate the equal protection clause.

Cleveland Board of Education v. LaFleur, 414 U.S. 632 (1974). Overturns a local Board of Education rule that required every pregnant teacher to take a mandatory leave of absence beginning five months before the expected birth of her child. The Court found the rule unconstitutional because it employs an "irrebuttable presumption" that all pregnant women are unfit to work. The Court declared that the Fourteenth Amendment required the school board to consider each woman individually and to permit each to continue working as long as she is capable of doing her job.

Kahn v. Shevin, 416 U.S. 351 (1974). Upholds a Florida law which granted property tax exemptions to widows but not to widowers. The Court interpreted the Fourteenth Amendment to allow sex classification to accomplish a remedial purpose, finding that women as a class are poorer than men.

Taylor v. Louisiana, 419 U.S. 498 (1975). Fifteen years after *Hoyt* (see above), the Court reversed itself and struck down a Louisiana law that permitted an automatic exemption of all women from jury service. A male criminal defendant had challenged his conviction on the ground that his jury had not been drawn from a fair cross section of the community and that his constitutional right to a fair trial had therefore been violated. The Court agreed and struck down the automatic exemption, an action that forced all other states with similar laws to repeal those laws.

Weinberger v. Wiesenfeld, 420 U.S. 636 (1975). Overturns a provision of the Social Security Act that granted automatic benefits to wives but not husbands of deceased wage earners who have the responsibility of caring for children. The Court found that the provision discriminated against men like the plaintiff, a father whose wife had died in childbirth, because of his sex as well as against female wage earners whose contributions to Social Security did not buy the same benefits for their surviving families as similarly situated males.

General Electric Company v. Gilbert, 429 U.S. 125 (1976). The Court rejects a claim that a private employer's insurance plan that provided disability benefits to its employees for all disabilities except those arising from pregnancy violated Title VII of the Civil Rights Act of 1964, which prohibits sex discrimination in employment. As in *Geduldig* (see above), the Court reiterates that discrimination based on pregnancy is not discrimination based on sex. Two years later, Congress amended Title VII to expressly prohibit discrimination based on pregnancy.

Craig v. Boren, 429 U.S. 190 (1976). Declares that an Oklahoma statute prohibiting the sale of alcoholic beverages to males under the age of twenty-one and females under the age of eighteen unconstitutionally discriminated against males between the ages of eighteen and twenty. In this decision, for the first time, the Court held that laws containing classifications based on gender must satisfy a stricter standard of judicial review—namely, that such classifications serve important governmental objectives and be substantially related to the achievement of these objectives.

Orr v. Orr, 440 U.S. 268 (1979). Holds that an Alabama statute requiring husbands, but not wives, to pay alimony upon divorce violated the equal protection provisions of the Fourteenth Amendment.

Rostker v. Goldberg, 448 U.S. 1306 (1980). Declares male-only draft registration to be constitutional, upholding the 1980 draft law. Deviating from the pro-women equal protection decisions of the previous decade, the Court found that the Constitution grants Congress broad authority in national defense matters and that it is not within the Court's power to question Congressional authority in this area.

Mississippi University for Women v. Joe Hogan, 73 L. Ed 2d 1090 (1982). Rules that the policy of a state-supported School of Nursing which limits enrollment to women violates the equal protection clause of the Fourteenth Amendment.

Further Reading

General

Women and the Law, by Eve Cary and Kathleen Peratis, National Textbook Company, Skokie, Illinois (1977). This book traces the development of women's rights in our legal system and provides the reader with key excerpts from landmark Supreme Court opinions and other historic documents.

Women's Rights Law Reporter is published quarterly at Rutgers Law School, 15 Washington Street, Newark, NJ 07102. Each issue contains full-length articles and student notes and comments on all areas of the law affecting women's rights and sex discrimination. Published since 1971, it is the oldest continuously published legal periodical in the country which deals exclusively with women's rights.

Harvard Women's Law Journal is published annually at Harvard Law School, Cambridge, MA 02138. It contains articles about the impact of law on women and the impact of women on the legal profession.

Babcock, Freedman, Norton & Ross, *Sex Discrimination and the Law*, 2nd edition 1981, Little, Brown and Co.

Davidson, Ginsburg & Kay, *Sex-Based Discrimination* (1974), and Ginsburg & Kay, Supplement (1978), West Publishing Co.

Tribe, *American Constitutional Law*, The Foundation Press, Inc., Mineola, New York (1978).

"Sex Equality and the Constitution," by Ruth Bader Ginsburg, in *Women's Rights Law Reporter*, Spring 1978.

National Directory of Women Elected Officials, National Women's Political Caucus, 1411 K Street, N.W., Washington, D.C. 20005.

What Women Want, by Caroline Bird, Simon and Schuster, New York (1979); an account of the history and recommendations of the National Women's Conference of 1977.

ERA

The ERA Impact Project, a joint project of the NOW Legal Defense and Education Fund and the Women's Law Project, is located at 132 West 43rd Street, New York, NY 10036. The project's purpose is to interpret and implement state ERAs through education and litigation. Among its available publications are: *Legal Reference Guide to State ERAs; ERA Impact Project Information Kit; Summary and Analysis of State ERA Experience* (presents, for each of the sixteen states that have ERAs, a detailed analysis of judicial decisions, and highlights legislative activity triggered by the amendment; updated regularly); texts of the sixteen state equal rights provisions; "Litigation Packets" designed for attorneys who want to raise ERA claims.

The Equal Rights Amendment, A Lifetime Guarantee, pamphlet published by the ACLU, 132 West 43rd Street, New York, NY 10036.

"The Equal Rights Amendment: A Constitutional Basis for Equal Rights for Women," by Barbara A. Brown, Thomas I. Emerson, Gail Falk, and Ann E. Fredman, in 80 *Yale Law Journal* 871 (1971).

"Gender and the Constitution," by Ruth Bader Ginsburg, in 44 *Cincinnati Law Review* (1975).

"Equal Rights Amendments," *Women's Rights Law Reporter*, Summer 1978 (Special Issue).

"Equal Rights For Women: A Symposium on the Proposed Constitutional Amendment," with articles by Norman Dorsen, Susan Deller Ross, Thomas I. Emerson, Paul A. Freund, Philip Kurland, and Pauli Murray, in *Harvard Civil Rights-Civil Liberties Law Review*, Vol. 6, No. 2, March 1971.

Marital Rape

Marital Rape Exemption Packet, National Center on Women and Family Law (1981), 799 Broadway, New York, NY 10003.

National Clearinghouse on Marital Rape (NCOMR), Women's History Research Center, 2325 Oak Street, Berkeley, CA 94708, an independent, nonprofit foundation which provides information, research, and legislative information on marital rape issues.

Four issues of the *Women's Rights Law Reporter* were devoted to the subject of rape: December 1976, Spring/Summer 1977, Spring 1980, and Summer 1980. A separate publication, *Rape Chart*, published in 1981, is an analysis of all legislation on rape in the United States. All are available from Rutgers Law School, 15 Washington Street, Newark, NJ 07102.

Against Our Will: Men, Women and Rape, by Susan Brownmiller, Bantam Books, New York (1975).

Insurance

Sex Discrimination in Insurance, a Guide for Women, published by the Women's Equity Action League (WEAL), 805 15th Street, NW, Washington, DC 20005. WEAL also has information on the substance and status of a federal bill to prohibit sex discrimination in insurance. This organization monitors Congress on a regular basis and has current information on a variety of women's rights proposals pending in Washington.

Testimony of Isabelle Katz Pinzler, Director of the Women's Rights

Project of the ACLU, in support of the Fair Insurance Practices Act (S.2204), before the Senate Committee on Commerce, Science and Transportation, July 15, 1982. Available from the ACLU.

Brilmayer, et al., "Sex Discrimination in Employer-Sponsored Insurance Plans: A Legal and Demographic Analysis," 47 *U.Chi. L.Rev.* 505, 536 n.157 and accompanying text (1980).

State Agencies for Women

ALABAMA: Alabama Women's Commission, No. 9 Office Park Circle, Suite 106, Birmingham, Alabama 35223

ALASKA: Alaska State Commission for Human Rights, 2457 Artic Boulevard, Suite 3, Anchorage, Alaska 99503; State Court Building, Pouch AH, Juneau, Alaska 99811

ARIZONA: Arizona Women's Commission, 1624 W. Adams, No. 305, Phoenix, Arizona 85007

ARKANSAS: Governor's Commission on the Status of Women, Room 001, State Capitol Building, Little Rock, Arkansas 72201

CALIFORNIA: California Commission on the Status of Women, 926 J Street, Room 1003, Sacramento, California 95814

COLORADO: Colorado Commission on the Status of Women, Room 600 C, 1525 Sherman Street, State Services Building, Denver, Colorado 80203

CONNECTICUT: Permant Commission on the Status of Women, 6 Grand Street, Hartford, Connecticut 06115

DELAWARE: Council for Women, 630 State College Road, Dover, Delaware 19901

DISTRICT OF COLUMBIA: D.C. Commission of the Status of Women, Room 204, 14th and E Streets, N.W., District Building, Washington, D.C. 20004

FLORIDA: Governor's Commission on the Status of Women, Office of the Governor, The Capitol, Tallahassee, Florida 32304

GEORGIA: Georgia Commission on the Status of Women, c/o Office of the Governor, State Capitol, Atlanta, Georgia 30334

HAWAII: Hawaii State Commission on the Status of Women, 250 S. King Street, Room 500, Honolulu, Hawaii 96813

IDAHO: Idaho Commission on Women's Program, Statehouse, Boise, Idaho 83720

ILLINOIS: Illinois Commission on the Status of Women, 1166 Debbie Lane, Macomb, Illinois 61455

INDIANA: Fort Wayne Women's Bureau, P.O. Box 554, Fort Wayne, Indiana 46801

IOWA: Iowa Commission on the Status of Women, 507 10th Street, Des Moines, Iowa 50319

KANSAS: Mayor's Commission on the Status of Women, Mayor's Office, City Hall, 215 E. 7th Street, Topeka, Kansas 66612

KENTUCKY: Kentucky Commission for Women, 212 Washington Street, Frankfort, Kentucky 40601

LOUISIANA: Bureau on the Status of Women, 150 Riverside Mall, Baton Rouge, Louisiana 70801

MAINE: Maine Commission for Women, State House, Augusta, Maine 04333

MARYLAND: Maryland Commission for Women, 1100 North Eutaw Street, Baltimore, Maryland 21201

MASSACHUSETTS: Governor's Commission on the Status of Women, Room 1105, 100 Cambridge Street, Boston, Massachusetts 02202

MICHIGAN: Michigan Women's Commission, 815 Washington Square Building, Lansing, Michigan 48933

MINNESOTA: Women's Advisory Committee, Department of Human Rights, 200 Capitol Square Building, St. Paul, Minnesota 55101

MISSISSIPPI: Mississippi Governor's Commission on the Status of Women, 1315 Camp Street, Hattiesburg, Mississippi 39401

MISSOURI: Missouri Commission on the Status of Women, c/o Department of Labor and Industrial Relations, 421 E. Dunklin Street, Jefferson City, Missouri 65101

MONTANA: Montana Status of Women Advisory Council, Power Block Building Annex, Room 2, Helena, Montana 59601

NEBRASKA: Nebraska Commission on the Status of Women, 619 Terminal Building, Lincoln, Nebraska 68508

NEVADA: Governor's Commission on the Status of People, c/o Dr. Felicia Campbell, University of Nevada, Department of English, Las Vegas, Nevada 89154

NEW HAMPSHIRE: Commission on the Status of Women, 3 Capitol Street, Room 301, Concord, New Hampshire 03301

NEW JERSEY: New Jersey Department of Community Affairs, Division on Women, 363 West State Street, Trenton, New Jersey 08625

NEW MEXICO: New Mexico Commission on the Status of Women, 600 Second Street, N.W., Albuquerque, New Mexico 87102

NEW YORK: Women's Division, Executive Chamber, State of New

York, 1350 Avenue of the Americas, New York, New York 10010

NORTH CAROLINA: North Carolina Council on the Status of Women, 526 N. Wilmington Street, Raleigh, North Carolina 27604

NORTH DAKOTA: Governor's Council on Human Resources, Commission on the Status of Women, 13th Floor, State Capitol, Bismarck, North Dakota 58505

OHIO: Ohio Women's Advisory Council, Women's Services Division, Ohio Bureau of Employment Services, 145 S. Front Street, Columbus, Ohio 43216

OKLAHOMA: Commission on the Status of Women, Governor's Office, State Capitol, Oklahoma City, Oklahoma 73105

OREGON: Oregon Governor's Commission on the Status of Women, P.O. Box 40011, Portland, Oregon 97240

PENNSYLVANIA: Pennsylvania Commission for Women, 512 Finance Building, Harrisburg, Pennsylvania 17120

RHODE ISLAND: Permanent Advisory Commission on Women in Rhode Island, 235 Promenade Street, Providence, Rhode Island 02908

SOUTH CAROLINA: South Carolina Commission on the Status of Women, P.O. Box 11467, Columbia, South Carolina 29201

SOUTH DAKOTA: South Dakota Commission on the Status of Women, State Office Building, Illinois Street, Pierre, South Dakota 57501

TENNESSEE: Tennessee Commission on the Status of Women, 1212 Andrew Jackson Building, Nashville, Tennessee 37219

TEXAS: Dallas Commission on the Status of Women, c/o Dallas Public Library, 1954 Commerce Street, Dallas, Texas 75201; San Antonio Mayor's Commission on the Status of Women, 235 Yolanda Drive, San Antonio, Texas 78228

UTAH: Governor's Commission on the Status of Women, 118 State Capitol, Salt Lake City, Utah 84114

VERMONT: The Vermont Governor's Commission on the Status of Women, 2nd Floor, Pavilion Office Building, Montpelier, Vermont 05602

VIRGINIA: Virginia Commission on the Status of Women, 4th Floor, 4th Street Office Building, Richmond, Virginia 23219

WASHINGTON: Washington State Women's Council, 313 Insurance Building, Olympia, Washington 98504

WEST VIRGINIA: West Virginia Commission on the Status of Women, Box 446, Institute, West Virginia 25112

WISCONSIN: Wisconsin Governor's Commission on the Status of Women, 30 W. Mifflin Street, Room 210, Madison, Wisconsin 53703

WYOMING: Wyoming Commission on the Status of Women, Office of the Labor Commissioner, Barrett Building, Cheyenne, Wyoming 82002

4 / GAY RIGHTS

Court Decisions

The following is a brief listing of the major court decisions affecting gay rights on the state and local level:

Consensual Sodomy Statutes

Doe v. Commonwealth's Attorney, 403 F. Supp. 1199 (E.D. Va. 1975), affirmed without opinion, 425 U.S. 901 (1976). Declares constitutional Virginia's statute making consensual sodomy a crime.

People v. Onofre, 51 N.Y. 2d 476, 434 N.Y.S. 2d 947, 415 N.E. 2d 936 (1980), cert. denied, 451 U.S. 987 (1981). New York's consensual sodomy statute violates federal constitutional guarantees of privacy and equal protection.

Commonwealth v. Bonadio, 490 Pa. 91, 415 A. 2d 47 (1980). Pennsylvania's Voluntary Deviate Sexual Intercourse statute exceeds the proper bounds of the state's police power and violates the constitutional guarantee of equal protection.

Baker v. Wade, F.Supp. (N.D. Tex. 1982). Texas's statute outlawing "homosexual conduct" violates both the right to privacy and the right to equal protection.

Other Criminal Statutes

Pryor v. Municipal Court, 25 Cal. 2d 238, 158 Cal. Rptr. 330, 599 P.2d 636 (1979). California's disorderly conduct statute must be limited to conduct involving touching of the genitals, buttocks or female breast for purposes of sexual arousal, gratification, annoyance or offense that takes place in public.

Commonwealth v. Sefranka, 414 N.E. 2d 602 (Mass. 1980). Massachusetts statute prohibiting "lewd, wanton or lascivious behavior" is unconstitutionally vague.

State v. Tusek, 52 Or. App. 997, 630 P.2d 892 (1981). Oregon statute outlawing solicitation to engage in deviate sexual intercourse violates First Amendment.

Public Employment

Norton v. Macy, 417 F.2d 1161 (D.C. Cir. 1969). The federal government must demonstrate a "rational basis" for any decision to dismiss a tenured employee, including homosexuals.

McConnell v. Anderson, 451 F.2d 193 (8th Cir. 1971), cert. denied, 405 U.S. 1046 (1972). A university library may refuse to hire a homosexual who actively and openly fought for gay rights.

Singer v. U.S. Civil Service Commission, 530 F.2d 247 (9th Cir. 1976), vacated as moot, 429 U.S. 1034 (1977). The federal government may dismiss a homosexual employee who engages in "open and public flaunting or advocacy of homosexual conduct."

Van Ooteghem v. Gray, 628 F.2d 488 (5th Cir. 1980), affirmed en banc, 654 F.2d 304 (5th Cir. 1981), cert. denied, 102 (1982). County may not fire employee for addressing public body on the subject of civil rights for homosexuals.

Public School Teachers

Morrison v. State Board of Education, 1 Cal. 3d 214, 461 P.2d 375, 82 Cal. Rptr. 175 (1969). The state may not rescind a teaching license on the basis of homosexual conduct unless it demonstrates that the teacher is unfit to teach.

Acanfora v. Board of Education, 491 F.2d 498 (4th Cir. 1974), cert. denied 419 U.S. 836 (1974). Homosexual teacher's public statements in favor of gay rights are protected by the First Amendment, but he may be dismissed for failure to disclose his activities to his employer when asked.

Board of Education v. Jack M., 19 Cal. 3d 691, 566 P.2d 602, 139 Cal. Rptr. 700 (1977). Reaffirmation of *Morrison* standard for gay teachers, cited above.

Gaylord v. Tacoma School District No. 10, 88 Wash. 2d 286, 559 P.2d 1340, cert. denied 434 U.S. 879 (1977). Mere fact of teacher's homosexuality is enough to support dismissal, even without evidence of overt homosexual acts.

First Amendment Rights

Acanfora v. Board of Education, cited above.

Gay Students Organization v. Bonner, 509 F.2d 652 (1st Cir. 1974). State university must permit gay organization to hold social functions on campus.

Gay Lib v. University of Missouri, 558 F.2d 848 (8th Cir. 1977), cert. denied *sub. nom. Ratchford v. Gay Lib*, 434 U.S. 1010 (1978). State university must grant formal recognition to gay student group.

Fricke v. Lynch, 491 F. Supp. 381 (D.R.I. 1980), vacated 627 F.2d 1088 (1st Cir. 1981). Gay high school student's attempt to take another male to the school prom is symbolic speech protected by the First Amendment.

ben Shalom v. Secretary of Army, 489 F. Supp. 964 (E.D. Wis. 1980). Army regulation allowing discharge of a soldier merely because he "evidences homosexual tendencies, desire or interest" violates the First Amendment and the constitutional right to privacy.

Department of Education v. Lewis, 416 So. 2d 455 (Fla. 1982). State law denying funds to any university that gives formal recognition or assistance to a group that "recommends or advocates sexual relations between persons not married to each other" violates the First Amendment.

Van Ooteghem v. Gray, cited above.

National Gay Task Force v. Board of Education,   F.Supp.   (W.D. Okla. 1982). Oklahoma statute permitting the discharge of a teacher for "advocating, soliciting, imposing, encouraging or promoting public or private homosexual activity" is constitutional.

Private Discrimination

Kramarsky v. Stahl Management, 92 Misc. 2d 1030, 401 N.Y.S. 2d 943 (1977). A landlord may discriminate so long as he or she does not do so for a reason specifically forbidden by law.

DeSantis v. Pacific Telephone and Telegraph Co., 608 F.2d 327 (9th Cir. 1979). A federal statute barring private discrimination on account of sex does not cover employees fired or otherwise discriminated against because of affectional or sexual preference.

Gay Law Students Association v. Pacific Telephone and Telegraph Co., 24 Cal.3d 458, 595 P.2d 592, 156 Cal. Rptr. 14 (1979). A public utility which has a quasi-governmental character may not discriminate against gay people.

Same-Sex Marriages

Baker v. Nelson, 291 Minn. 310, 191 N.W.2d 185 (1971). Two homosexuals have no right to marry one another under either Minnesota law or the federal constitution.

Jones v. Hallahan, 501 S.W.2d 588 (Ky. Ct. App. 1973). Kentucky analogue to *Baker v. Nelson*, above.

Singer v. Hara, 11 Wash. App. 247, 522 P.2d 1187 (1974). Washington State analogue to *Baker v. Nelson*, above.

Cohabitation Agreements

Marvin v. Marvin, 18 Cal. 3d 660, 557 P.2d 106, 134 Cal. Rptr. 815 (1976). Property agreements, even if not express or in writing, between cohabiting but unmarried heterosexual men and women may be enforced.

Jones v. Daly, 176 Cal. Rptr. 130 (1981). A gay male is not entitled to a portion of his deceased lover's estate under *Marvin* because rendition of his sexual services was an "inseparable part" of the alleged agreement between them.

Child Custody and Visitation

People v. Brown, 49 Mich. App. 358, 212 N.W. 2d 55 (1973). A lesbian relationship in and of itself does not render a household an unfit place for children.

In Re Jane B., 85 Misc. 2d 515, 380 N.Y.S.2d 848 (1976). A lesbian mother must relinquish custody to the father of their eleven-year-old daughter because her home environment is not a "proper atmosphere" for raising a child.

M.P. v. S.P., 169 N.J. Super. 425, 404 A.2d 1256 (App. Div. 1979). Homosexuality *per se* is not a sufficient ground for removing children from the custody of their mother.

Doe v. Doe, 222 Va. 736, 284 S.E.2d 799 (1981). Homosexuality *per se* does not make a parent unfit.

Further Reading

Rivera, "Our Straight-Laced Judges: The Legal Position of Homosexual Persons in the United States," 30 *Hastings L.J.* 799 (1979); a thorough and very useful survey of the law to date.

Rivera, "Recent Developments in Sexual Preference Law," 30 Drake L. Rev. 311 (1980-81); a supplement to the *Hastings Law Journal* article.

Bell & Weinberg, *Homosexualities: A Study of Diversity Among Men and Women,* Simon & Schuster (1978); a publication of the Alfred C. Kinsey Institute for Sex Research.

Bell, Weinberg & Hammersmith, *Sexual Preference: Its Development in Men and Women,* Indiana University Press (1981); a publication of the Alfred C. Kinsey Institute for Sex Research.

Brown, *Familiar Faces, Hidden Lives: The Story of Homosexual Men in America Today,* Harcourt Brace Jovanovich (1976); a moving account of the author's own acceptance of his homosexuality together with stories about gay men with other backgrounds and approaches to their homosexuality.

Knutson, ed., *Homosexuality and the Law,* Haworth Press (1980); a collection of articles that appeared originally in the *Journal of Homosexuality.*

Stoddard, *et al.*, *The Rights of Gay People* (second edition), Bantam (1983); ACLU paperback on legal rights written for non-lawyers.

Vida, ed., *Our Right to Love: A Lesbian Resource Book*, Prentice-Hall (1978); a rich and varied compendium of articles and essays on all aspects of lesbianism.

Weinberg, *Society and the Healthy Homosexual*, Anchor (1973); a psychoanalyst's sympathetic view of homosexuality.

The National Gay Task Force, 80 Fifth Avenue, New York, New York 10011, publishes several pamphlets on homosexuality that are available for a nominal amount. Particularly useful as an introduction to the subject is a brochure entitled "Twenty Questions About Homosexuality."

Selected National Gay Organizations

Gay and Lesbian Advocates and Defenders
2 Park Square
Boston, MA 02116
(617) 426-2020

Gay Rights Advocates
540 Castro Street
San Francisco, CA 94114
(415) 863-3622

Gay Rights National Lobby
930 F Street, N.W.
Suite 611
Washington, DC 20004
(202) 462-4255

Lambda Legal Defense and Education Fund
132 West 43rd Street
New York, NY 10036
(212) 944-9488

Lesbian Mothers National Defense Fund
2446 Lorentz Place, N.
Seattle, WA 98109
(206) 282-5798
(206) 284-2290

National Federation of Parents and
  Friends of Gays
5715 16th Street, N.W.
Washington, DC 20011
(202) 726-3223

National Gay Task Force
80 Fifth Avenue
Suite 1601
New York, NY 10011
(212) 741-5800

*Statement by Lee Dreyfus, Governor of Wisconsin, upon his signing of
the first statewide prohibition against discrimination based on sexual
orientation (February 25, 1982):*

AB 70 prohibits discrimination in employment, housing, and
public accommodations based on sexual orientation. This bill has a
controversial history, and my office has been under heavy pressure to veto it. It also, however, has the support of a wide-ranging
group of religious leadership, including leadership of the Roman
Catholic Church, several Lutheran synods, and the Jewish
community.

I have decided to sign this bill for one basic reason: to protect
one's right to privacy: As one who believes in the fundamental
Republican principle that government should have a very restricted involvement in people's private and personal lives, I feel
strongly about governmentally sanctioned inquiry into an individual's thoughts, beliefs, and feelings.

Discrimination on sexual preference, if allowed, clearly must
allow inquiries into one's private life that go beyond reasonable
inquiry and in fact invade one's privacy. No one ought to have the
right and no one ought to be placed in the position of having to
reveal such personal information when it is not directly related to
an overriding public purpose.

Be certain to understand that the clear and stated intent expressed by the legislature is that this policy will not require affirmative action or quotas. That was vital to my decision to sign this

bill. I was also influenced by the fact that Madison, Dane County, and the City of Milwaukee have ordinances similar to this legislation. The problems associated with them which many predicted just have not arisen.

Let me firmly state that this restriction on discriminatory actions or decisions does not imply approval or encouragement any more than the restriction on discrimination because of a religion or creed implies approval or encouragement of certain religions or creeds.

As to the relationship of this subject to the process of education, I feel very strongly that one's sexual preferences, either homosexual or heterosexual, have absolutely no place for expression in our classrooms generally, and should not be tolerated.

5 / MARIJUANA AND OTHER DRUG LAWS

Court Decisions

Gashkin v. Tennessee, 414 U.S. 886 (1973). Rejects the claim that a state may not prohibit a person's use of marijuana when that use is asserted to be for religious reasons.

Record Revolution v. City of Parma, 638 F.2d 916 (6th Cir. 1980). Declares unconstitutional a city's drug paraphernalia law that was based on the Drug Enforcement Administration's Model Act.

Casbah, Inc. v. Thone, 651 F.2d 551 (8th Cir. 1980), and *Hegira Corp. v. MacFarlane*, 660 F.2d 1356 (10th Cir. 1981). Upholds drug paraphernalia laws based on the DEA's Model Act.

Village of Hoffman Estates v. The Flipside, 50 US Law Week 4267 (1982). Upholds a local drug paraphernalia law that was not based on the DEA's Model Act.

Ravin v. State, 537 P.2d 494 (Alas. 1975). Ruled state law unconstitutional.

New England Accessories Trade Association v. Nashua 679 F.2d 1 (1st Cir. 1982). Upheld DEA model law.

Further Reading

The National Organization for the Reform of Marijuana Laws (NORML) publishes a wide variety of materials on the subject of marijuana and drug laws, including materials with extensive bibliographies.

For further information or assistance, contact NORML, 2035 P. Street, NW, Washington, D.C. 20036, (202) 331-7363. A brief bibliography follows:

Anderson, *High In America: The True Story Behind NORML and the Politics of Marijuana*, Viking Press, 1981.

Domestic Cultivation on Public Lands, hearings before the Senate Agriculture Subcommittee on Forestry, Water Resources and the Environment, Government Printing Office, September 30, 1982.

Barnett, "Who'd Profit From Legal Marijuana?," *Playboy*, March 1980.

Bonnie, *The Marijuana Conviction*, University Press of Virginia, 1973.

Bonnie, *Discouraging Unhealthy Personal Choices: Reflections on New Directions in Substance Abuse Policy, Journal of Drug Issues*, Vol. 8, No. 2, Spring 1978.

Brecher, *Licit and Illicit Drugs*, Little, Brown, 1972.

Commission of Inquiry Into the Non-Medical Use of Drugs, Final Report (LeDain Commission), Ottawa, Canada, 1973.

Evans, et al. *The Regulation and Taxation of Cannabis Commerce*, December 1981, second edition, November 1982 (published by NORML).

The Facts About Drug Abuse, Final Report of the Drug Abuse Council, *The Free Press*, New York, 1980.

Grinspoon, *Marijuana Reconsidered*, Harvard University Press, 1971, second edition 1977.

Kaplan, *Marijuana: The New Prohibition*, World Publishing Co., 1970.

National Academy of Sciences, "An Analysis of Marijuana Policy," National Academy Press, June 1982.

National Academy of Sciences, "Marijuana and Health," National Academy Press, February 1982.

National Commission on Marijuana and Drug Abuse, "Models and Statutory Schemes for Controlling Marijuana," reprinted from Technical Papers of the First Report of the Commission, March 1972.

National Commission on Marijuana and Drug Abuse, "Toward a Coherent Social Policy," from *Drug Use in America: Problems in Perspective*, Second Report of the Commission, March 1973.

Zinberg, *Drugs and the Public*, Simon and Schuster, 1972.

MARIJUANA DECRIMINALIZATION LAWS

State	Max. Fine Imposed	Max. Amount Possessed	Classification of Offense	Effective Date
Oregon	$100	1 oz.	Civil	Oct. 5, 1973
Alaska[a]	$100	Any amount in private for personal use or 1 oz. in public	Civil	Sept. 2, 1975
Maine	$200	Any amount[b] for personal use	Civil	March 1, 1976
Colorado	$100	1 oz.	Class 2 petty offense—no criminal record	July 1, 1975
California	$100	1 oz.	Misdemeanor— no permanent criminal record	Jan. 1, 1976
Ohio	$100	100 grams (approx. 3½ oz.)	Minor misdemeanor— no criminal record	Nov. 22, 1975
Minnesota	$100	1½ oz.	Civil	April 10, 1976
Mississippi	$250	1 oz.	Civil	July 1, 1977
North Carolina	$100	1 oz.	Minor misdemeanor	July 1, 1977
New York	$100	25 grams (approx. ⅞ oz.)	Violation—no criminal record	July 29, 1977
Nebraska	$100	1 oz.	Civil	July 1, 1978

[a]The Supreme Court of Alaska ruled in 1975 that the constitutional Right of Privacy protects the possession of marijuana for personal use in the home by adults. This decision invalidates the $100 fine for simple possession in the home. In 1982 the Alaska legislature placed amount restrictions on possession.

[b]There is a rebuttable presumption that possession of less than 1½ oz. is for personal use and possession of more than 1½ oz. is with an intent to distribute.

Note: Distribution of marijuana by gift, or for no remuneration, is treated the same as simple possession in four states: California, Colorado, Minnesota, and Ohio (for up to 20 grams).

Only one state, Mississippi, has a mandatory minimum fine—$100 for first offense and $250 for second offense within a two-year period—but state judges can suspend payment of these fines.

In five states—Minnesota, Mississippi, New York, North Carolina, and Nebraska—subsequent offenses are subject to increased penalties.

6 / CENSORSHIP

Court Decisions

Queen v. Hicklin, 3 Q.B. 360 (1868). Establishes the definition of obscenity that prevailed in Britain and the United States for more than half a century.

United States v. One Book Entitled Ulysses, 72 F.2d 705 (2d Cir. 1934). Rejects *Hicklin* test and declares James Joyce's "Ulysses" not obscene.

Roth v. United States, 354 U.S. 476 (1957). Declares that obscenity is not protected by the First Amendment and begins the Supreme Court's unending effort to define that term.

Freedman v. Maryland, 380 U.S. 51 (1965). Establishes procedural requirements for any system of prior censorship of materials.

Memoirs v. Massachusetts, 383 U.S. 413 (1966). Finds the novel *Fanny Hill* to be not obscene and continues the Supreme Court's effort to define that term.

Ginsberg v. New York, 390 U.S. 629 (1968). Approves a "variable" and less stringent definition of obscenity when the intended recipients are children.

Stanley v. Georgia, 394 U.S. 557 (1969). Strikes down as unconstitutional a state law that made it a crime simply to possess obscene materials in one's home.

Miller v. California, 413 U.S. 15 (1973). The Supreme Court's most recent attempt to define "obscenity," including the use of "local standards," together with exhaustive dissenting opinions by Justices William J. Brennan and William O. Douglas.

Paris Adult Theater, Inc. v. Slaton, 413 U.S. 49 (1973). Rejects the view that consenting adults have a First Amendment right to obtain obscene materials for their private use and enjoyment.

Kaplan v. California, 413 U.S. 115 (1973). Holds that materials that contain no pictorial matter and consist only of printed words can nevertheless be found obscene.

Hamling v. United States, 418 U.S. 87 (1974). Declares that the states may use either statewide "community standards" or the standards "of the community or vicinage" from which the jurors come in determining the obscenity of a given work.

Jenkins v. Georgia, 418 U.S. 153 (1974). Overturns a lower court ruling finding the film *Carnal Knowledge* to be obscene.

Erznoznik v. City of Jacksonville, 422 U.S. 205 (1975). Declares unconstitutional a city ordinance making it a public nuisance for a drive-in theater to exhibit films containing nudity when the screen was visible from the street.

Young v. American Mini Theaters, 427 U.S. 50 (1976). Upholds Detroit's zoning scheme to disperse establishments providing "adult" materials and entertainment.

F.C.C. v. Pacifica Foundation, 438 U.S. 726 (1978). Upholds an F.C.C. sanction against a radio station that broadcast in the afternoon a monologue containing "seven dirty words" even though it was admittedly not obscene.

Schad v. Borough of Mount Ephraim, 452 U.S. 61 (1981). Severely limits the scope of the *Young* decision by holding that zoning laws cannot be used to restrict First Amendment freedoms.

American Booksellers Association, Inc. v. McAuliffe, 533 F.Supp. 50 (N.D. Ga. 1981). Declares unconstitutional a state law prohibiting the display of materials for sale to adults if the materials are within the view of children.

Home Box Office, Inc. v. Wilkinson,   F.Supp.   (D Utah 1982). Declares unconstitutional a state law that made it a crime to present on cable television certain non-obscene programming.

Further Reading

As might be expected, a great deal has been written on the subject of the censorship of obscenity and pornography. Each year the American Library Association publishes an excellent annotated bibliography of materials written on the subject during the previous year; copies of the most recent edition, as well as earlier editions, can be obtained by writing the Association at 50 East Huron Street, Chicago, Illinois 60611. Similarly, the Freedom of Information Center at the School of Journalism of the University of Missouri at Columbia regularly publishes an annotated bibliography of materials concerning free speech and freedom of information.

A useful index of current developments in the law of obscenity, although published by a pro-censorship group, is the "Obscenity Law Bulletin," issued six times a year by the National Obscenity Law Center, a project of Morality in Media, Inc., 475 Riverside Drive, New York, N.Y. 10025. In addition, an exhaustive bibliography of publications dealing with the subject of censorship over the past two decades may be found in McCoy, *Freedom of the Press: A Bibliocyclopedia,* Southern Illinois University Press, 1979.

Other selected works include:

Boyer, *Purity in Print: Book Censorship in America,* Charles Scribner's Sons, 1968.

Chandos, ed. *"To Deprave and Corrupt . . .": Original Studies in Nature and Definition of "Obscenity,"* Association Press, 1962.

Cox, *Freedom of Expression in the Burger Court,* Harvard University Press, 1981.

Crowther, "Movies and Censorship," Public Affairs Pamphlets, No. 332, 1962.

Haight & Grannis, *Banned Books,* R.R. Bowker, 4th ed., 1978.

Haiman, *Speech and Law in a Free Society,* University of Chicago Press, 1981.

Hentoff, *The First Freedom,* Delacorte, 1980.

Jennison, "Freedom to Read," Public Affairs Pamphlets, No. 344, 1963.

Kalven, "The Right to Publish," in *The Rights of Americans: What*

They Are—What They Should Be, edited by Norman Dorsen, Pantheon Books, 1971.

Kuh, *Foolish Figleaves? Pornography in—and Out of—Court,* Macmillan, 1967.

Lewis, *Literature, Obscenity and the Law,* Southern Illinois University Press, 1976.

Norwick, "Pornography: The Issues and the Law," Public Affairs Pamphlets, No. 477, 1972.

Rembar, *The End of Obscenity,* Random House, 1968.

Report of the Commission on Obscenity and Pornography, Bantam Books, 1970.

St. John-Stevas, *Obscenity and the Law,* London: Secker & Warburg, 1956.

Schauer, *The Law of Obscenity,* Bureau of National Affairs, 1976.

Schwartz and Ernst, *Censorship: The Search for the Obscene,* Macmillan, 1964.

Sharp, ed., *Commentaries on Obscenity,* Metuchen, N.J.: The Scarecrow Press, 1970.

Strom, *Zoning Control of Sex Businesses,* Clark Boardman, 1977.

7 / SAMPLE MATERIALS FOR THE CITIZEN-LOBBYIST

The following materials, referring to the various substantive issues discussed in this book, are provided as examples of the kinds of materials citizen-lobbyists might use in connection with their own lobbying efforts. Obviously, these materials should be revised to reflect the actual situation to which the materials are to be addressed.

CHECKLIST FOR FORMING COMMUNITY ORGANIZATIONS

Forming a local community organization to lobby on an issue can be one of the most effective tools available to the citizen-lobbyist. The following steps should help ensure that your organization gets off to the best possible start:

1. Select a convenient time and place for the first meeting. If you are in doubt as to the time and place, check with a friend or community leader who has had experience holding such meetings.

2. Announce the meeting long enough in advance so that people can arrange to come—usually, a week's notice is the minimum you should provide. Post notices of the meeting as widely as possible, especially in those places where they are most likely to be read by people who agree

with you, including libraries, churches, bar associations, school faculty rooms, bookstores, and theaters. Also, personally contact specific members of the community who you feel might be particularly interested in the issue, including clergy, psychologists and psychiatrists, political leaders and public officials, educators, lawyers, journalists, doctors and nurses, and other civic leaders.

3. Prepare a short program for the meeting. Have someone briefly discuss the background of the issue, and have someone else discuss the specific issues and timetable for the current lobbying campaign in your state.

4. Have a resolution ready to be introduced, discussed, and then proposed for adoption by the members.

5. Ask for volunteers to help work on the lobbying effort. If appropriate, form committees to handle such matters as publicity, finances, and coordination of lobbying.

6. Set a definite time and place for the next meeting. Urge everyone who attended to discuss the issue within their own organizations and communities and to report at the next meeting the names of additional groups and individuals who will be joining the lobbying effort.

7. Follow up this first meeting with personal contacts with those who attended, making sure they discuss the issue with others and attend the next meeting.

SAMPLE RESOLUTION FOR COMMUNITY ORGANIZATIONS

(State Equal Rights Amendment)

WHEREAS, the Constitution of this State does not contain an Equal Rights Amendment; and

WHEREAS, the laws and policies of this State are permeated with a double standard that provides different rights for men and women; and

WHEREAS, the existence of such a double standard results in discrimination against women and the perpetuation of a legal system that treats women as inferior to men; and

WHEREAS, an Equal Rights Amendment to the State Constitution will prevent the State from categorizing people solely on the basis of their sex, will require the State to remain neutral with respect to the roles men and women play in society, will mean that men and women

will be equal before the law, and will foster a legal system in which each person will be judged on individual merit and ability; and
WHEREAS, at least sixteen other States have added Equal Rights Amendments to their State Constitutions without any of the dire consequences often predicted by the opponents of such Amendments; and
WHEREAS, this State should wait no longer to commit itself fully and firmly to the principle of equality under the law for people of both sexes;

NOW, THEREFORE, be it

RESOLVED, that the ⎯⎯⎯⎯⎯ hereby endorses the adoption of an Equal Rights Amendment to the State Constitution and calls upon every member of the State Legislature to take all steps necessary to enable the people of this State to approve such an Amendment at the earliest opportunity.

SAMPLE PETITION (Against Censorship)

The undersigned citizens of ⎯⎯⎯⎯⎯ call upon every member of the State Legislature to oppose and defeat all bills that would perpetuate or enhance the power of the state to censor what we can read or view. We recognize that some books and magazines and films and works of art can be offensive and disturbing to many people, but we also believe that it is even more offensive and disturbing—and dangerous to our precious individual liberties—for the state to try to protect those persons through governmental censorship of those materials. We also believe that it is inherently impossible to define and enforce obscenity laws without at the same time seriously infringing on many other materials that are fully protected by the First Amendment, and that that is much too high a price to pay for whatever benefits can be derived from censoring what does qualify as obscene.

Accordingly, we call upon the legislature to defeat all bills that would continue any form of censorship and to support those bills that would repeal all existing censorship laws.

⎯⎯⎯⎯⎯⎯⎯⎯⎯⎯   ⎯⎯⎯⎯⎯⎯⎯⎯⎯⎯
⎯⎯⎯⎯⎯⎯⎯⎯⎯⎯   ⎯⎯⎯⎯⎯⎯⎯⎯⎯⎯
⎯⎯⎯⎯⎯⎯⎯⎯⎯⎯   ⎯⎯⎯⎯⎯⎯⎯⎯⎯⎯
⎯⎯⎯⎯⎯⎯⎯⎯⎯⎯   ⎯⎯⎯⎯⎯⎯⎯⎯⎯⎯
⎯⎯⎯⎯⎯⎯⎯⎯⎯⎯   ⎯⎯⎯⎯⎯⎯⎯⎯⎯⎯

SAMPLE PRESS ADVISORY FOR PRESS CONFERENCE
(Drug Laws)

PRESS ADVISORY
Date:
Contact:
Phone:

An important press conference concerning the current legislative battle over the proposed repeal of the state's marijuana laws will be held at 10:00 A.M. on Wednesday,   , at the offices of   . The purpose of the conference will be to announce the formation of a new community organization to lobby in favor of the proposed repeal. The leaders of the new organization, including
,   , and   , will be present at the conference.

SAMPLE PRESS RELEASES FOR COMMUNITY ORGANIZATIONS

(Censorship)

A. *Challenge*

Contact:
Phone:
For Immediate Release

CHALLENGE ISSUED FOR CENSORSHIP DEBATE

The   has challenged all local groups favoring strict censorship laws to debate the merits of censorship at a public forum on the issue to be held on
at   . The challenge was issued by
chairperson of the Free Speech Committee.

In a statement issuing the challenge,
said, "The power of government to censor what we can read and view is one of the greatest threats to freedom and democracy. We believe the case against censorship is so strong that we challenge all groups who favor censorship to debate the issue with us in a forum open to the general public. Only through a full and free discussion of the whole

censorship question can each member of the public reach his or her own conclusion on this subject, and we expect this debate to provide that kind of open and uninhibited discussion."

The forum will be chaired by   and will also include a discussion of the members, procedures, and sessions of the state legislature. The forum has been scheduled to coincide with the introduction into the legislature of a number of bills dealing with the censorship issue.

The Free Speech Committee was formed in to work toward the preservation of the First Amendment freedoms of speech and press against encroachments by all censorship laws. The committee has over   members from   .

The forum will begin at 8:00 P.M. and admission is [free/ $] per person.

B. *Award*

For Release:

CIVIC LEADER TO BE HONORED
FOR FREE SPEECH ROLE

                    , the noted civic leader, will be honored on   by the organization "for his outstanding leadership and contribution to the cause of free speech." [Mr./Ms.] will be the recipient of the organization's "Medal of Recognition" award at its annual dinner, to be held at   .

In announcing the award,   , chairperson of the organization, said the civic leader was chosen "because [his/her] tireless efforts for the cause of free speech have served as an example and an inspiration to everyone who believes that governmental censorship must be resisted if our fundamental First Amendment freedoms are to be preserved. His eloquent advocacy and dynamic leadership in behalf of free speech have made an indelible impression on everyone who has come in contact with him and have made an immeasurable contribution to that cause."

The award will be presented by the Honorable   , a member of the state legislature. [Mr./Ms.]   will serve as master of ceremonies for the evening's program.

Tickets for the dinner may be obtained from
and cost $ each.

C. *Endorsements*

For Immediate Release

CIVIC LEADERS ENDORSE ANTI-CENSORSHIP BILL

Three leading local community leaders,   ,
                            , and   ,
announced today that they were "in complete agreement with" and
"fully supported" the bill in the state legislature to repeal all state
censorship laws.

In a joint statement addressed to every member of the legislature,
the three leaders stated that they had "become convinced that all
efforts to censor so-called obscenity and pornography cannot succeed
without at the same time encroaching upon basic First Amendment
freedoms," and that "the time has come for the state to put its faith in
the ultimate taste and judgment of the people to decide for themselves
what is or is not obscene."

With their announcement, the three leaders joined more
than   other civic and community leaders who have previously
endorsed Bill   , introduced by   ,
which would adopt the main recommendations of the U.S. Commis-
sion on Obscenity and Pornography as the law of this state. That bill is
presently under review in the
committees of each house of the state legislature. Among those who
have previously endorsed that bill are   ,
                            , and   . For fur-
ther information contact:

Name:

Phone:

LETTER TO THE EDITOR (Gay Rights)

To the Editor:

The State Legislature is now considering a bill that would prohibit discrimination in employment, housing and public accommodations on the basis of sexual orientation.

I strongly urge the enactment of this bill for civil rights for gay people.

There are many misconceptions about this bill. The bill would *not* give special recognition to gay people; it would simply extend to gays the same civil rights already guaranteed to most other citizens of this state. The bill would *not* constitute an endorsement of homosexuality; it would merely establish the rule that people are entitled to fair treatment in vital public services regardless of sexual orientation. It would *not* force employers to hire any gay man or woman who happened to apply for a job; it would only bar an employer from making employment decisions on the basis of sexual preference rather than professional competence.

Gay people have suffered terribly in this country. As a class, they have encountered scorn, derision, and hatred of a special kind. Until 1970, there was little acknowledgment that they even existed.

This bill cannot undo the injustices of the past. But it can help to bring forth a new spirit of tolerance toward a large and significant portion of our population.

Very truly yours,

TESTIMONY TO LEGISLATIVE COMMITTEE (Gay Rights)

My name is   . I am Chairman of
                              . I am here today to express our strong
support for   , the bill to extend civil rights
to gay people.

This bill would ban discrimination on the basis of sexual orientation in the areas of employment, education, public accommodations, and housing. Existing law already forbids discrimination in these areas on account of race, creed, color, national origin, and, to a limited degree, physical handicap and marital status. Thus, the bill would merely add a new category of protection to an already existing statutory scheme.

We view this bill as essential to fulfillment of the state's historic commitment to equal protection under the law. There are many thousands of lesbians and gay men in our state. Under present law and under most circumstances, they have no protection whatever against an arbitrary employer or landlord or shopkeeper. A gay person may be denied a job, an apartment, or a vital good or service, *on the mere suspicion* that he or she is homosexual. This is appalling and—in a state that prides itself on diversity, tolerance, and concern for individual rights—totally unacceptable.

There was a time when employers and landlords were given full discretion to determine with whom they would or would not deal. In fact, in this state, until recently, employers and landlords were entirely free to pick and choose among applicants on the basis of race or ancestry or religion. Then came the civil rights revolution, and legislative bodies throughout the country, including this legislature, voted to set limits on this discretion in the furtherance of a higher value—equal justice for all. It is the same principle that is at stake with this bill.

Indeed, the reasons to vote in favor of this bill are the same reasons that prevailed two decades ago with regard to racial or ethnic discrimination. There are at least three.

First, discrimination on the basis of sexual orientation, like discrimination on account of race and sex, is, at heart, irrational. There is no evidence of any kind that indicates that homosexuals make less responsible employees or less reliable tenants than anyone else. There is no sociological data that suggests that they are, as a class, less intelligent or hard-working or loyal. Yet the myth persists: Homosexuals prey on children, homosexuals like to proselytize, homosexuals are sexually predatory, homosexuals are unstable and insecure.

These fears are utterly groundless, as study after study has proven. They have no more substance than earlier canards about other groups—that blacks are "shiftless," that Jews are "Shylocks," or that women have "no head" for business. They are products of fear and ignorance and must not be permitted to forestall a serious consideration of this important issue.

But the irrationality of the discrimination is not the only reason to vote for this bill. Even more important is the suffering that is hard to document on a large scale. Most gay people are invisible; they pass for straight. They exist within all classes, segments, and races. Generally speaking, they are identifiable as gay only if they reveal themselves to be gay. Consequently, most never encounter overt discrimination. And those who do often fail to complain even when they do encounter overt discrimination because they know that the law as it now stands offers no remedy or recourse.

But we know—all of us, almost instinctively—that the suffering does exist. Our group has some sense of the problem from the complaints we receive from the numerous lesbians or gay men who have lost their jobs or apartments. But these complaints are undoubtedly just a shadow of the problem. As a class, gay people have been deeply loathed and feared in this country ever since its founding; so much so that until ten years ago their problems, indeed their mere existence, were never discussed openly. Homosexuality is now, at long last, a subject fit for the pages of the *New York Times* and *Time* magazine, but the overwhelming number of lesbians and gay men are still too fearful to reveal themselves. Can there be any doubt whatsoever that if, by some sinister magic, every lesbian and gay man in this state suddenly became identifiable to friends, neighbors, employers, and landlords, we would immediately see an avalanche of pink slips and eviction notices? The prejudice runs too deep to expect anything else.

The third reason for passage of this bill follows logically from the first two. Discrimination against gays is simply wrong. Just as it is wrong to punish someone for the color of his skin or the nature of his religious belief or the language spoken by his ancestors, it is wrong to chastise someone on account of a sexual and emotional makeup that happens to be different from that of the majority of the people. It is wrong to make decisions that affect people's lives on the basis of a group label or stereotype. Gay people, like everyone else, should be given the chance to rise or fall on individual merit, without fear of categorization or unfounded assumption.

Again, our group urges the passage of this important bill.

I appreciate having the opportunity to testify today.

Thank you very much.

LETTER TO COMMITTEE MEMBER
(Reproductive Freedom)

Dear   :

My family and I have lived in your district for many years now, and we have always supported you in your election campaigns. We believe you have shown commendable leadership and courage in the legislature, and we hope you will continue to do so.

We understand that you are a member of the
committee, and that a number of bills dealing with the availability of

safe, legal abortions in this state are now being considered by that committee. Speaking for my [husband/wife] and, I might add, for a great many of our friends and neighbors, I want to urge you to oppose all those bills that would restrict the availability of abortions in our state, and particularly bills

, and

In our view, the decision whether or not to bear a child—even after a pregnancy has commenced—is a uniquely personal decision in which the state should not interfere. We are aware that many people believe that abortion is wrong. However, many other people—including the members of our family and virtually all of our friends—do not share that view. People who oppose abortions should not have them, but they also should not try to prevent those others from having the right to make a different decision.

We urge you to stand up for the right of privacy and reproductive freedom of every person in this state—and especially the poorest and least sophisticated, who would be most directly affected by these bills—by vigorously opposing all these bills.

Sincerely,

About the Contributors

Janet Benshoof is a lawyer who has served since 1977 as Director of the Reproductive Freedom Project of the American Civil Liberties Union. She has been involved in numerous cases concerning reproductive freedom and abortion rights, including the crucial Supreme Court cases *Harris v. McRae* and *City of Akron v. Akron Center for Reproductive Health*. She also coordinates the project's public education program and has appeared on radio and TV programs across the nation, and on panels and at seminars discussing issues of reproductive choice. She is a graduate of the Harvard Law School.

Barbara Shack is a consultant on legislation to the New York Civil Liberties Union. She served as the NYCLU's Legislative Director and principal lobbyist from 1976 to 1982, representing the organization before the New York State Legislature, the Governor's office, and state agencies. From 1971 to 1975, she was director of the NYCLU's Women's Rights Project. She has written, testified, and lectured on women's issues and a broad range of civil liberties subjects.

Thomas B. Stoddard is currently Legislative Director of the New York Civil Liberties Union, the New York State branch of the American Civil Liberties Union. He serves on the adjunct faculty of the New York University School of Law, where he teaches a course on the rights of gay people, and he also maintains a private law practice in New York City. He has written and lectured extensively on civil rights and civil liberties, particularly gay rights, abortion rights, First Amendment rights, and criminal justice.

George L. Farnham is currently National Director of the National Organization for the Reform of Marijuana Laws (NORML). He has written numerous articles and appeared in public forums and on television to support drug law reforms. A graduate of George Washington University's law school, he is also active in prison reform and in Americans for Democratic Action.

About the Editor

Kenneth P. Norwick is a practicing lawyer in New York City and the author of numerous works on legal and political subjects. He is a co-author of *The Rights of Authors and Artists*, to be published by Bantam Books in 1983, and the editor of *Your Legal Rights: Making the Law Work For You*. He has served as Legislative Director of the New York Civil Liberties Union and as Special Professor of Law at Hofstra Law School. He is a 1965 graduate of the University of Chicago Law School, where he was a member of the editorial board of the *Law Review* and the founder and editor-in-chief of the law school's newspaper.

Index

Index